DATE			

British
RESEARCH
AND
DEVELOPMENT
Aircraft

SEVENTY YEARS AT THE LEADING EDGE

British RESEARCH AND DEVELOPMENT Aircraft

SEVENTY YEARS AT THE LEADING EDGE

Ray Sturtivant

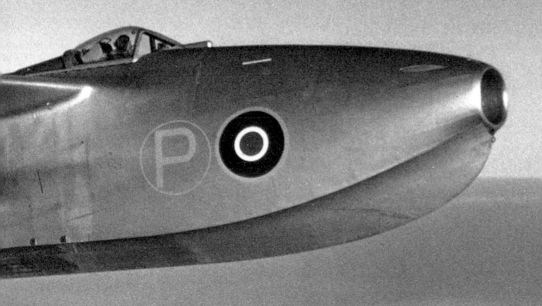

Foulis

Haynes

A **Foulis** Aviation Book

First published 1990

Published by:
Haynes Publishing Group
Sparkford, Nr. Yeovil, Somerset
BA22 7JJ, England.

Haynes Publications Inc.
861 Lawrence Drive, Newbury Park,
California 91320, USA.

British Library Cataloguing in Publication data
Sturtivant, Ray
British research & development aircraft.
1. Great Britain. Aeronautical engineering. Reseach
projects
I. Title
629.130072041

ISBN 0-85429-697-2

Library of Congress catalog card number 90-80218

Editor: Mansur Darlington
Page design: Chris Hull, Peter Kay and Alan Hobday
Printed in England by: J.H. Haynes & Co. Ltd.

Contents

Introduction 6

Acknowledgements 8

Chapter 1
First World War Experimental Designs 9

Chapter 2
Research after the First World War 15

Chapter 3
Central Engine Rooms 21

Chapter 4
All-metal Construction 24

Chapter 5
Early Rotorcraft 29

Chapter 6
Flying Wings and Things 43

Chapter 7
Aspects of Inter-war Research 50

Chapter 8
Flying Boat Developments 55

Chapter 9
The Quest For Height 60

Chapter 10
The Quest For Distance 64

Chapter 11
Military Experiments 69

Chapter 12
Wartime Wing Experiments 75

Chapter 13
Birth of the Jet 97

Chapter 14
Second Generation Jets 100

Chapter 15
Tailless Aircraft Research 108

Chapter 16
Laminar Flow Wing Research 116

Chapter 17
Delta Research 120

Chapter 18
The Miles M.52 128

Chapter 19
Transonic Delta Research 130

Chapter 20
Prone Pilot Research 140

Chapter 21
Commercial Ventures 142

Chapter 22
Vertical Take-Off & Landing 147

Chapter 23
Wing Experiments 154

Chapter 24
Naval Aviation Research 160

Chapter 25
Third Generation Jets 165

Chapter 26
Small Rotorcraft 170

Chapter 27
Large Rotorcraft 176

Chapter 28
Rotary wing variations 184

Chapter 29
The Flying Boat Fighter 190

Chapter 30
Supersonic Success Story 194

Chapter 31
The TSR.2 Saga 199

Chapter 32
Promises Unfulfilled 203

Chapter 33
For The Future 208

Index 210

Introduction

Over the years, numerous varied designs have emerged from the drawing offices of British aircraft manufacturers, both large and small. Many were produced specifically to test some new theory or line of research which might lead to a significant advance in aviation technology. A number of books have explored different aspects of this type of research, but the present work is the first attempt to bring together the history of such developments in this country. Space limitations preclude the detailed analysis of every possible candidate for inclusion, but the aircraft and designs dealt with cover most of the more important aspects of British aircraft research and development over a period spanning some seven decades.

The first few formative years of British aviation were a period of much experimentation, already detailed in other publications. This volume therefore commences at the point, late in the First World War, where aircraft manufacturers were granted special licences to pursue particular lines of research for which there was no current official requirement. In the event, none of the aircraft produced under such licences led to production orders, being either produced too late in the war to be needed, or being largely swept aside in the post-war contraction of the industry.

After the Armistice, many aircraft manufacturers went into oblivion, but some managed to survive, though not necessarily those whose designs had become the best known. A reputation for good workmanship helped, but finance was usually a more important factor. The highly respected Sopwith company, for instance, fell foul of an exorbitant Treasury claim for Excess War Profits Duty and had to go into liquidation, though in this case the phoenix was able to emerge almost immediately from the ashes, to become the equally famous Hawker company.

The next twenty years saw research into every aspect of aeronautical theory. Although finance was never plentiful, production of prototype and research aircraft was, by present day standards, relatively inexpensive. As a consequence, even within the limited budgets then available, it was possible for new aircraft to be officially sponsored on a numerical scale which would be quite impracticable today. Most of the costly technological wonders which are now part and parcel of even the most humdrum aircraft today were then unknown, and this less advanced state of the art allowed relatively cheap and varied research and development, often entirely at the expense of the firms concerned.

The origins of many of the more recent advanced concepts can be traced back to this period. The large faired-in wing of the Westland Dreadnought might, for instance, be regarded as a forerunner of that used on such types as the Avro Vulcan bomber. The pioneering work undertaken by the series of Westland-Hill Pterodactyls proved invaluable when the appearance of jet engines led to this layout becoming a practical proposition for fast new aircraft in both the military and commercial fields. Rotating wing aircraft also became a reality, with both autogiros and helicopters beginning to emerge from the theoretical stage, and one can only conjecture as to what might have emanated from the unique brain of Se§nor Cierva, had he not been so sadly killed in an accident to a fixed-wing aircraft.

Many of the early experimental and research aircraft had been produced to Air Ministry Specifications. In 1927 it became the practice to prefix such Specification numbers with a letter (or letters) denoting the type category of aircraft required, but it was not until shortly after the commencement of the Second World War that such a prefix was adopted for pure research aircraft. The British designs of the last half century covered in this book are largely those produced to such Specifications.

The demands of the Second World War, like those of its predecessor a quarter of a century earlier, led to a great expansion and speeding-up of aviation research and development. The most important advance, however, that of jet propulsion, was not to become a widespread practical reality until the post-war period. The first British jet-powered aircraft to fly, and the first design to be produced to an E-prefixed Specification, was the Gloster E.28/39, a purely experimental machine, which was flying within eighteen months of concept, and which led to the ubiquitous Gloster Meteor, flown not only by the Royal Air Force, but by many other air forces. Its equally famous contemporary, the de Havilland Vampire, stemmed from another experimental prototype, being initially known by the code name 'Spider Crab', produced to official Specification E.6/41.

Research into rotating wing aircraft produced less happy results. The autogiro has only been developed on a small scale, the main emphasis being on helicopters, though with no real lasting success for purely British designs. The Cierva W.9 and Air Horse designs led down blind alleys, the promising Fairey Gyrodyne was lost in one of the periodic Defence cuts and the noisy Rotodyne from the same stable disappeared in a Government-induced rationalisation of the British aircraft industry. Several other British designs enjoyed an ephemeral success, until the mergers resulted in rotating wing manufacture being centred on Westlands, who then ceased to be involved with fixed-wing aircraft. Most aircraft since produced by that firm have, however, been largely based on designs produced by American, and to some extent French and Italian, designers.

In the fixed wing field, the results of British design work have been on the whole much happier, though not without their frustrations and setbacks. One can only surmise what might have followed, had successive Governments not pulled the plug on, for instance, the Miles M.52, the Bristol 188 or the TSR.2. These and others all had their faults, and would undoubtedly have needed considerable

and costly development, but some or all might well have given this country a lead in their respective fields, which in the event went by default to other nations.

Nevertheless, many varied research aircraft were allowed to proceed, producing much invaluable information. A few were developed directly into successful production aircraft, whilst others provided vital information needed for later successful designs. Varied wing shapes were, for instance, explored by such types as the Armstrong Whitworth A.W.52/G flying wing glider and the jet-powered A.W.52, the swept wing de Havilland Swallow and the delta-winged Avro 707. Research into transonic flight was undertaken by designs from Fairey and Boulton & Paul. The low speed characteristics of slim-delta wings were tested on the Handley Page H.P.115, whilst the same firm produced the H.P.88 to test the crescent wing for its Victor bomber. Variable sweep was tested on the Short SB.5, which was also tried with both high and low tailplanes.

One field in which Britain gained and has held the lead is that of vertical take-off and landing, other than by rotors. This concept only became a real possibility with the availability of powerful jet motors capable of generating sufficient lift for take-off without forward movement of the aircraft. Initial trials were carried out at Hucknall on the Rolls-Royce 'Flying Bedstead', and the concept was later tested on the Short SC.1, built specially for VTOL research. The Hawker P.1127 was the first, and very successful, attempt at a practical subsonic VTOL aircraft, and this progressed through the Kestrel to become the much-vaunted Harrier and Sea Harrier, to which much of the British success in the Falklands War can be credited.

The heyday of pure research aircraft now appears to be over, at least in Britain, the cost having become prohibitive, and most of the vital questions posed in the early days of jet power, and later supersonic and vertical flight, having been largely overcome. Nevertheless, there is some scope for further practical flying research, as evidenced by the British Aerospace EAP, which has produced advanced technological information likely to be invaluable in the development of the European Fighter Aircraft, or EFA.

Acknowledgements

The author would like to acknowledge the generous assistance he has received from a large variety of sources, both official and private. Information has been provided from records held by the Air Historical Branch of the Ministry of Defence, the Royal Air Force Museum, the Fleet Air Arm Museum, the Museum of Army Flying, the Public Record Office and the archives of the Yeovil Branch of the Royal Aeronautical Society. Invaluable help has been given by Eric Myall in the area of rotary wing development; he also helped to check the original manuscript, as did Chris Ashworth, Fred Balham, Mick Burrow and Jim Oughton, who all gave considerable help and advice

As ever, many thanks are due to Mike Keep for the excellent drawings, which are up to his invariably high standard. The assistance is also acknowledged of the following, this being quite substantial in some instances: Rick Barker, Jack Bruce, Peter Green, Mike Hooks, Philip Jarrett, Richard King, Stuart Leslie, Angus McMillin, Eric Morgan, Brian Pickering, Mike Stroud, Dave Watkins and Ray Williams.

Some of the aircraft involved have proved quite difficult to research, since so much valuable material has been lost over the years. A number of books and publications have therefore proved invaluable in filling gaps, notably the excellent Putnam series of company histories as well as *British Aeroplanes 1914-1918* (J.M. Bruce), *Cierva Autogiros* (Peter W. Brooks) and *Project Cancelled* (Derek Wood). In addition numerous issues have been consulted of various magazines, including *The Aeroplane*, *Aeroplane Monthly*, *Air Enthusiast*, *Flight* and *Royal Air Force Flying Review*.

Chapter 1
FIRST WORLD WAR EXPERIMENTAL DESIGNS

In the early days of flying, nearly every aircraft design was of an experimental nature. During the First World War, however, it gradually became necessary to concentrate scarce resources on those aircraft which appeared likely to stand a good chance of meeting specific official requirements. On 30th March 1917 therefore, it was pronounced that under the Defence Regulations it would henceforth be an offence to produce an experimental aircraft without official authority. A system was instigated, which in essence still appertains today, whereby requirements would be drawn up and aircraft firms then invited to submit appropriate designs. If the requirement still existed when these were received, one or more firms would be contracted to produce up to three prototypes, sometimes in competition with each other.

It was recognised, however, that a designer might come up with an original idea which either did not meet a specific official requirement, or approached the problem somewhat differently, and which had sufficient merit to justify further investigation. Provision was therefore made for a limited number of the more promising designs to be produced as private ventures under licence. Materials were made available for this purpose, and they were regarded as experimental aircraft, meriting a serial number in a special 'X' range.

The system was relatively short-lived, and documentation of 'X' serial number issues is therefore incomplete, but it is known that at least ten different designs were considered, with serials ranging from X1 to X25. Of these ten, two were never built, serial X1 being allocated to a proposed Glendower design, and serials X12 and X13 to an intended new British Nieuport fighter powered by a 230 hp Bentley B.R.2 engine. Serials X21 to X24 were earmarked for the Siddeley Sinaia bomber, but the first two of these were completed as J6858 and J6859, and X23 and X24 were cancelled.

The 'X' series continued for a while after the Armistice, seemingly on the lines of the later Class 'B' registrations. It is known, for instance, that Vickers were granted licences in respect of 35 V.I.M.s, or Vickers Instructional Machines, (X41 to X75), these being reconditioned F.E.2Ds for China, fitted with Vimy instruments, and delivered between 2 May and 15 June 1920.

SOPWITH BULLDOG

The earliest numbered 'X' serials to materialise were X2 to X4, allocated to the Sopwith Bulldog (though X2 has also been suggested for the prototype Martinsyde F.3). With the maker's type number 2.F.R.2, this became a contender for Air Board Type A.2(a) Specification for a two-seater fighter reconnaissance aircraft to replace the Bristol Fighter. Similar in general appearance to the Sopwith Snipe single-seat fighter, the first machine was fitted with single-bay wings and had a 200 hp Clerget 11Eb engine. Serial numbers H4422 and H4423 were also allocated to the other two machines, but never taken up, and X3 was completed as the Bulldog MkI with 33 ft 9 in span two-bay wings, whilst X4 was the Mk II of similar configuration but with a 360 hp ABC Dragonfly Ia engine.

SOPWITH RHINO AND HIPPO

Licence No.14 under the experimental system was granted for another Sopwith design, the 2.B.2 Rhino, serials X7 and X8 being issued. Intended as a two-seat day bomber to meet Type A.2(b) Specification, and powered by a 230 hp B.H.P. engine, it emerged in October 1917 as a rather ugly looking triplane, and trials proved it to have a poor performance. Equally unsuccessful was the Sopwith 3.F.2 Hippo two-seat fighter, authorised under Licence No.16.

Above: The third prototype Sopwith Bulldog at Brooklands in June 1918. (via J.D. Oughton)

Below: Bulldog MkII 2.F.R.2 takes off – complete with divot attached to the tail skid. (via J.D. Oughton)

One of the Sopwith Rhino prototypes prior to receiving its serial number. Here it is seen with balanced ailerons. (via J.D. Oughton)

Sopwith Hippo prototype X10 seen at Brooklands on 13 September 1917 during engine tests. Sopwith can be seen in the cockpit. (via J.D. Oughton)

Two machines were built, numbered X10 and X11, both powered by a 200 hp Clerget 11Eb engine. X10 first flew on 13 September 1917. The 38 ft 9 in two-bay wings had backward stagger, somewhat similar to that in the Dolphin from the same stable, but the aircraft's performance was below that of the Bristol Fighter, which was already in service and, unsurprisingly, no production orders were forthcoming. X11 was renumbered H4420, and another machine which would have been serialled X18 became H4421 instead.

SAUNDERS T.1

Licence No.13 was granted for the Saunders T.1, a two-seat biplane serialled X14 and fitted with a fixed synchronised Lewis gun for the pilot and a Scarff ring-mounted Lewis gun for the observer. The power plant was originally intended to be a 200 hp Hispano-Suiza, but in the event a 150 hp Sunbeam Nubian was fitted. Some problems were experienced with the engine cooling system, but before these could be overcome the designer, H.H.Thomas, had

The only known photograph of the Saunders T.1. (via Chaz Bowyer)

The first prototype of the Austin Osprey triplane fighter. (RAF Museum P.3659)

The first prototype of the somewhat snub-nosed Armstrong Whitworth Armadillo. (MAP)

the misfortune to be one of the huge number of victims of the 1918 influenza epidemic and the design consequently fell into abeyance.

AUSTIN OSPREY

Next came serials X15 to X17, given under Licence No.17 to the Austin Motor Co., for its A.F.T.3 triplane fighter, later named the Osprey. Powered by a 230 hp Bentley B.R.2 engine, it was designed to meet the Type A.1(a) Specification for which the Sopwith Snipe was the successful contender. In the event, only the first machine was completed, its first flight taking place in February 1918, work on the other two being abandoned.

ARMSTRONG WHITWORTH ARMADILLO

Licence No.18 was issued to Armstrong Whitworth for their rather tough looking F.M.4 design, soon named the Armadillo and first flown in April 1918. Also powered by a 230 hp Bentley B.R.2 engine, serials X19 and X20 were allocated to this armoured trench fighter. It was another of the many machines intended to meet the Type A.1(a) Specification, but visibility was poor, especially for ground attack work, and the firm turned its attention to the Ara, an improved design to the same requirement, which had in the meantime become R.A.F. Type I Specification.

BOULTON & PAUL P.6

Finally in this series came the Boulton and Paul P.6, numbered X25. Unlike the remainder of the X-series, however, this had the distinction of being a purely experimental aircraft, and therefore the earliest example of the special type of aircraft which form the main theme of this book. It was intended for full-scale aerodynamic research, especially in relation to the characteristics of aerofoil sections. Its design was quite simple and straightforward, much of the fuselage consisting of standard Sopwith Camel components. The power provided by its 90 hp R.A.F.1a engine was adequate for the purpose, and the 25 ft span single-bay wings were basically of R.A.F.15 section. Much research work was undertaken, and the experience gained proved invaluable in the design of the post-war P.9, of which about 20 were sold, helping to lay the foundations of what was to become a prominent company in the British aircraft industry.

After the war, the aircraft took on civil guise, first as K120, then later as G-EACJ.

The only example built of the Boulton & Paul P.6 prior to receiving civil markings. (Dowty Boulton Paul Ltd)

Chapter 2
RESEARCH AFTER THE FIRST WORLD WAR

During the four years of the First World War, the barriers of aeronautical research were of necessity pushed back considerably, so that those aircraft in use at its end were considerably more sophisticated than the stick and string designs which were in service at its beginning. Much was still to be learned, however, even about the basics, and the 1920s became a period of considerable experimentation, which manifested itself in many ways. This chapter deals with the efforts of three British manufacturers in this field, the last of which was destined to make a great impact on aviation all over the world.

ARMSTRONG WHITWORTH APE

Air Ministry Specification 48/22 called for a two-seater biplane to be used for aerodynamic experiments at the Royal Aircraft Establishment. It was thought by the boffins of the time that solutions might be found to some of the problems then confronting them if a machine could be

The second example of the rather ungainly Armstrong Whitworth Ape. Note the mechanism for changing the position of the empennage, and the elaborate landing gear. (via M.J. Hooks)

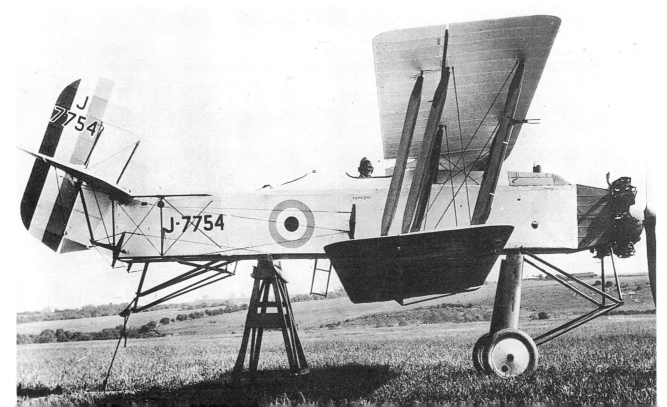

constructed in such a form as to be infinitely adjustable – variable geometry in modern parlance.

With not much enthusiasm, John Lloyd, the Chief Designer of Armstrong Whitworth, took on the task of producing three machines. His resulting design incorporated a fuselage of rectangular profile, untapered apart from the rear four feet. Of tubular steel construction, it could be extended by inserting up to four additional sections immediately aft of the rear cockpit. Two other sections could be inserted in the forward fuselage so that the engine could be moved forward to adjust the centre of gravity.

In addition, it was possible to fit three different sizes of tailplane and rudder in different positions, and the pilot had a lever in his cockpit with which he could alter the angle of incidence of the tailplane. No provision was made, however, for sweepback, nor for operating the machine as a monoplane. The possibility of heavy landings during experiments was taken into account by fitting an extremely large long-travel oleo undercarriage and a rather elaborate tailskid.

The first machine, J7753, made its initial flight on 5 January 1926, powered by a 215 hp Armstrong Siddeley Lynx III in place of the planned Viper. It reached Farnborough on 1 June, after evaluation by the manufacturers, but tests on control at low speeds proved unfruitful due to poor performance, which was not surprising in view of the low power provided by the specified engine. This aircraft crashed on take-off on 8 May 1928, but was rebuilt by the makers and re-engined with a 350 hp Jaguar III

before returning to Farnborough. The other two machines (J7754 and J7755) were both were delivered to Farnborough on 9 November 1926, but poor performance was still a problem, increased engine power having been counterbalanced by additional weight, and in any event both were soon lost in crashes.

BRISTOL 92

In 1923, Bristols were experiencing cooling difficulties with the Jupiter engines fitted to their Bullfinch, Badger and Type 62 Ten-seater aircraft. If the cylinders were left exposed they automatically received sufficient airflow to keep them cool, but paid a penalty in drag, which was becoming a significant factor as the speed of aircraft increased. Early attempts to produce some form of streamlining resulted in overheating.

Wind tunnel tests had been carried out on models, but Frank Barnwell, the firm's Chief Designer, considered that a full scale aircraft was required, and put forward a proposal to the Air Ministry. It was accepted that there was a case for such a machine, and a contract was awarded in April 1924 for a single aircraft. The design of the Type 92, as it became, was very soon under way, and as it was purely a research machine it was kept very basic. The slender high-mounted fuselage took the form of a rectan-

The Bristol 92 was specially built to overcome engine overheating problems. (via J.D.Oughton)

gular box of square cross-section tapering aft of the two cockpits to a horizontal knife edge rather like the Bristol Fighter, and on this was mounted an angular fin and rudder with a tailskid. At the front end of the fuselage there was provision for different circular fairings. The widely spaced wings were of rectangular shape, and under them were two main wheels mounted well outboard of the fuselage, directly underneath the two innermost of the four pairs of interplane struts.

The aircraft was ready for testing by 13 November 1925, having been fitted with a Jupiter VI on loan by the Air Ministry. Although it was allocated the constructor's sequence number 6920, it had not been given an RAF serial number. It was not eligible for a civil registration, and the system of allotting Class B registrations to manufacturer's experimental machines was not introduced until 1929, so it remained without any visible form of identification.

The original intention had been to have five different engine fairings, varying in size from 3 ft to 5 ft. Cost ruled this out in practice, however, and the Type 92 took to the air with a 3 ft fairing, it being generally referred to as the 'Laboratory' machine. A number of trial flights were made, and it was not until 1928 that a 5 ft engine fairing was fitted, but this had not been long installed when the undercarriage collapsed after landing at Filton. The expense of rebuilding the machine was considered unjustified, as by then the Townend ring had appeared on the scene to largely solve the drag and cooling problems the Type 92 had been designed to investigate, and in any case cylinder design had also improved.

The Handley Page H.P.17 was a surplus D.H.9 fitted with slats along the leading edges of the wings. The hastily rigged pitot head boom was fitted, presumably, to cater for the unusually slow speeds and high angles of attack. (via A. McMillin)

HANDLEY PAGE SLOTS

Wing design was early recognised as being one of the main keys to successful flying, as can be seen from articles and letters in contemporary aviation magazines. One of those who adopted a scientific approach to the problems involved, was Frederick Handley Page, who in April 1911 read to the Aeronautical Society of Great Britain, as it then was, a paper attempting to relate lift to the angle of incidence of a wing. It had been found that a wing of moderate aspect ratio (6.25:1) increased in lift up to about 10 degrees angle of attack before lift levelled off, whereas a square wing, with an aspect ratio of 1.0:1 could be inclined to about 40 degrees before this phenomenon occurred. He put forward the suggestion that high-pressure air escaping from beneath a high incidence wing was responsible for the loss of lift, as wind tunnel experiments had shown that as this air went past the trailing edge of the wing it was swept up into the suction area above the wing, creating an effect known as 'burbling'.

Handley Page continued his studies in this direction and, using a wind tunnel at his firm's Kingsbury works, he and his aerodynamicist R.O. Boswell developed the idea of building into a wing a full length slot along its leading edge to draw off some of the air which would have otherwise continued beneath the wing. The laboratory results were spectacular, lift being increased by between 25 and 50 per cent, depending on the wing section being tested, and the 'burbling' effect was delayed until reaching an angle of 25 degrees.

The great advantage of the Handley Page slot was that it smoothed out the airflow over the top of the wing and delayed the onset of 'burbling' and so allowed a greater angle of attack to be attained before the lift broke down completely as the aircraft stalled. Use of the slot on the outer sections of the wing therefore prevented the wing tips stalling first, which could cause the wing to drop and allow a spin to develop. Low speed flying was therefore made much safer and landing speeds could be safely reduced.

The newly-discovered principle was kept secret for a time, until patents had been taken out in both Great Britain and the United States, then in February 1920 the company bought a surplus D.H.9 biplane (H9140) for practical research into the subject. Both mainplanes were soon fitted with slats mounted ahead of the leading edges, the gap between wing and slat being covered with fabric which was then doped. On 31 March the machine took the air in this form for the first time, to begin a series of trials in each of which more of the doped fabric was removed.

These tests quickly demonstrated that the theory was well founded, the aircraft being able to land very slowly and very steeply by the time the last of the fabric strip was removed. After an official demonstration on 22 April the undercarriage height was raised by 12 inches to increase the angle of incidence. By August further patents had been taken out, covering control gear, slot mechanisms and multiple slots. The Air Ministry now began to take an interest, and trial flights were made with H9140 both at Farnborough and Gosport, as well as flying on and off the deck of the carrier HMS *Argus*, then anchored off Spithead. In January 1921 comparative tests were carried out at Farnborough between H9140 and a standard D.H.9 machine (D5755).

Meanwhile, for proposed trials on HMS *Eagle*, the Air Ministry agreed in late 1920 to pay for the cost of a D.H.9A (F1632) being fitted with slots and variable incidence, the new serial number J6906 being allotted. The firm could not manage this in the time-scale proposed, however, and instead suggested converting the aircraft to a thick-section high-wing monoplane. The resulting machine was given the company designation X.4B, it being later retrospectively styled H.P.20 under a standardised system of nomenclature by which H9140 became known as the H.P.17.

The squared-off cantilever wings of the X.4B were

The Handley Page H.P.20 was basically a D.H.9A fuselage fitted with a thick new high wing for slat trials. (via A. McMillin)

fitted with movable slats extending along the whole of the leading edge, these being connected to the ailerons so that the slats opened automatically when the ailerons were lowered. Still serialled F1632, initial trials with the slats sealed were undertaken between 24 February and 11 March 1921. By October the aircraft was ready to go to Farnborough for official trials, the fresh serial number J6914 being allotted, and Air Ministry Specification 13/21 issued. Unfortunately it made a heavy landing on its first flight there, a bottom longeron being cracked.

By now the basic principle had been proved, however. The firm incorporated slots in its Hanley and Hendon torpedo bombers, though neither of these gained contracts. The system was gradually improved throughout the decade, and from 1928 automatic leading-edge slots were installed as standard near the upper wing-tips of all RAF aircraft, with a consequent reduction in accidents. The air forces of many other countries soon followed this lead, and Handley Page slots became a universally accepted device.

As a postcript, Handley Page submitted a specially designed aircraft for a Safe Aircraft Competition promoted in America by the wealthy Guggenheim family. Designated H.P.39, it was later named Gugnunc, inspired by a catchword in the contemporary newspaper strip cartoon 'Pip, Squeak and Wilfred.' The aircraft took to the air on 27 April 1929 with the civil registration G-AACN, powered by a 155 hp Armstrong Siddeley Mongoose engine. Of sesquiplane configuration, it had a span of 40 ft, length was 26 ft 9 in, height 9 ft 5 in and wing area of 293 sq ft. To meet the requirements for a short landing and take-off, both upper and lower wings were fitted with full-span leading-edge

The Handley Page Gugnunc was an unsuccessful contender for the 1929 Guggenheim Competition for a safe aeroplane. (via A. McMillin)

The Gugnunc demonstrating why it should have won the competition! (via J.D. Oughton)

The Gugnunc at Mitchell Field in October 1929, now with revised engine cowling. (via J.D. Oughton)

slots and trailing-edge flaps. There were 27 entries for the competition, but only half of these began the official trials, of which only the Gugnunc and the Curtiss Tanager were eventually permitted to complete the safety tests. The $100,000 prize was awarded to the Tanager, which incorporated Handley Page slots – for which no permission had been given, nor royalties paid. To add insult to injury, Handley Page were not awarded the consolation 'Safety Prize' of $10,000, but they had the last laugh as the Tanager was burnt out on the ground soon afterwards, whereas the Gugnunc went on to be used at Farnborough for experimental work, with the serial number K1908, until being presented to the Science Museum in 1934. The machine remains in existence to this day, being now in that Museum's Air Transport Collection at Wroughton.

Chapter 3

CENTRAL ENGINE ROOMS

Shortly after the First World War, the Directorate of Research became interested in the possibilities of medium-sized aircraft powered from a central engine room, with the propellers mounted externally in the wings and driven by means of shafts and gears. The idea was evidently thought to have some merit, as three separate Specifications were drawn up, and contracts for prototype machines were awarded to three different firms: Boulton & Paul, Bristol and Parnall. The principal attraction of the concept was the avoidance of assymetric flying in the event of engine failure.

The first Specification, and in fact the first to be issued under the new post-war numbering system, was 1/20, which was officially described as being for a spares carrier, this being based on Specification D of R Type 11 issued under the old system. It was followed later in 1920 by Air Ministry Specifications 9/20 for a postal machine, and 11/20 for a military conversion.

BRISTOL TRAMP

The Bristol contribution stemmed from a line of research started by that firm's submission to the Air Board's Type VIII Specification for a bomber able to carry out retaliatory raids against Germany in response to Gotha raids on London. The first of three prototypes of the B.1 triplane, later named the Braemar, flew on 13 August 1918. The final machine was completed as a civilianised commercial aircraft and renamed the Pullman.

In the early post-war period Bristols had been looking into the possibility of fitting a flying boat version of this aircraft with 1,500 hp steam turbine engines. The Air Ministry would not agree to finance a full size machine, but did award a contract for two landplane machines, the so-called 'spares carriers'. These were named the Tramp, maker's Type number 37 being allotted under the retrospective post-war numbering system. Allotted serials J6912 and J6913, they were to cost £23,000 each, which included £7,500 for four 240 hp Siddeley Puma engines to be housed in a central engine room and driving two outboard tractor propellers through Siddeley-Deasy gearboxes and transmission shafts.

Laid down with respective constructor's numbers 5871 and 5872, both J6912 and J6913 were completed by the end of 1921. The wings had a span of 96 ft and an area of 2,284 sq ft, the length being 60 ft and height 20 ft. Empty weight was 12,809 lb and all-up they weighed 18,795 lb. Intended to have a crew of three, they never flew, due to insoluble problems with the transmission system, the clutches being particularly troublesome. Both machines found their way to Farnborough, where they were used as ground test rigs, and the steam turbine idea was abandoned. A projected commercial flying boat version, the Tramp Boat, or Bristol Type 44, received no official support, and never left the drawing board.

BOULTON & PAUL BODMIN

Meanwhile Specifications 9/20 and 11/20, both of which originated in Specification D of R Type 3, had produced the Boulton & Paul Bodmin and the Parnall Possum, both very similar in concept, and both designed in two versions to meet both Specifications. The Bodmin had maker's number P.12, and again two machines were ordered, to be given serial numbers J6910 and J6911. Power was provided by two 450 hp Napier Lion II engines mounted in tandem within the fuselage, and in this case each drove an outboard pair of tractor/pusher airscrews. This was

The second of two examples of the Bristol Tramp, neither of which ever took to the air. (via J.D.Oughton)

The second prototype of the Boulton & Paul Bodmin.

exactly the opposite arrangement to the Tramp, in which four engines drove only two propellers.

The Bodmin, which was initially to have been named the Bodeigre, was largely of metal construction, the fuselage having a length of 53 ft 4½ in, and the unstaggered wings being 1,204 sq ft in area with a span of 70 ft. The main undercarriage consisted of a central pair of main wheels, a smaller pair under the long nose, and a tail skid. The first machine, J6910, was completed as the civil or postal version, to meet Specification 9/20, and had its maiden flight in July 1922 at Norwich at the hands of Captain Frank Courtney, the firm's test pilot. It was flown until it suffered undercarriage failure while taxiing at Martlesham Heath in April 1924, following which it was soon scrapped. Its place was taken by J6911 which nominally met Specification 11/20 as the military version, but which did not fly until 8 July 1925, and which was put up for disposal only six months later.

The power arrangement was rather complex, with two engines driving four airscrews mounted between the wings in tandem, but this proved much more satisfactory than that of the Tramp. Each Lion drove a cross-shaft, which in turn drove an airscrew shaft, the front engine driving tractor airscrews and the rear engine driving pusher airscrews. Access was possible to both engines whilst in flight, and a single engine failure presented no problems as the aircraft was capable of flying on either engine. No rudder adjustment was necessary if one engine failed, and the pairs of airscrews rotated in opposite directions relative to each other, and also relative to the other pair, thus eliminating any problems which might have been caused by the slipstreams or torque. Horizontal streamlined ducted radiators were fitted around the forward driving shafts, and they were designed to be able to cope with possible tropical use.

Much thought was also given to other aspects of the design, especially reliability. For instance the gravity fuel tank was duplicated, and the main fuel tanks, which were mounted between the front and rear airscrews, were interconnected in such a way that each could be isolated independently. The engines were watched over in flight by a mechanic, effectively an early example of a Flight Engineer, who sat between them and was provided with all the equipment necessary for starting and controlling them. Empty weight was 7,920 lb and loaded it weighed 11,000 lb. Its top speed was 116 mph at sea level, the service ceiling was 16,000 ft and it took 8.9 minutes to climb to 6,500 ft.

PARNALL POSSUM

The third in this trio of aircraft, the Parnall Possum, although produced to the same two Air Ministry Specifications as the Bodmin, adopted a rather different format. Again, two prototypes were ordered, to be given serial numbers J6862 and J6863, but in this case a single 450 hp Napier Lion II engine was to power a triplane of somewhat smaller dimensions than the Bodmin, the length being 39 ft and the wings having a span of 46 ft and an area of 777 sq ft. The engine was housed around the centre of gravity, with the tops of the cylinder blocks exposed. The two airscrews, which counter-rotated and were driven by shafts concealed within the central wing, turned so slowly at cruising speed that the individual blades could be distinguished. Like the other two designs, a crew of three was carried. J6862 was first flown at Filton on 19 June 1923, but had several taxiing accidents before being scrapped in March 1925. J6863 was then completed, flying at Filton on 27 April 1925, but it was probably tested for the last time about a year later, at Martlesham Heath, by which time official interest in this concept was at an end.

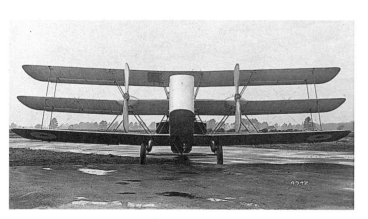

Several views of the second Parnall Possum, taken at Martlesham Heath early in 1926. The amidships position of the three-bank Napier Lion engine can clearly be seen.

Chapter 4
ALL-METAL CONSTRUCTION

Early attempts at building metal-framed aeroplanes had met with problems. The structure needed to be strong but light. The difficulty was that lightweight mild steel tubing was prone to buckling during ground handling. On the other hand the type of aluminium alloys available at that time could not be soldered or brazed, and soon became corroded. Frames were therefore of necessity largely wooden in construction. By the middle of the First World War, however, available stocks of the necessary

Grade A silver spruce were rapidly diminishing and, though undesirable, Grade B was often substituted where it was felt that there would be no great reduction in safety.

The first prototype of the metal-framed Bristol M.R.1 (A5177) showing clearly its unusually smooth construction method. Here it is seen fitted with the initial conventional wings. (via J.D. Oughton)

BRISTOL M.R.1

Around that time Bristols decided to tackle the problem of a two-seater reconnaissance aircraft operating primarily in tropical climates, where there was also likely to be limited enemy air opposition. Frank Barnwell, the Chief Designer, saw metal construction as the answer, and work commenced on the M.R.1, which was later given the type number 13.

This had a number of similarities with the famous Bristol Fighter, which was being developed around the same time, although the dimensions of the M.R.1 were a little larger. The fuselage comprised four sections, the first of which carried the engine and fuel tanks, the second the pilot, the third the observer and his Lewis gun on a Scarff ring, and finally a tapered boom to which the tail surfaces were attached. The machine could easily be built as a single-seater by omitting the third section.

A contract was awarded on 2 November 1916 for two machines, to be numbered A5177 and A5178, but these were only for evaluation and mechanical test. Due to the need to concentrate on planning production of the Bristol Fighter, Barnwell had to delegate the design to W.T. Reid. The fuselage was built of double-skinned duralumin, the inner skin being corrugated lengthways whilst the outer skin was smooth. Drawing on Barnwell's early experience in the ship-building industry, a protective top quality marine varnish was applied to reduce the risk of corrosion.

Wing design was a problem, the first attempt at a duralumin structure adapted from the normal wood techniques proving too flexible. The work was therefore sub-contracted to The Steel Wing Company of Gloucester, who had already produced wings made of rolled high-tensile steel strip for test on the Avro 504 and B.E.2d. This took time, however, and it was decided to fit the prototype with conventional wings of wooden construction for its initial tests and, with a 140 hp Hispano-Suiza engine, it flew suc-cessfully in the autumn of 1917, being handed over to the Air Board on 23 October.

The metal wings did not materialise until about a year later, and A5177 consequently did not fly until around the time of the Armistice, fitted with a 170 hp Wolseley Viper engine. It was the first aircraft of all-metal construction to be completed in Britain. On 19 April 1919 it was ferried to Farnborough by Captain Barnwell, but unfortunately he struck a tree on arrival, and the damage was found to be too great to be worth repair. In the meantime tests on the structure of A5178 continued, the machine being repainted with the spurious serial number 'A.58623', this being based on the fuselage component numbers, and a considerable amount of valuable data was obtained on the practicality of this form of construction.

SHORT COCKLE

Short Bros. was another firm taking an active interest in metal construction. Its Silver Streak biplane of 1920 pioneered metal structure and skinning, having a semi-monocoque duralumin fuselage and the wing construction comprising duralumin covered tubular steel spars.

The firm went on to produce a series of marine air-craft of metal construction, but in the immediate post-war period, the diminutive Short Cockle, or Type S.1 under their newly-introduced numbering system, laid claim to have been the first all-metal flying boat in the world. A single-seat machine, it was of high-wing layout, powered by two standard 697 cc Blackburne Tomtit modified motor-cycle engines. Due to centre of gravity considerations

The diminutive Short Cockle flying boat, fitted with the original V-twin Blackburne engines, on the Medway alongside the firm's Rochester works. (MAP)

these had to be mounted well back on the wings, the tractor propellers being driven directly through extension shafts and hand-started from a lever in the pilot's open cockpit.

The Cockle was originally to have been called the Stellite, being one of a pair of small experimental aircraft, its landplane equivalent being the Satellite, or S.4. The wings had a span of 36 ft and an area of 210 sq ft, overall length being 24 ft 8½ in and height 5 ft 8 in. Built at Rochester under constructor's number S.638, it was intended for delivery to Lebbeus Hordern, but never reached him.

Carrying civil registration G-EBKA, the aircraft was first tested by J. Lankester Parker on 18 September 1924 but, not surprisingly, proved to be underpowered at an all-up weight of 880 lb, and failed to get off. He eventually managed a straight flight on 17 October after wing incidence had been increased to 7 degrees. At take-off the indicated air speed was 27 mph, and its maximum speed in level flight was only 57 mph. Initial climb was of the order of 250 ft/min, and with a struggle it could on occasion climb above 2,000 ft – provided Parker first took off such unnecessary items as jacket and shoes.

Few problems were experienced with the metal structure, which showed no signs of leakage or corrosion. A new fin and rudder were fitted in January 1925, and two months later the Air Ministry decided to purchase it, under Contract No.572165/25, for trials at Felixstowe, the service number N193 being then applied. MAEE soon found that it was difficult for the weightier pilots to get it off the water unless they stripped down to bathing costumes, but once airborne it was able to achieve a fair amount of flying.

Power was increased in 1927 by fitting two 35 hp horizontally-opposed Bristol Cherub III engines, with which it flew extremely well from 14 June onwards, though with some loss of its former smoothness, its acceptance test being undertaken by Parker at Felixstowe on 3 October 1927. It was then relegated to corrosion exposure tests, following which it is believed to have ended its days as a ground instructional machine at Cranwell.

BEARDMORE INFLEXIBLE

At the other end of the scale, by 1923 the Air Ministry were taking an interest in the ideas of a German designer, Dr Adolf Röhrbach, for a large all-metal monoplane, and decided to place an order for a trials machine to be built under licence in the United Kingdom. Specification 18/23 was issued, and a contract placed with the large shipbuilding and engineering firm of Sir William Beardmore & Co. Ltd. at Dalmuir. Over the previous decade Beardmores had built a number of aircraft under sub-contract, as well as producing a series of abortive designs of their own, and the firm's interest in aircraft manufacture was maintained for a time in the early post-war years.

The design team was headed by W.S. Shackleton, and they had a difficult task, especially as Röhrbach withdrew his help after a disagreement, leaving them to finish his design unaided. Model tests in the Farnborough wind tunnel had shown the need for considerable modification to the original design, including enlargement of the control surfaces, which in turn brought a need for servo assistance and vibration dampers for the resulting larger rudder.

The machine was given the Type Number BeRo.1, and in December 1925 was allocated the civil registration

The all-metal Short Silver Streak soon after construction. (Short Bros & Harland Ltd)

The large Beardmore Inflexible seen at Martlesham Heath around the time of its first flight there in March 1928. The stability noted in tests may well have been induced in part by the substantial mainplane dihedral.

G-EBNG, though this in fact was never taken up. When it eventually emerged in 1928 it carried the military serial number J7557, and with a span of 157 ft 6 in was the largest aircraft in the world at that time, and also proved to be the largest British aircraft for many years to come. Power was provided by three 650 hp Rolls-Royce Condor engines, mounted one under each wing and one in the nose, each with an independent throttle. The aircraft was of stark appearance, with a rectangular section fuselage and rectangular wings and tail surfaces. It had a length of 75 ft 6 in, and the wings, which were mounted at the top of the fuselage, had an area of 1,967.25 sq ft. The two main Dunlop wheels had a diameter of 6 ft and were fitted with independently operated hydraulic brakes, which worked automatically as soon as the tailwheel touched down through a connection to a piston in the tailwheel bracket.

Construction took five years, and when the machine eventually emerged it had to be shipped from the Clyde in sections. From there it sailed to Felixstowe, where it was transported by road to Martlesham Heath, having its first flight there on 5 March 1928 in the hands of Squadron Leader J. Noakes. The RAE tests having indicated that the machine might be tail heavy, he allowed as much space as possible, starting his flight early in the morning from just inside the aerodrome boundary, but to his surprise it took to the air before he had reached the main aerodrome. Subsequent tests showed the machine to be quite stable, with very few vices, being described as 'a perfect lady'. Its only real fault was lack of sufficient power for its size, and at an all-up weight of 44,800 lb it could only achieve a top speed of 109 mph.

Trials were later made with Squadron Leader de Haga Haig at the controls, and the machine appeared at the annual RAF Display at Hendon in June of that year, bearing the New Types Park number '9', which it still carried when it showed up at air displays at Norwich and Cambridge the following summer. A number of modifications were made, but the weight of the structure was such that no military load could be carried. Soon afterwards the project was abandoned, and in January 1930 the engines were removed and the machine placed in storage, eventually being broken up.

BEARDMORE INVERNESS

Mention must also be made of another large Beardmore-Röhrbach all-metal design built to an Air Ministry order. This was a twin-engine flying boat, designated RoIV by its designer, but given the British designation BeRo.2. Under a contract awarded in November 1924 it was constructed at Dalmuir to Specification 20/24, being given the serial number N184, and was named the Inverness.

This too was a high wing monoplane, with a span of 93 ft 6 in and a loaded weight of 14,100 ft, being fitted with a hand rail to assist handling on the water. Power was provided by two 360 hp Rolls-Royce Eagle IX engines, but details of its performance appear not to have been published. The gestation period was only marginally less than that of its landplane counterpart, the first flight being made at Felixstowe on 30 November 1928. Tests had already been carried out there on an imported machine of the same type (N183), flown from Copenhagen on delivery on 18 September 1925 and also powered by two 450 hp Napier Lion V engines, but neither was considered a success, N184 being scrapped the following year.

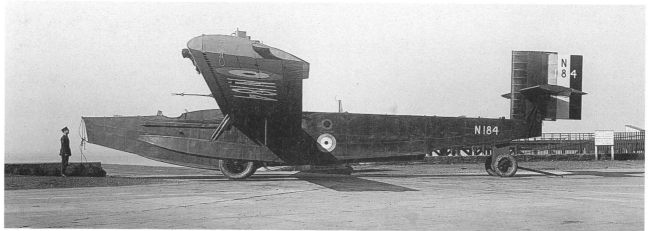

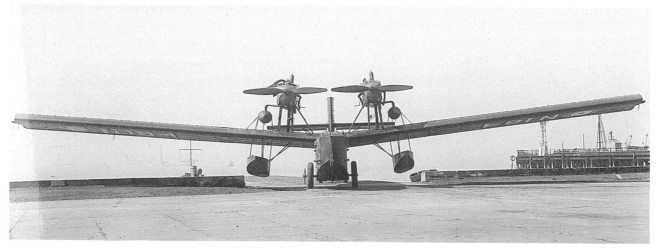

Several views of the Beardmore Inverness flying boat during trials at the Marine Aircraft Experimental Establishment at Felixstowe in early 1929.

Chapter 5

EARLY ROTORCRAFT

The early development of practical rotary wing flying in Britain is a complex story, characterised by different approaches to this aspect of flying, with the consequent production of a series of designs by different manufacturers.

The successful stage of the story effectively began with demonstrations of the Cierva C.6 autogyro at Farnborough in October 1925. Coincidentally, this was the same month in which the British-built Brennan helicopter crashed after some six years of trials and development, probably confirming the British authorities' view that the development of a practical helicopter was, for the time being, impossible, thus leaving the field clear for Cierva.

BRENNAN HELICOPTER

Louis Brennan was a noted inventor who had designed a successful torpedo. In 1916 he had interested the Ministry of Munitions in a helicopter proposal, but little progress had been made with this by the end of the First World War, and the project had passed to the Air Ministry in 1919.

Brennan's helicopter was a large machine with a two-bladed 62 ft rotor diameter and a massive 6 ft rotor chord. It was powered by a centrally placed 230 hp Bentley BR.2 rotary engine, driving two four-bladed propellers at the rotor tips. This complex layout proved very difficult to develop, and practical assistance was soon required from Armstrong Whitworth Aircraft personnel, as construction continued at the Royal Aircraft Establishment, Farnborough. Costs were also a matter of continuous concern. Louis Brennan has been described as 'imperious', and personal relationships, particularly over finance, were seldom good in the project team.

Engine runs commenced in November 1921, and in March 1922 the machine lifted its pilot plus four men during indoor trials inside the balloon shed at Farnborough. It was not until May 1924, however, that control problems had been overcome to the stage where the helicopter could be moved into the open. During the next 18 months it made around 200 'flights', but never went more than eight feet off the ground, and the longest flight was only about 600 yards. An estimated £55,000 had been spent on the project up to 2 October 1925, when disaster struck on a demonstration flight. The machine crashed and was damaged to the point where the project was finally abandoned.

CIERVA BRITISH AUTOGYROS

Señor Cierva's rotary-wing experiments had commenced in his native Spain in 1920, and the Cierva C.6 was his first practical design. In 1925 he was invited to England by the Director of Scientific Research at Farnborough, H.E. Wimperis, and, uniquely, an Air Ministry Specification (14/25) was issued for a 'Demonstration Flight of La Cierva Autogyro', presumably to cover the cost of transportation and other related expenses.

There is some doubt as to the correct designation of the actual aircraft brought to Farnborough by Cierva, but it is generally supposed to have been C.6A. A second machine remained in Spain and is believed to have been designated C.6B. Both were based on an Avro 540K fuselage.

The autogyro concept of Juan de la Cierva was an attempt to overcome the gyroscopic effects of a rotor driven by engine power (as in the case of the helicopter), by the substitution of a freely rotating rotor for lift, with forward speed being provided by a separate tractor

Two views of the Brennan Helicopter, showing it with and without cockpit, rudder and 'gear'. (via Eric Myall)

propeller driven by a forward mounted engine. This is a simplified description of a complicated process; the solution of the many associated problems involved in progress towards practical rotary-wing flight is a tribute to the perseverance and immense practical engineering ability of Cierva.

The demonstrations of Cierva's C.6 were most successful, being soon followed by the issue of two further Specifications, for the construction of autogyros in this country. The first of these, 3/26, covered a 'Gyroplane with Clerget engine', and 4/26 covered a 'Light Gyroplane with Armstrong Siddeley Genet engine'. Meanwhile the original C.6 brought to England from Spain had crashed twice and was written-off in the second of these, but this had no detrimental effect on the programme.

The first Specification produced two autogyros built by Avros at Hamble under licence from Cierva; one military and one civil machine, reflecting the dual responsibilities of the Air Ministry at that time for both military and civil aviation. The serial J8068 was given to the Cierva C.6C, while the similar civil aircraft was designated C.6D and received the civil registration G-EBTW, Avro designations being respectively 574 and 575. J8068 crashed at Hamble on 7 February 1927, having first flown some eight months earlier on 19 June 1926. The C.6D flew shortly afterwards on 29 July.

The second 1926 Specification was met by the Avro Type 576/Cierva C.9, to which the serial J8931 was applied. Built under Contract number 698108/26, this first flew in September 1927 and was tested at Farnborough for at least a year, finally being withdrawn from use in 1930.

A further Cierva-designed autogyro with a Genet engine also appeared, but this time manufactured by George Parnall & Co of Yate. Designated C.10, it was allocated the serial J9038, being completed in January 1927. It suffered some damage when it blew over during taxiing at Yate on 26 April 1928, then was more substantially damaged when it again overturned on attempting its ini-

tial flight at Andover on 5 November 1928, never being rebuilt.

Meanwhile a further Specification was issued (11/26) for a two-seat autogyro with a 180 hp Armstrong Siddeley Lynx engine. This produced another Avro design (Type 611) with Cierva designation C.8L-I, which initially incorporated the rudder from J8068, although the aircraft was given serial number J8930. Flown for the first time in the summer of 1927, J8930 was delivered to Farnborough on 30 September 1927 and remained there for about three years. It crashed at Andover in May 1930.

The sequence of serial allocation of these early autogyros is somewhat puzzling, as the proximity of J8930/J8931 belies the fact that they were allocated to Specifications issued in 1926 and 1927 respectively. Simi-

Señor Juan de la Cierva and his model C.6C autogiro, shortly before it crashed at Farnborough in September 1926.

This view of the Cierva C.6C, here being displayed at Farnborough by Frank Courtney on 10 October 1925, clearly shows the Avro 504K fuselage on which it was based. (via J.D. Oughton)

larly, the Parnall/Cierva C.10 had a Genet engine and was produced under contract 642578/25 in response to Specification 4/26, but bears a serial (J9038) issued much later than the comparable Avro design.

Autogyro design continued at a rapid pace in the late 1920s, and the first production autogyro was Cierva's C.19 design (Avro Type 620), which first flew in July 1929 with a 80 hp Genet II engine, later machines being fitted with a 100 hp Genet Major I. To continue military interest in

the development of the autogyro, two examples of the C.19 Mark III were purchased by the Air Ministry, these being K1696 (ex G-AAYO) and K1948 (ex G-ABCM) taken on charge for tests at the Royal Aircraft Establishment at Farnborough in late 1930. K1696 had a comparatively short service life, having had a forced landing on Laffans Plain on 10 September 1930 and being struck off charge on 21 February 1931. But K1948 survived until also being struck off charge on 14 March 1934.

All of the foregoing machines may be regarded as experimental, given the state of the art of rotary wing flying

The Cierva C.8L J8930, fitted with the rudder from the ill-fated C.6C J8068. (T. Taylor collection via M. Stroud)

A flying shot of Cierva C.8L J8930. (T. Taylor collection via M. Stroud)

at that time. While the occasional crash or two curtailed some of the test flying, the slow-speed characteristics of these early autogyros were such that repairs were fairly easily effected. Military interest remained high and led to the issue of two further Specifications in the mid-1930s. These were 16/35 and 2/36, and covered the Cierva Rota I and II. They were given the Cierva designations C.30 and C.40 respectively, but while the C.30 was primarily a civil design of which the Rota I was a variant, the C.40 (or Rota II) was more orientated to the military requirements of the Royal Air Force. Eventually all the C.40s were acquired by the RAF, though by then the country was at war and any civil aspirations of the Cierva company towards the C.40 had been stifled for various reasons.

The C.40 was the culmination of Cierva's lengthy experiments in autogyro development, and possessed a jump-start capability which almost matched the vertical take-off ability of the true helicopter. It was fitted with a 180 hp Salmson engine and had an enclosed cabin. Sadly, Cierva was not there to see this achievement, as he died in a take-off crash of a K.L.M. DC-2 in fog at Croydon on 9 December 1936. Cierva remained convinced, until his

The Avro-built Cierva C.9. (via P.W. Brooks)

The short-lived Parnall-built Cierva C.10 shortly before its attempted first flight.

The Cierva C.10 after coming to grief on 26 April 1928.

Cierva C.19 MkIII K1696 bedecked in dragon markings for the Hendon Display in June 1932. (RAF Museum P101297)

Avro-built Cierva C.30A G-ACXR bearing a sherry advertisement. (RAF Museum)

death, that the autogyro could be refined and improved to the point where it could undertake all the tasks of a helicopter but would do so without requiring the latter's complexity or cost. With Cierva's death, however, a change of emphasis in British rotary-wing development inevitably came about, and two other designers came into prominence.

ISACCO HELICOGYRE

Senor Cierva's efforts were not the sole manifestation of continuing Air Ministry interest in the future prospects of rotorcraft. In 1928 it placed an order for a version of the autogyro designed by an Italian, Vittorio Isacco, which he named the Helicogyre. Isacco, who since 1917 had devoted himself entirely to solving the problems of practical helicopter flight, had already constructed two of these machines in France, though neither machine No.1 or No.2, had proved very successful. The British order for machine No.3 came whilst the second of these was still under test, and followed basically the same concept, but with some modifications.

His designs consisted of a fairly normal fuselage, complete with tailplane, fin and rudder, and fitted with two main wheels and a tailskid. Forward propulsion was provided by a medium-powered engine, but for lift he fitted a smaller engine to the ends of each of four large rectangular shaped rotor blades, describing this as the 'sustain-

The Hafner A.R.III gyroplane (G-ADMV), complete with inevitable small boy! (M.J. Hooks)

The Cierva C.40 Rota II was fitted with a partially enclosed cabin. (RAF Museum P.104637)

ing system'. Each blade had an aileron fitted in its trailing edge, enabling the pilot to control incidence and therefore be able to adapt the machine to different flight conditions. To reduce the risk of the aircraft's overturning, the rotors were articulated at the hub, this also serving to avoid rotor damage during transition. By doing away with the need for a rotor transmission system, Isacco sought appreciable weight savings, which he calculated would more than offset the total weight of the four small engines.

Construction of the British machine was covered by Specification number 2/28, and was entrusted to S.E. Saunders Ltd at East Cowes, Isle of Wight, this company being renamed Saunders-Roe Ltd before the machine was completed. Changes from the first two machines included fitting a passenger seat, and providing an auxiliary control rotor with four flaps, this being attached rigidly to a longer hub to improve lateral control. The forward propulsion engine in this case was a 100 hp Armstrong Siddeley Genet, and the rotor engines were 35 hp Bristol Cherubs, though the latter were unsuited to this task.

The completed machine, which was allocated the serial number K1171, had a maximum weight of 2,920 lb, its fuselage length being 28 ft 4 in, and the rotor diameter 48 ft 2 in. On testing, trouble was soon experienced with the rotor motors, the Cherubs being badly affected with

Above: **The Weir W.1, which also had the Cierva type number C.28. (via Eric Myall)**

Below: **A fine 'period' photograph of the Weir W.2, fitted with a geared ABC engine. (RAF Museum)**

the centrifugal forces, which starved the inner cylinders of oil whilst choking up the outer ones. The Saro engineers never really overcame this problem, but they made a number of modifications which improved matters sufficiently for the engines to be run for short periods. The machine was then sent to Farnborough for ground testing inside a balloon shed. There were, however, some misgivings about the effect of one of the rotor engines failing, especially if it should shed one of its components in the process, with possible lethal results to anyone standing nearby.

The tests were never completed, in fact, the machine being destroyed due to a worker failing to release one of the four rotors from a wire attached to the ground at the moment the rotation had to start. No.3 was broken up without any attempt to rebuild it. Isacco continued his researches, however, his No.4 machine being built and tested for the Soviet Government between 1932 and 1936, after which he concentrated for seven years on developing a rotating-wing parachute whose design won the technical approval of the British Government in 1936, but was

The Weir W.2 in flight. (RAF Museum P.102085)

Starboard ground view of the Weir W.3. (RAF Museum)

subsequently tested in model form in Paris during the German occupation. After the liberation he was called to England to develop the concept, the work of developing and testing models being entrusted to the firm of Bevan Brothers of Rettendon Common, near Chelmsford, lorry tests being carried out at Boreham aerodrome on 15 April 1947. Around that time Isacco was also engaged in work on a projected jet-powered Helicogyre No.5, or Jetcopter, which had the technical approval of both the French and British Governments, the latter formulating Specification E.1/48 for a proposed machine fitted a small jet at each rotor tip, to have been built by Bevan Brothers. Nothing came of this, however, nor of plans for much larger commercial machines.

EARLY HAFNER HELICOPTERS

Raoul Hafner had experimented with helicopters in his native Austria, where he produced his R.I and R.II Helicopter Revoplane models, and also a design study for the R.III with two contra-rotating rotors. In 1932 he moved to England, taking his R.II with him for use as a rotor test rig. He learned to fly the Cierva C.19 and C.30, and is believed to have had permission from Señor Cierva to make use of the latter's patents.

His first 'British' design was an autogyro, the A.R.III

The Weir W.3 was fitted with a two-blade jump take-off rotor. (RAF Museum)

(A.R. = Auto Rotation). Only one machine was built, being designed at Hanworth by A.R.III Construction (Hafner Gyroplane) Ltd and built by Martin-Baker Aircraft Ltd of Denham. Bearing the civil registration G-ADMV, it was first flown at Heston in September 1935, powered by a 80 hp Pobjoy Cataract engine. It had a fuselage length of 17 ft 10 in, and a rotor diameter of 32 ft 10 in. It was similar in layout to the 'classic' Cierva design, but with significantly different rotor-head control features. Following a landing accident at Farnborough, it was rebuilt as the MkII version, being first flown on 6 February 1937 refitted with a 95 hp Pobjoy Niagara III. It was flown for some time at Farnborough, being given the military serial number DG670 in April 1941, but was struck off charge on 11 April 1942, following the last of several accidents.

Specification S.29/37 was issued in 1937 for some kind of Hafner Gyroplane for the Fleet Air Arm, being possibly a derivative of the A.R.III. The designation A.R.9 has been suggested for this, though it may not be correct, and in any event nothing came of the proposal.

WEIR AUTOGYROS AND HELICOPTERS

Scotland became increasingly involved in the pre-war British rotary-wing scene when the Weir organisation, which already had a controlling financial interest in the Cierva company, established their own design and production facility. Between 1933 and 1937 four autogyro designs were turned out, designated the W.1, W.2, W.3 and W.4. However, Weirs were not entirely happy with Cierva's contention that

the autogyro would be the only practical method of rotary wing flight, and in December 1937 decided to embark on a programme of helicopter design and construction.

The first to be produced were a small single-seat helicopter, the W.5, and a two-seater machine, the W.6, both of which had twin side-by-side rotors and were flown successfully. The W.5, which had a 50 hp Weir engine, was the first British helicopter to fly successfully, on 6 June 1938, two years ahead of the American Sikorsky VS-300, and was given the wartime designation Experimental Aeroplane No.116. The W.6 first flew on 27 October 1939 with a 205

The Weir W.4 was wrecked on the ground before it could make its first flight. (via Eric Myall)

The Weir W.5 had twin rotors powered by a single engine. (via M.J. Hooks)

hp de Havilland Gipsy Six II engine, and had the wartime designation Experimental Aeroplane No.119, the serial R5269 being allocated to it. Purchased under contract B.968953/38, R5269 eventually went into storage at Weirs on 12 March 1941, being transferred to Cierva at Southampton for further storage until being struck off charge on 3 November 1949. A proposed wartime W.8 project would have had a similar engine, but was a quite different design, being in effect a forerunner of the post-war W.9 with reactive jet torque control (see Chapter 26).

The W.2 has survived and is currently in the Museum of Flight at East Fortune, Lothian.

LATE PRE-WAR ROTORCRAFT
During the late thirties, the Air Ministry issued a flurry of Specifications for rotary-wing designs. The first of these was 43/36 for a 'Gyroplane for the Fleet Air Arm'. This followed naval interest in the fleet-shadowing and convoy protection capabilities of the autogyro, which manifested

itself in extensive trials on the Cierva C.40/Rota II during 1939. This particular Specification did not apparently result in specific projects, although it was very likely aimed at a development of the C.40, and was probably 'lost' in the events leading up to the transfer of naval aviation from the Royal Air Force to the Fleet Air Arm. Another possible contender for this abortive Specification, incidentally, was David Kay, another pre-war Scottish designer of gyroplanes and helicopters, only two of whose designs were actually built.

Specification S.22/38, which covered an 'Experimental Rotating Wing Aircraft' and was issued on 20 March 1939, appears, however, to have superseded 43/36, and both Cierva and Hafner were requested to produce designs. In addition, Weirs produced the W-7 design based on the W.6 and, interestingly, Fairey also did some project design work on this Specification. Finally, in 1939, Specification 10/39 was issued to Hafner to cover his P.D.6 helicopter (P.D. = Power Driven).

The Chief Designer at Ciervas was, by this time, Dr

The Weir W.6 was a larger machine which developed the twin-rotor concept. (via M.J. Hooks)

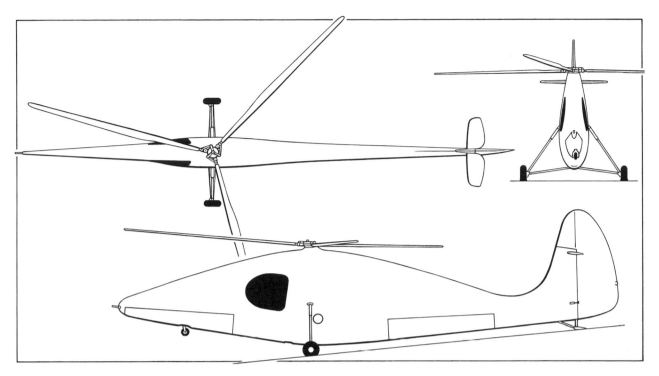

Three-view of the Hafner P.D.6, the Wellsian shape of which, it was hoped, would overcome the torque of the power-driven rotors.

Three-view of the Hafner A.R.VG, the last autogyro from this fertile mind.

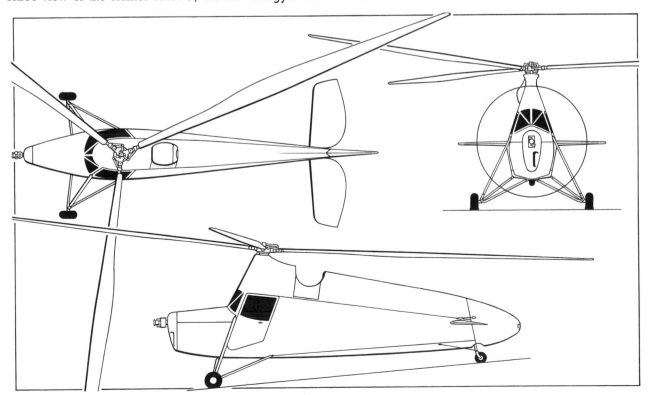

The unsuccessful Isacco Helicogyre. (via Eric Myall)

J.A.J. Bennett, and although Cierva's put forward an autogyro solution to this Specification (allegedly designated C.39), Dr Bennett had begun to think along the lines of a convertiplane approach to the subject. Consequently the firm also put forward a design which he called 'Gyrodyne', to which the Cierva designation C.41 may have been applied, both of these machines being planned around a 600 hp Rolls-Royce Kestrel engine.

Hafner's response to this Specification was designated A.R.V and was a continuation of his work on autogyros, although, as can be seen, his earlier interest in helicopters had manifested itself by 1939 when Specification 10/39 was issued.

The Hafner P.D.6 was a unique approach to the solution of 'helicopter' problems, whereby the aircraft's fuselage was shaped like an aerofoil, thus counteracting the torque effects of the power-driven main rotor. The serial T3005 was allocated to the P.D.6, which was purchased under contract 972107/38, and serials V8906 and V8909 to the A.R.V prototypes which were ordered under contract 541316.

Cierva's autogyro design to Specification S.22/38 may have been allocated the serials P9635 and P9636, which were issued for two direct take-off machines ordered under contract 968954/38, although one of these numbers finally appeared on one of their ex-civil C.40/Rota IIs. The position is far from clear, but the Air Ministry were cer-

tainly minded to order two additional C.40's in 1939, to incorporate certain unspecified improvements/modifications from the production batch of five machines ordered against Specification 2/36. No serial allocation can be traced for Cierva's 'Gyrodyne' machine.

Within a short period after the outbreak of war, however, this significant programme had collapsed. Ciervas never really recovered from the early death of Juan de la Cierva, while Weirs seemed to have lost interest in the Cierva company, both technically and financially. In 1940 Weir's ceased all development of their helicopters, claiming that the company's resources should be put to better use in the war effort. Raoul Hafner was interned as an alien, and his intended association with Pobjoy Aero Engines was cancelled, bringing the preliminary production of machines at Rochester to an end.

This association had been promoted by the Air Ministry to put sufficient resources behind Hafner, whose A.R.III Construction company had run on a very tight financial rein. Similarly, David Kay had been advised that no Ministry support would be forthcoming unless he could find major financial/technical backing. An attempt to form the Scottish Aircraft Manufacturing Co in the late 1930s was abortive, and there the matter rested.

Hafner was soon to be released and continue his activities at the Airborne Forces Experimental Establishment, but it was not until 1943 that Cierva/Weir again became active in the rotary-wing field.

Chapter 6
FLYING WINGS AND THINGS

Aircraft development in the United Kingdom during the First World War had largely concentrated on biplane construction. This was partly due to an unfortunate series of accidents to early military monoplanes, which had engendered distrust of this configuration, but mainly due to the fact that the biplane was considered the most suitable for wartime mass production. Two separated wings connected by interplane struts, and strengthened by internal and external wiring, resulted in a light but strong structure which was adequate for the speeds and stresses likely to be met at that stage of evolution. Post-war needs were likely to be much different from those of the four years of conflict, and research was now necessary to meet future requirements.

WESTLAND DREADNOUGHT
One idea which interested the Air Ministry's Directorate of Technical Development was that of a Russian inventor, Voyovodsky, who proposed a single deep aerofoil section incorporating both the fuselage and the wings: in effect a very early flying wing concept. Not only would the upper wing be abolished, but there would be no external bracing, the thickness of the wings allowing this to be provided internally.

The Directorate gave serious thought to the proposition, and early in 1921 issued Specification number 6/21 for a mail-carrying machine based on this configuration. Various proposals were made, and extensive wind tunnel tests were carried out, which suggested that the best layout should have 69 ft 6 in span wings fitted with two engines, the undercarriage to be retractable. Wing area would be 840 sq ft and length 56 ft.

The Specification was updated in mid 1922 as number 29/22, and on 13 January 1923 contract No 382430/23 was awarded to Westlands for the construction of a single development machine on these lines, to be given serial number J6986. As work progressed it was decided to replace the twin engines with a single nose-mounted Napier Lion II giving 450 hp, and the retractable undercarriage gave way to the more normal fixed chassis.

Advanced construction techniques were employed, including drawn metal panelling and corrugated metal panels, anticipating the later standard stressed skin construction. The wing, which had a root chord of 18 ft and was the first of its type to be constructed by a British manufacturer, was of multi-spar design of fabric-covered metal construction, incorporating early Frise-type ailerons. Each of the two wing roots incorporated four rectangular windows and could accommodate five passengers, two circular windows being also incorporated above the centre of the fuselage.

Work progressed well in the firm's shop, which had previously been used to construct Vickers Vimy bombers under sub-contract, and the aircraft was rolled out in late April 1924. The futuristic shape seemed attractive for that period, and taxiing trials by Captain Stuart Keep attracted considerable interest. On occasion the machine was briefly airborne for a few yards, and the omens seemed good.

In the afternoon of 9 May, Keep took her off smoothly and all appeared to be going well, when suddenly the machine went out of control whilst near the factory buildings. It stalled from a height of 100 feet , and as it struck the ground squarely the cockpit section broke away. The pilot was seriously injured, losing both legs, though he survived to continue with a technical and advisory career in the aviation industry.

The aircraft was evidently ahead of its time, but the

Above: The Westland Dreadnought seen before its dis-astrous attempt at a maiden flight in May 1923. (via M.J. Hooks)

Below: The unmarked Hill Pterodactyl prototype seen early in 1926, fitted with underwing rudders.

Directorate lost interest in pursuing the concept and in trying to overcome the practical aerodynamic problems involved.

THE PTERODACTYLS

Westland also became involved in a series of experiments which followed on from the ideas of John W. Dunne who in the early years of this century had built a series of tailless gliders and powered machines in an attempt to produce an inherently stable layout for a fixed wing aeroplane. Such a machine would in theory be controllable even below stalling speed, and therefore not be subject to the fatal spins which were then only too common. His designs adopted a V-shaped wing configuration, extending fore and aft of the centre of gravity.

The First World War put an end to Dunne's experiments, but when peace returned the concept was taken up by Captain (later Professor) Geoffrey Hill, his first attempt being a tailless monoplane glider which flew in December 1924. In place of the usual control surfaces, the outer 7 ft 6 ins of the wings acted as 'controllers' – elevons in modern parlance. Operated in unison they worked as elevators, or if used differentially they became ailerons. Some distance inboard of each controller was mounted a small rudder beneath the wing acting slightly out of unison, so that they could provide yaw by inducing drag on the inner one but inhibit it on the other. This novel form of control led to the aircraft being named Pterodactyl after the prehistoric flying reptile.

The successful flights showed that the machine had sufficient promise for the Air Ministry to take an interest in possible military applications. With this official support,

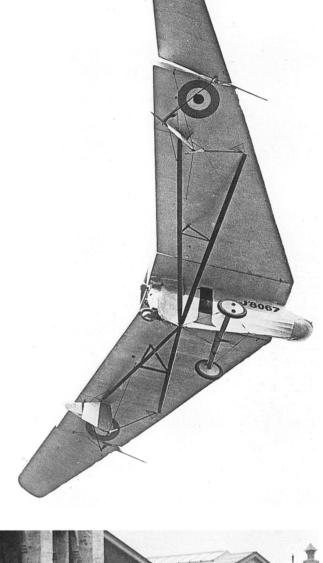

Right: **A flying shot of the Hill Pterodactyl, bearing New Types No.1 for its appearance in the 1926 RAF Display at Hendon. (via M.J. Hooks)**

Westland-Hill Pterodactyl J9251 in its Mk. IB form. (via M.J. Hooks)

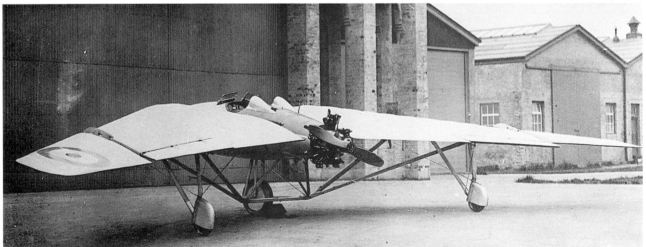

the machine was given serial number J8067 and fitted with a 35 hp Bristol Cherub III motor driving a pusher propeller. In this configuration it was assembled at Farnborough, where taxiing trials were carried out on 28 October 1925, followed by its first flight on 2 November. The powered machine was later demonstrated before the then Secretary of State for Air, Sir Samuel Hoare, and also appeared at the RAF Display at Hendon on 3 July 1926, bearing the New Types Park number '1'. It was eventually presented to the Science Museum in Kensington, to be preserved for posterity, and can still be seen there.

If the line of research was to be pursued further, proper design and manufacturing facilities would be necessary, and Hill was therefore invited to join the staff

Westland-Hill Pterodactyl J9251 in its final form as the Mk IC. (via P. Jarrett)

The Westland-Hill Pterodactyl IV featured an enclosed cabin. (Westland Helicopters Ltd)

The Westland-Hill Pterodactyl V open-cockpit two-seat fighter.

of Westlands. Air Ministry Specification 23/26 was then drawn up, and in 1927 the firm received a contract for a new machine for research purposes, to carry serial number J9251. Known as the Westland-Hill Pterodactyl IA, it was again to be powered initially by a Cherub III engine, but a number of changes were made to the design. The fuselage would accommodate a crew of two in side-by-side seating, and a form of tricycle undercarriage was fitted, with a large nose-wheel under the centre fuselage and faired balancing wheels situated half way along each wing, all on struts. The underwing rudders gave way to double-split trailing-edge flaps, then referred to as 'electroscopic rudders' by analogy with the gold leaf electroscope used to detect electricity. If used together they acted as air brakes, but if used differentially provided directional control. Overall length was 17 ft and span was 45 ft 6 in.

The machine was taken to Andover for trials, and the first flight was made there in June 1928. Its novel controls took a little mastering, but otherwise it proved fairly easy to fly. Power was increased by fitting a 70 hp Armstrong Siddeley Genet II engine, and in this form it became the Pterodactyl IB. The single main wheel showed its shortcoming when it collapsed after a rather heavy landing, and it was then replaced by two central main wheels in tandem, the forward wheel being steerable, a feature which was

continued on later machines. With this modification it became the Pterodactyl IC, making its last flight from Farnborough on 31 July 1930.

It had become apparent that heavier machines were a practicable proposition, and Westlands then proposed two fighter versions of the concept. The Mks II and III would both have had a gull-winged configuration, but whilst the MkII continued the pusher engine tradition, the MkIII was to have been the first with a tractor engine. Their hopes were unfulfilled however, the Air Ministry believing that such an advance was too great at that stage of development.

Instead a further research machine was contemplated. Specification 16/29 was issued towards the end of 1929, resulting the following year in a contract for a larger machine, to be given serial number K1947 and named the Westland-Hill Pterodactyl IV. The cabin was now to be fitted with an enclosed cockpit, with the crew of two seated ahead of an inverted pusher 120 hp de Havilland Gipsy III engine.

The wings were high-set and were effectively of variable geometry, it being possible by means of a special gear to alter their sweep angle by a range of $4\frac{3}{4}$ degrees. This facility enabled the aircraft to be flown without difficulty as either a single-seater or a two-seater. Alterations could be made in flight, and it enabled the aircraft to be trimmed when different loadings affected the position of the centre of gravity. The wings were of wooden construction, and

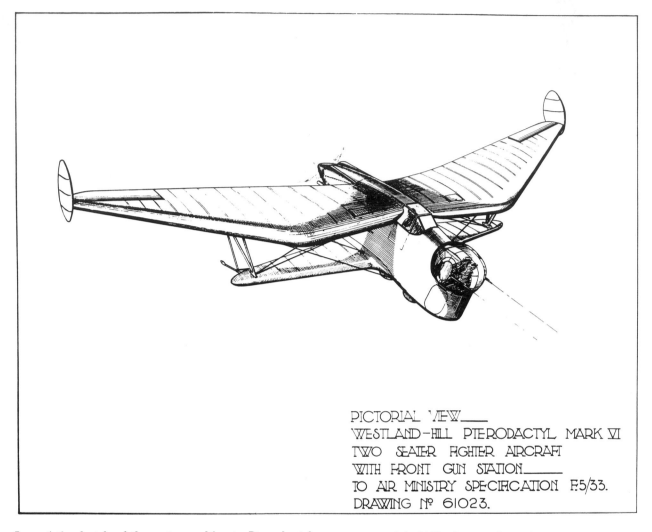

PICTORIAL VIEW____
WESTLAND-HILL PTERODACTYL MARK VI
TWO SEATER FIGHTER AIRCRAFT
WITH FRONT GUN STATION____
TO AIR MINISTRY SPECIFICATION F.5/33.
DRAWING № 61023.

An artist's sketch of the antepenultimate Pterodactyl, the MkVI.

the wingtip controllers were replaced by true elevons fitted in the outer portions of the trailing edges. The undercarriage consisted of two central tandem wheels, with outer support being provided by skids mounted on fabric covered V-struts.

K1947 was first flown by Louis Paget in March 1931, and proved to be an advance on the earlier versions, the only significant problem being in yaw control. This was cured by replacing the trailing-edge flaps and fitting an elliptical rudder at each wingtip. The machine now became very manoeuvrable, and frequently performed aerobatics, including spins. For the 1932 RAF Display it was programmed as 'Terror MkI' and adorned with a startling sharks-teeth colour scheme, 'Terror MkII' being a similarly adorned Hawker Hart. Piloted by George Stainforth, who shortly afterwards gained the world's air speed record in a Supermarine S.6B seaplane, the Pterodactyl joined in repeated attacks against barrage balloons made up to resemble striped hippopotamuses. It was eventually

scrapped in 1938 after much testing.

The last of the line to materialise was the Pterodactyl V. This time Westlands were allowed to produce a two-seat fighter, albeit an experimental one, and Specification F.3/32 was drawn up for the purpose. Allocated serial number K2770, it generally carried the Class B registration P8 and was bigger and much heavier than its predecessors. For the first time a tractor engine was fitted at the front of the fuselage nacelle, in this instance a 600 hp steam-cooled Rolls-Royce Goshawk driving a two-bladed propeller. At the rear of the nacelle were two open cockpits, one for the pilot, who could operate two synchronised Vickers guns, and behind him one for the gunner, fitted to carry an electrically operated turret fitted with one or two Lewis guns.

The main wing, which was raised above the nacelle on struts, was rather different in shape from earlier Pterodactyls, the centre section having a straight forward edge, with the outer panels being swept back at an angle of 42.5 degrees. The trailing edges were swept from the centre at a lesser angle, and the usual elevons were fitted, as were an elliptical rudder at each wing tip. In addition,

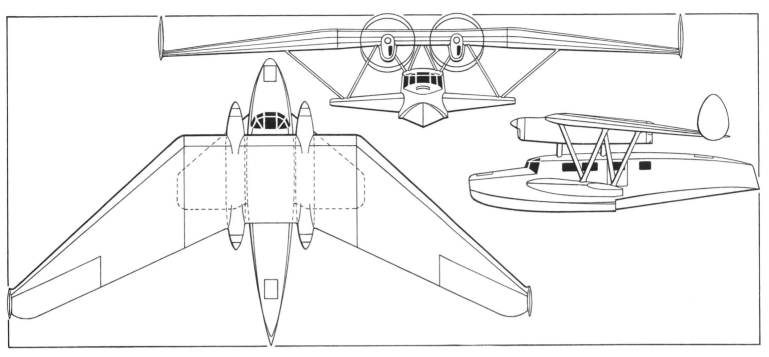

A three-view of the Pterodactyl MkVII which was to have been a tailless flying boat fitted with four engines.

two stub wings were attached to the nacelle sides immediately below the pilot, turning the aircraft into a sesquiplane. Interplane N-struts were extended downwards to form an undercarriage with two supporting skids, one under each wing, the main undercarriage consisting of the now usual two tandem wheels, in this case half buried in the nacelle, the front one being steerable and the rear one fitted with brakes.

By February 1933 the aircraft was ready at Yeovil for taxiing trials. It was then partially dismantled and taken to Andover by road for its first flight. After reassembly, however, it was given a further taxiing trial, when the port outer wing suddenly collapsed. Investigation revealed that the slide rule calculations had erred, and the interplane struts were insufficiently stressed for the upward load imposed on the ground by the balancing skids. Correcting the fault occupied more than a year, so that it was not until May 1934 that the machine returned to Andover for another attempt. Five taxiing runs were safely achieved before Harald Penrose took off for the delayed first flight, which lasted 20 minutes.

Whilst the aircraft was not without promise, there were evidently a number of problems to be overcome, not least with the engine. The Goshawk turned out to be something

of a disaster, its steam cooling system, which worked by evaporation, being very unreliable, and only a small number were built before production was stopped. The engine also gave rise to ground handling problems due to its torque, and these were never really overcome, despite alteration to the undercarriage, including offsetting the main wheels and fitting small outer wheels to the balancing skids. Various other modifications were tried, mainly to the wings, these including enlarged wingtip rudders incorporating fins, and additional fins underneath the wings, inboard of the elevons.

Around this time, Geoffrey Hill left Westlands to take up the Kennedy Chair of Engineering Science at the University of London. After curing most of its faults the Pterodactyl V went to Farnborough for evaluation, but it was not considered sufficiently advanced in comparison with other designs by then on the drawing board.

Three further Pterodactyls were contemplated, but came to nothing. The MkVI, designed to meet Specification F.5/33, would have been very similar to the MkV, but with a pusher engine and a nose turret, being intended to act as forward escort for bombers, in conjunction with the MkV acting as rear escort. The MkVII would have been a tailless flying boat fitted with four Gipsy Six engines in tandem, to which outline Specification 1/33 was drawn up but not pursued. Finally, an airliner variant would have been the MkVIII, with passenger accommodation inside the wing.

Chapter 7
ASPECTS OF INTER-WAR RESEARCH

During the year immediately before the outbreak of the Second World War, experimentation was taking place into many aspects of aircraft design. Some of these were eventually developed to become of partial use, whilst others led down blind alleys or were too far ahead of their time in terms of the resources and materials then available. Dealt with here are five varied aspects of this work.

PARNALL PARASOL

During 1928, Specification 15/28 was issued for an aircraft on which full-scale tests could be carried out on airflow over wings. The small firm of George Parnall & Co Ltd of Yate, Gloucestershire, was awarded the contract, being asked to produce two machines, numbered K1228 and K1229.

The aircraft was to be of parasol monoplane construction, and was consequently referred to as the Parnall Parasol. The wing mounting was designed so that the wing could move slightly in relation to the fuselage. These movements were fairly restricted, and the wing-supporting system incorporated a dynamometer to enable the forces exerted on the wing to be measured at any angle of incidence. The Air Ministry gave its blessing to possible foreign sales of this type of machine, but these failed to materialise.

It was essential for the machine to have clean lines to minimise interference with the free flow of air over the wings, and this was achieved with composite wood and metal construction. The swinging cradle supporting the wing was built of high tensile steel, as were the outboard wing-bracing struts, the latter being in the shape of a deformable parallelogram.

Both machines first flew in 1929 powered by a supercharged 225 hp Armstrong-Siddeley Lynx IV engine. For test purposes, the observer sat in the front cockpit, which was equipped with a dynamometer, whilst the pilot in the

rear cockpit had a lever with which he could actuate a hydraulic brake on the airscrew. When a reading was required, the pilot stopped the engine and applied the brake to stop the propeller windmilling. The observer then took his dynamometer reading while the aircraft was in gliding flight, thus preventing any of the wing being in the slipstream of the engine and thereby affecting the readings. After completion, the engine could be restarted by means of its R.A.E. Gas Starter MkII.

K1228 was taken on charge at R.A.E. Farnborough on 20 August 1930, and K1229 on 15 October. Both machines were fitted with RAF 28-section wings, that of K1228 initially having full-span ailerons, whilst that of K1229 was fully slotted and square tipped with parallel chord. Full details of their history appear not to have survived, but it is apparent that wings of various section and type were fitted at different times. In 1934 K1229 was fitted with a new wing of RAF 28-section, built by Avros under their type designation 661, and fitted with Zap flaps. These were split flaps which moved bodily rearwards when lowered and thus increased the effective wing area as well as the lift coefficient. Zap flaps were later used in the Blackburn Skua, and were somewhat similar in operation to the Fowler flaps, but proved less efficient as they did not have an aerofoil shape. K1229 reverted to its previous wing in August 1935, making its last flight on 31 March 1936 when it made a forced landing.

Facing page top: **The Parnall Parasol wing research aircraft at Martlesham Heath. The wing support cradle and arrangement for longitudinal movement can be seen clearly.** *52*

Bottom: **Parnall Parasol K1228 with tufted wings and tail-mounted camera for airflow tests. (via J.D. Oughton).***53*

MONOSPAR-WINGED F.7/3m

On the staff of Sir William Beardmore & Co Ltd during 1926 and 1927 was a Swiss-born technician, H.J. Stieger, who was then involved in the development of the Röhrbach-designed Inflexible. Using his experience with the heavy metal wing structure of this aircraft, he went on to devise a completely new type of wing of cantilever construction, which would be suitable for monoplane designs but without invoking the penalty of excessive weight characteristic of the German designs. His wing was based on a Warren girder-type spar able to absorb flexural wing loads and having a pyramidal tie-rod bracing system to take torsional loads.

The Air Ministry were interested in his ideas, and in 1929 placed a contract for a specimen wing to undergo strength tests, this being built by Gloster at Hucclecote and displayed that year in the Aero Exhibition at Olympia. Stieger lost his job when Beardmore closed its aviation department, but he then decided to set up a private company in partnership with a fellow ex-student of Imperial College. The Air Ministry were still keenly interested, and the new Mono-spar Wing Company was awarded a contract for a further wing, for flight testing on the tri-motor Fokker F.VIIA/3m J7986, which had been purchased in 1925. The original wing was given the designation ST.1, and the new wing was also built at Hucclecote and given the type number ST.2, J7986 having its maiden flight on 16 December 1931.

The ST.2 wing was some 560 lb lighter than the original Fokker wing, from which it differed in planform by having a more pronounced taper, though the span and area were identical. At a gross weight for the aircraft of 8,000 lb it was calculated that the payload could be increased from 1,405 lb to 1,935 lb, equivalent to three extra passengers.

J7986, which was powered by three 215 hp Armstrong Siddeley Lynx engines, remained at Hucclecote for some time, test flights being carried out there from time to time by RAE pilots in addition to Gloster's own trials. It was then flown for a time by Avro at Woodford, before going to Farnborough on 27 June 1933, though it does not seem to

have been used there very much, if at all.

Having proved the principle, the firm set up business at Croydon, and produced several more designs before being taken over in October 1934 by General Aircraft Ltd, which formed specifically to take over the business and world patent rights, acquiring premises at Feltham. Over the next few years they constructed a number of aircraft on the Stieger principle, Stieger himself leaving the company in 1935. The fuselage of J7986 was last heard of in September 1935, being then in use at Canvey Island as a coffee stall.

MILES PEREGRINE BLS

During 1936 Phillips and Powis Aircraft Ltd received an order for a special version of their Miles M.8 Peregrine, for use as a flying laboratory at Farnborough, where it was to be used to undertake research into boundary layer suction on wings. The theory was that by exerting suction on the boundary layer of air immediately above the top surface of a wing, turbulence would be prevented, and a number of consequent benefits would ensue: wing drag would be reduced, the stall delayed, and the climb rate improved, as well as producing a general increase in aerodynamic efficiency. The company had already done both theoretical and practical work on these lines, a Miles Whitney Straight (G-AECT) having been flown during 1937 with an aerofoil sleeve fitted over its wings, underneath which a large venturi had been mounted to induce the necessary suction, end plates preventing air from spilling over the BLS area.

The Peregrine had not gone into production, despite attracting some interest, due to the company's becoming preoccupied with large orders for both Magister and Master trainers, but they now set about building a modified version of their twin-engined, eight-seat light transport. The new machine, designated M.8A Peregrine II, flew on 30 March 1938 with the serial L6346, being powered by two 290 hp Menasco Buccaneer B.6S engines, which gave it a top speed of 194 mph at 4,500 ft. Its empty weight was 3,350 lb and loaded it weighed 5,700 lb. The cruising speed was 172 mph at 4,500 ft, and it could climb to 5,000 ft in 4.76 minutes and 10,000 ft in 10.53 minutes.

L6346 was the first metal-skinned aircraft produced by the company, and their first with a retractable undercarriage. Inside its fuselage was a 10 hp Ford motor engine driving a large vacuum pump, this being connected to a series of ducts extending internally along the span of the wing, the surface of which was perforated.

After initial trials at Woodley, the aircraft went in April 1939 to Farnborough, and tests proved quite promising. The Ford motor was required to remove less air than tests on models had suggested, and there was a considerable reduction in drag, as well as a marked increase in the rate of climb, which showed a 29 per cent improvement for the expenditure of only 8 hp. One can only conjecture where this line of research might have led, however, as it was discontinued shortly before the outbreak of war,

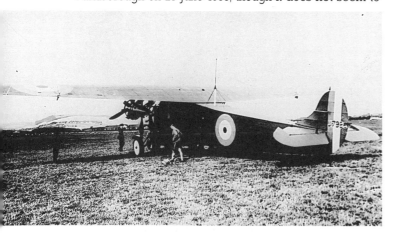

Fokker F.VII/3m J7986 fitted with a Monospar wing.

Miles Peregrine L6346 was adapted for boundary layer suction trials.

having no direct connection with the paramount need to expand the RAF.

G.A.L. MONOSPAR TRICYCLE
In April 1938 the Air Ministry ordered an adaptation of the General Aircraft Monospar light transport to test the characteristics of tricycle undercarriages, of which there was then little experience on modern aircraft. Generally referred to as the Monospar Tricycle, the aircraft was supplied the following month under Contract No.756507/38 and numbered N1531, having been previously flown with the maker's Class B registration T42.

The fuselage was basically a standard S.T.25 Monospar Universal fitted with two 95 hp Pobjoy Niagara IIIs, the standard undercarriage being replaced by a framework with the two main wheels under the wings and the nose wheel on bars extending forward some little way beyond the nose.

The aircraft was taken on charge at Farnborough on 22 August 1938, but undercarriage tests had not been under way very long before it had to return to the makers on 15 September for repair. These took six months, and it was not until 20 March 1939 that N1531 was back at RAE

for handling trials. On 28 July 1940, having completed the trials, the aircraft was placed in store with No.39 Maintenance Unit at Colerne.

Five months later N1531 was earmarked for 92 Squadron, but they would have been surprised and somewhat puzzled if it had arrived, as they were then operating Spitfire VBs from Biggin Hill. This was obviously an administrative error, the true destination being Middle Wallop, where No.93 Squadron were in the process of converting from Handley Page Harrows to tricycle-undercarriaged Douglas Bostons. The unit's task was to lay 'Pandora' Long Aerial Mine devices (generally referred to as LAM) in the path of German night bombers, though this concept had little success, soon giving way to radar equipment. N1531 arrived on 2 January 1941, and remained until going back into store on 11 June 1941, later being scrapped.

General Aircraft did derive some benefit from the experiment, however, tricycle undercarriages being fitted to other of their designs, including the Cygnet, GAL.38 fleet shadower and Owlet.

SPECIFICATION 35/35
Towards the end of 1935 the Air Ministry issued Specification 35/35 for an experimental high speed aircraft to meet the needs of Air Staff Requirement OR.30.

Ever since the time of the Schneider Trophy Races,

This General Aircraft-built Monospar was ordered by the Air Ministry for tricycle undercarriage trials. (via J.D. Oughton)

speed had been a matter of great importance but had gradually become submerged in the operational needs of various Air Staff Requirements. It was felt therefore that the time had arrived for a further step forward in this area with the object of stimulating high speed development, determining the limiting factors when applied to practical flying, and pointing the way to achieving the highest possible performance. The design would be essentially that of a fighter, though actual installation of armament was unnecessary except on a mock-up. It should be undertaken in such a way as to make it possible afterwards to turn it into quite a practical production aircraft, with only a slight mitigation of its most advanced characteristics.

Constructors were to be encouraged to use not only the fruits of existing research and technological development, but also to try and develop new design techniques which might otherwise be considered too advanced for ordinary service use. Boldness and originality were to be the keywords, not merely the reproduction of existing practice with increased engine power. The actual engine was not specified, except that it had to be British, and must have completed 50 hours of type test before delivery.

Maximum level speed at 15,000 feet was to be not less than 400 mph, and the aircraft had to be sound and safe to handle at high speeds, including diving and recovery. The pilot should have a reasonably good view for take-off and landing, and his cockpit must be enclosed, free from draught and preferably heated.

The requirement attracted some interest within the industry, and firms taking sufficient interest to produce designs included Airspeed (A.S.31), Bristol (Type 151), Fairey, General Aircraft (GAL.28) and Hawker. The specification certainly produced some original ideas. Airspeed came up with a wing-first twin-boom monoplane with the cabin in a tail pod, the engine being a 1,030 hp Merlin E. Bristol preferred their own Hercules power plant as did General Aircraft, the latter producing a design with a variable-area wing. Their efforts were in vain, however, as the demands of approaching war led to the idea being dropped.

Chapter 8

FLYING BOAT DEVELOPMENTS

During the 1914-1918 war, flying boat design in the United Kingdom had been most successfully undertaken by Col John C. Porte at the Royal Naval Air Station at Felixstowe. His ideas were developed from the 'Small America' and 'Large America' products of the Curtiss Company, which had been imported in some numbers until the home-built products became available late in the war.

Construction of these Felixstowe flying boats, as they were known, was entrusted to a number of firms, among them S.E. Saunders Ltd, Short Bros, Dick, Kerr & Co. Ltd and The Phoenix Dynamo Manufacturing Co. Ltd. All of these maintained their activities in this field after hostilities ceased, although the latter two ceased to be independent firms. Also to become involved was the Blackburn Aeroplane & Motor Co. Ltd, which had begun to take an interest in both flying boats and seaplanes late in the war.

Saro, otherwise Saunders-Roe, as S.E. Saunders became in 1929, was largely known at that time for the production of civil flying boats and amphibians, but did manage to get orders for its biplane London flying boat, and later for the Lerwick, a twin-engined aircraft built on somewhat similar lines to the larger Short Sunderland, which was not a great success. After the abandonment of aircraft design by the English Electric Company, however, the design and construction of flying boats for the RAF was largely shared between Blackburn and Shorts, gradually progressing from biplanes to monoplane designs. It was largely a story of steady progress, rather than experimentation, but there were exceptions, of which the following are of note.

EEC AYR

In 1918 the English Electric Company was established by amalgamating five varied electrical and mechanical engineering firms. Three of these firms, Coventry Ordnance Works, Phoenix Dynamo Co and Dick, Kerr and Co. had been engaged in aircraft manufacture, mostly sub-contract work on aircraft for the Royal Naval Air Service. An aircraft department was formed in the new company, its Chief Designer being W.O. Manning, who had previously held this position with two of the former firms.

During the latter part of the First World War, the Phoenix company, in addition to its sub-contract work on Felixstowe machines, had designed a series of seaplanes and flying boats, one of the latter, the P.5, being actually constructed and named the Cork. This nautical interest was continued by EEC in the early post-war period, and at the beginning of 1921 Manning began work on an experimental design of small single-engined four-seater reconnaissance flying boat to meet the requirements of Air Ministry Specification 12/21.

Two prototypes were ordered at a cost of £9,550 each in December 1921, to be numbered N148 and N149, both fitted with a 450 hp Napier Lion IIb. Before commencing construction a one-twelfth scale model of a preliminary design, the M.1, was tested at the National Physical Laboratory. A modified design, the M.2 was then considered, this being an amphibious variant, but that approach was soon abandoned and the design was completed as the M.3, later named the Ayr.

The most unusual external feature of the final design, for which Manning was granted two patents, was the configuration of the lower wings. These were given a high dihedral, and like the hull were built on the Linton Hope streamlined monocoque principle. This enabled them to act as partially submerged sponsons, in effect increasing the aircraft's beam as well as giving it lateral stability on the water, thereby doing away with the need for the more normal wing tip floats. The upper wings, whose ribs were of Warren-girder construction in compression, were somewhat longer, resulting in a sesquiplane layout, and had both sweepback and negative stagger but no dihedral. The wings were separated by strong N-shaped interplane struts, and few bracing-wires were necessary.

Construction was undertaken at the former Dick, Kerr works at Preston, and the first machine, N148, was transported to nearby Lytham St.Annes for final assembly, emerging there on 10 February 1925. Length was 40 ft 8 in, the upper wing having a span of 46 ft and the lower one 30 ft, the combined wing area being 466 sq ft. Estimated figures showed an empty weight of 4,406 lb and 6,846 lb, the maximum sea level speed being judged to be 127 mph, with a service ceiling of 14,500 ft.

The first attempt at flight came on 10 March when Marcus Manton taxied down the Lytham slipway. Initial water taxiing proved difficult because the machine tended to rock from one side to the other, with the lower wings being alternately submerged, but on reaching 10 mph there was sufficient lift for both wings to be kept out of the water. A new problem now arose, however, as the machine tended to veer off course, despite the use of a water rudder fitted under the base of the second step of the hull.

With difficulty, Manton kept the machine sufficiently straight to attempt a take-off, but yet another problem arose. As speed increased, the lower wings became submerged under the water being thrown up by the bows, and the aircraft immediately nosed down, so that the attempt had to be abandoned. Various expedients were tried to overcome the problems, such as putting ballast in the hull to make it settle deeper in the water, and removing the Scarff gun ring to reduce drag, but all to no avail.

In the meantime events had been moving against the company's aircraft department. Apart from a small development order for its contemporary Kingston flying boat, no production contract had been forthcoming and the cut-back in official expenditure outlined in the 1925 Air Force Estimates made it unlikely that there would ever be any for this comparatively small aircraft producer. Added to the apparently insurmountable problems with the Ayr, this led to the company ceasing to be involved in aircraft design from April 1926, despite local protests.

The second machine, N149, was still uncompleted when the end came. One of the Ayr hulls was sent to Farnborough for structural testing, and by the early thirties was

The sesquiplane configured English Electric Ayr at Lytham St. Annes in February 1925. The lower wings, designed to act as sponsons, caused insuperable problems because of their low position on the fuselage.

moored on the nearby Basingstoke Canal, along with Kingston N9712, also from Farnborough. On the outbreak of war they were both towed to Greatbottom Flash, Ash Vale, to obstruct possible German seaplane landings, the Ayr sinking there in 1951 when it finally disintegrated.

BLACKBURN B.20

At the beginning of 1936, the Air Ministry issued Specification R.1/36 for a small general purpose flying boat, and several firms took an interest in this, including Fairey, Saro and Blackburn. Saro received an order for their Lerwick design, but Blackburns, who had adopted a novel approach, continued to pursue this despite losing the main contract.

Designers of medium-sized sea-based aircraft face two major problems. One is the necessity to keep the propellers well clear of the water, this being usually achieved by adopting a high-wing layout. The other difficulty is to provide angles of incidence and suitable streamlining which are appropriate to both take-off conditions and level flight. Most flying boats tend to have the wings set at high angles of incidence in relation to the fuselage, in order to achieve the maximum possible lift for take-off, but once the aircraft has achieved height this produces excess drag.

To overcome these problems, Major J.D. Rennie, the chief seaplane designer of Blackburns, patented the idea of fitting a flying boat with a retractable planing bottom, and the firm set about producing the B.20 design based on this principle. A contract, number 498571/36, was awarded for a single aircraft, and this emerged from the firm's Dumbarton works early in 1940, only then being given the serial number V8914.

The all-metal aircraft had a length of 69 ft 8 in and was powered by two 1,720 hp Rolls-Royce Vulture II engines. The wing-tips incorporated floats which folded outwards, and with these retracted in flight the span was 82 ft 2 in, the wing area, including the floats, being 1,066 sq ft. The bottom of the fuselage consisted of a retractable pontoon which fitted tight to the main fuselage in the up position, so as to provide a good streamlined shape, but was so attached that when down it gave the optimum take-off attitude. The special hydraulics for the retraction mechanism caused some problems, but the Lockheed firm were able to design suitable equipment.

The hull had a depth of 16 ft $4\frac{1}{2}$ in with the pontoon lowered, but when this was retracted it reduced to 11 ft 8 in. For safety, the pontoon was constructed with five separate watertight compartments, each with bilge connections so that if one or two become holed the aircraft would have a chance of remaining afloat, the fuel tanks being housed in the midship compartment. Mooring was undertaken from the pontoon, which housed most of the necessary marine equipment, such as the anchor and its winch, and the boat hook mooring pennant and drogue. The pontoon was also used to gain access to the main hull by means of a hatch under the bomb aimer's compartment, further hatches being fitted under the wardroom and galley.

The design included defensive armament, consisting of a power-driven movable turret amidships and another in the tail, a crew of six being carried. An ingenious arrangement allowed bombs to be carried in the centre section of the mainplane, the retractable bomb-bay doors folding up into the wings. The prototype, however, was unarmed when it made its maiden flight in March 1940. A number of flights were made, and the aircraft appeared to fulfil its promise, the retractable pontoon proving very effective. Estimated maximum speeds were 280 mph at sea level and 322 mph at 15,000 ft, these being reduced respectively to 268 and 306 mph with the turrets fitted. Range was judged to be 1,500 miles at a cruising speed of 200 mph, but trials came to an abrupt end when the aircraft was lost in an accident on 7 April 1940.

Official interest was maintained, however, despite this setback, and very soon afterwards a new specification, R.13/40, was issued around the design. This called for a retractable-hull replacement for the Sunderland, able to do better and more economically what the Sunderland already did well, but not to perform duties beyond its powers, these being catered for by contemporary Specification R.14/40 for a much larger aircraft, eventually to emerge much too late as the Short Shetland.

By comparison with the Sunderland, the R.13/40 required at least an equal range, but the top speed would have to be better by 35-40 mph and the cruising speed by 25-30 mph. It would need heavier armament, and contain ample space for all equipment, plus living facilities for the crew of seven, but with no wasted space. Special equipment would be necessary for handling and access on the water. Power was to be provided by two Bristol Centaurus engines, whose output was likely to be equivalent to the four Pegasus engines in the Sunderland, which were now approaching the limits of their development potential. The requirements laid down in the specification as originally drawn included a normal cruising range of 1,500 miles, rising to 3,500 miles with overload tanks, a bomb load of 2,000 lb and maximum overload weight of 52,000 lb.

Blackburns set about meeting the new Specification, their type B.40 being awarded a contract for two prototypes in 1941, to be given serials ES966 and ES979. By November 1941 their design had progressed to a machine with a crew of eight and powered by two Centaurus II engines. Empty weight was to be 37,382 lb and all-up weight 60,000 lb. The maximum range without bombs was estimated at 3,050 miles, and with them 2,400 miles.

Officialdom was not impressed, however, especially in comparison with the Sunderland, being particularly critical of the 98 ft wing span which was some 15 ft less than that of its four-engined counterpart. Calculations showed that in the event of an engine failure the aircraft would only be able to continue with its task if the weight were reduced to 44,500 lb, and if such a failure were to occur more than 500 miles from base the aircraft would be unable to return.

The Blackburn B.20 retractable-hull flying boat at Brough early in 1940.

Blackburns were by then becoming discouraged by the lack of enthusiasm for the project, and said that they would much rather have their activities directed on to some other project more likely to be of use in the present war. They were told at first that as their design fell short of the range laid down in the Specification, the Air Staff now had no great interest in it, but that it was proposed to continue with the two prototypes as it was considered that there was a lot to be learned from the retractable hull principle.

What they were not told at this stage was that consideration was being given to diverting the firm's energies to a proposed single-seater fighter flying boat design with a retractable hull, the B.44 to Specification N.2/43. This was seen as enabling the Ministry to get themselves out of a jam they were already in with regard to the unsuccessful Spitfire floatplane. It was thought that much of the wing structure would be common to the Blackburn Firebrand, the first prototype of which was then nearing completion. Nothing came of this idea, however, and in January 1942 Blackburns were notified that the contract was cancelled.

SARO SHRIMP

The most successful flying boat design of the immediate pre-war period was the Short Sunderland, which was to

The underside of the Blackburn B.20 showing the pontoon in close-up.

be produced in quantity and in the event served throughout the Second World War and beyond. At the beginning of 1938, however, the Air Ministry began to look towards a possible replacement and Specification R.3/38 was issued, only to be superseded a year later when R.5/39 appeared on 22 April 1939, to meet a requirement for a large four-engined reconnaissance patrol flying boat.

Based on Air Staff Requirement OR.69, this new specification attracted the interest of Blackburn, Fairey, Short Bros and Saro. The latter firm tendered an updated version of their A.38 design, already submitted for the now defunct R.3/38. Saro decided that it would be advantageous to build a half-scale model, the A.37, so as to be able to assess both

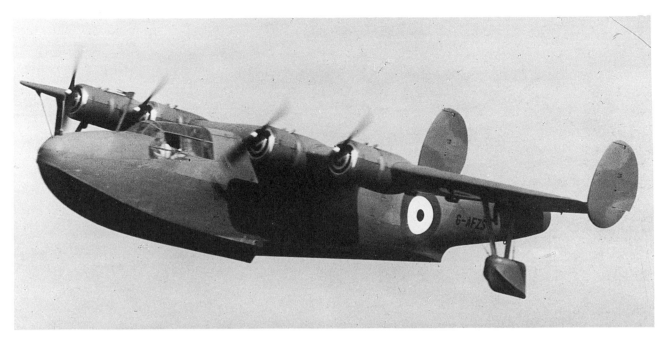

The Saro Shrimp flying in civil guise. (British Hovercraft Corporation)

aerodynamic and hydrodynamic problems before starting work on the full sized aircraft. It was essentially a private venture, but tests were carried out at Farnborough in relation to the design, and Specification R.5/39/2 was drawn up to cover the project.

The firm quickly got to work, and the aircraft, which was given constructor's number A.37/1, had its maiden flight at Cowes in early October 1939 bearing the civil registration G-AFZS and a rather hastily painted camouflage scheme. Powered by four 95 hp Pobjoy Niagara III engines, it had a wing span of 50 ft, length was 42 ft 8¾ in and wing area 340 sq ft. The all-metal hull had a single step, the wings being of plywood and fabric covered wood, and it was fitted with twin fins and rudders. Empty weight was 4,362 lb, and fully loaded it weighed 6,200 lb. Tests gave the maximum speed as 152 mph at sea level, with a cruising speed of 114 mph.

The 'Shrimp', as it was nicknamed, was later given the wartime designation Experimental Aeroplane No.126. It had very smooth lines, and viewed from a distance its four engines helped to give it the appearance of a much larger machine. It was a credit to its builders, proving to have very few vices, but it had the misfortune to be overtaken by events, because by the time of its completion official thinking had again changed, and the R.5/39 requirement had been suspended. It was replaced in July 1940 by a further update, however, numbered R.14/40, for which both Saro and Shorts were again contenders.

The vulnerability of its Cowes works led Saros to set up a factory at Beaumaris, on the Menai Straits, and in August 1940 the A.37 was sent there, before being transferred early in 1941 to the Marine Aircraft Experimental Establishment, which had already been similarly moved, to Helensburgh on the Clyde. The results of tests here were excellent, with very favourable comments on both water handling and flying qualities. The only real criticisms were a tendency for a wing to drop when the machine was stalled without the use of flaps, and heaviness of the rudder handling.

The R.14/40 Specification was finalised on 23 March 1942, and the Ministry of Aircraft Production made the unusual proposal, with which both Saro and Shorts agreed, that this should be a shared project. It went ahead under the Shorts type number S.35, eventually becoming the Shetland, and it was agreed that the A.37 be used to test scale reproductions of various components.

On 22 April 1942 the 'Shrimp' went to Helensburgh for test with a new hull, returning to Saro at Beaumaris on 13 November 1942 for extensive modification.

In February 1944 it was flown at Helensburgh with a scaled-down Shetland hull, and in June 1944 it was allocated the serial number TK580 on being taken over by the Ministry of Aircraft Production under contract Acft/1371/C.20(b). On 8 September 1944 it returned once again to the makers and in later trials it was fitted with Shetland-type single fin and rudder, floats and elevators. The varying effects of scaling meant that not every type of test was equally valid, but some useful work was undertaken.

On 7 July 1945 TK580 was despatched once more to the MAEE, this unit returning to its pre-war home at Felixstowe the next month, the A.37 following it, being later fitted with a revised Shetland-type hull bottom. This, however, proved most unsatisfactory, considerable skipping being experienced during both take-offs and landings. The aircraft was eventually sold for scrap in February 1949, having achieved very little. The Saro A.38 for which it started life never materialised, and only two examples of the Shetland were ever built.

Chapter 9
THE QUEST FOR HEIGHT

The 1930s was a time for pushing back frontiers and creating records. Many different nations were involved, and creating a new record, or achieving a world first, became a matter of national pride. The quest for greater height was but one aspect of this, and two quite different British aircraft became involved, but for differing reasons.

WESTLAND P.V.3

During the late 1920s the Westland design team had produced the successful Wapiti which served with a number of RAF squadrons, especially in India. They also produced the unsuccessful C.O.W. (Coventry Ordnance Works) gun fighter, but were then left with little work to do. To fill the gap, the company decided to embark on a private venture version of the Wapiti, able to undertake army co-operation and general purpose work as well as, it was hoped, meeting naval requirements for a torpedo bomber.

As was the practice with a number of pre-war manufacturers of such aircraft it was given a private venture designation, in this case P.V.3. Many Wapiti components were incorporated, and the overall dimensions were therefore similar. In view of the proposed Fleet Air Arm use, the wings were hinged to facilitate folding to enable the aircraft to fit an aircraft carrier's lift, the folded width being 20 ft 4 in. The undercarriage was also redesigned to accommodate a 1,000 lb torpedo.

The prototype emerged early in 1931, bearing the Class B registration P3, based on its PV number, fitted with a 575 hp Bristol Jupiter XFa engine. It was test flown by Louis Paget in January and had an excellent performance, including a service ceiling of 26,000 ft. No RAF orders were forthcoming, however, and naval use was ruled out as the torpedo it had been designed to accommodate had been superseded by a larger one which the P.V.3 was incapable of carrying. The aircraft was therefore relegated to experimental flying. Fortune was to take a hand, however, and give the one-off P.V.3 a permanent place in aeronautical history.

In March 1932 the Royal Geographical Society received a proposal to mount a flight over Mount Everest, which at that time had not been conquered by climbers. The main object was to survey the peak accurately for the benefit of future mountaineering attempts, but at the same time it would provide some welcome publicity for the British aircraft industry.

Three months later it had been decided that a supercharged version of the successful Bristol Pegasus engine would be most suitable for the task of clearing the 29,000 ft summit, a choice which was vindicated when on 16 September 1932 a new world altitude record of 43,976 ft was established by Cyril Uwins, Bristol's chief test pilot, flying a Vickers Vespa VII powered by a 550 hp Pegasus I.S.3 engine.

Few machines then available were suited to the task, which would need several requirements to be met. It had to be a two-seater with plenty of space for the observer and all his photographic equipment, as well as sufficient room for him to be able to manoeuvre them within the confines of his cockpit. To avoid the cost of adaptation it had to be an existing machine already designed for a radial engine and, because of the need for a specially large propeller to cope with the thin air at the extreme altitude, a tall undercarriage was required.

The P.V.3 met all these requirements, it was readily available, and would only require minimal modification to bring it up to the necessary standard. All that was required

Westland P.V.3 G-ACAZ about to fly over Mount Everest, viewed from the accompanying Wallace G-ACBR.

was the removal of the wheel spats and military equipment to reduce weight, enclosing of the observer's rear cockpit, and replacement of the tailwheel by a tailskid. The engine would be fitted with a Townend ring.

For the attempt, the P.V.3 was renamed the Houston-Westland, thus acknowledging the fact that financial backing for the expedition was being provided by Lady Houston, a philanthropist who was always keen to advance the cause of British aviation. It would be accompanied by a back-up aircraft in the shape of a converted Wallace from the same stable. The civil registration G-ACAZ was allocated to the P.V.3, the Wallace becoming G-ACBR.

The P.V.3 was ready early in 1933, and on 25 January, fitted with a 580 hp Pegasus II.S.3, it flew from Yeovil aerodrome to prove that it could achieve the necessary height. Piloted by Harald Penrose, with Air Commodore Fellowes, leader of the expedition, it climbed to around 35,000 ft.

Two weeks later both aircraft were aboard SS *Dalgoma* en route to Karachi. On arrival the machines were transported to Lilbalu aerodrome, near Purnea in northeast India, where they were reassembled, then test flown on 29 March. Maps for the area were known to be unreliable, and as an added complication the Nepal Government

refused to allow flying near Everest, except for the actual attempt. In addition, the Tibetan Government would not permit them to fly nearer than 100 yards to the summit. However, a Puss Moth was used two days later by Air Commodore Fellowes and Lieutenant Colonel L.V.S. Blacker to practice infra-red photography in the region of Kanchenjunga, which rises to over 28,000 ft. Further flights were made near the Nepalese frontier each dawn in this machine, the Westland machines being prepared in case the weather was suitable for the attempt, but strong winds and cloud cover prevailed.

On 3 April the weather report was good, and after a preliminary flight by the Puss Moth, at 8.25 am the two machines took off. The Houston-Westland was piloted by Lord Clydesdale with Lt Col Blacker observer. In the other machine was Flt Lt D.F. McIntyre accompanied by Gaumont-British photographer S.R. Bonnett. They reached the summit in good visibility at 10.05, and were able to spend around 15 minutes in the vicinity taking pictures. No significant problems had been encountered with either of the machines or their Pegasus engines, and they landed safely at 11.25 am. When developed, not all of the photographs had come out as well as hoped, and on 19 April a second flight was made, with the approval of the Government of Nepal, but without the knowledge of Air Commodore Fellowes, uninsured, and against the wishes of Lady Houston. All went well, however, and some useful photographs were taken which were to prove invaluable for future attempts to climb the summit.

The two aircraft then flew to Karachi for shipment home, and the Houston-Westland ended its days as a test-bed for Bristol engines.

BRISTOL 138

During the late twenties and early thirties a number of record-breaking high altitude flights were made by various countries, several using machines powered with Bristol Jupiter and Pegasus engines made either by the parent company or under licence. Among these were Unwins' record-breaking flight and the aerial conquest of Everest.

These achievements sparked the interest of the Air Ministry, who foresaw the future need for high flying in the event of future hostilities. In November 1933 Frank Barnwell of Bristols put forward a proposal for a purpose-built high flying machine, to be designated Type 138. This was to be a large single-seat low-wing monoplane with a rearward-retracting undercarriage, powered by a development of the engine used in the P.V.3 for its Everest flight.

The design attracted some official interest, and in June 1934 the company received an invitation to tender for Specification 2/34. At that time the world's absolute height

record stood at 47,352 ft, established at Rome in a Pegasus-powered Caproni 161 on 11 April 1934. The Specification required a research machine capable of reaching at least 50,000 ft, with a wing-loading not exceeding 9 lb per sq.ft and a span-loading of not more than 1.4 lb per sq.ft.

To meet the Specification, Barnwell revised his drawings to produce a single-seat machine, convertible to a two-seater, with a simple lightweight fixed undercarriage. Designated Type 138A, it was powered by a special version of the Pegasus incorporating a two-stage supercharger. The design was finalised by September 1934, and work began four months later on a full-sized mock-up. A single machine was then built under contract 348467/34, serial number K4879 (constructor's sequence number 7840), and this made its first flight from Filton at the hands of Cyril Uwins on 11 May 1936, powered at this stage by a Pegasus IV fitted with a three-bladed propeller. The aircraft had a span of 66 ft and a length of 44 ft, the wing area being 568 sq ft. For lightness the machine was of wooden construction, with an empty weight of 4,391 lb and loaded would weigh 5,310 lb for the record attempt, the difference being comprised of 180 lb for the pilot, 30 lb for his pressure suit, 20 lb for his parachute, 40 lb for the oxygen apparatus, 100 lb for special instruments and 549 lb for fuel and oil, the latter being 65 gallons of fuel and 10 gallons of oil. The loading aspects of the Specification had been achieved, with a wing-loading of 8.53 lb per sq ft and a span-loading of around 1.22 lb per sq ft.

The wooden Bristol 138A K4879, seen here fitted with Bristol Pegasus VI.S. (via M.J. Hooks)

After further flights on 22 May and 16 July it went to Farnborough in August to test a specially developed oxygen pressure-helmet, following which it returned to Filton to be refitted with the 500 hp Pegasus P.E.VI.S engine. Returning to Farnborough, the upper surfaces of the wings and fuselage had been painted black to reduce glare. The machine took off at 07.30 hrs on 28 September 1936 at the hands of Sqn Ldr F.R.D. Swain, reaching an indicated height of 51,000 ft in 70 minutes. For the attempt, the pressure in the suit was set at an atmospheric equivalent of somewhere between 32,000 and 35,000 ft. Shortage of oxygen on the way down however, caused him to begin to fly erratically and, unable to release any of the levers or fastenings, he had to resort to hacking out the helmet window of his pressure-suit with a knife which had been hung within reach for such an emergency. By this

time he was down to 14,000 ft and near Yeovil, so he steered east in the direction of Salisbury, to land safely at Netheravon after a flight of two hours, with only two gallons of fuel left in the tank. The height attained, after making allowance for temperature and barometric pressure, was later ratified as a new world's record at 49,967 ft or 15,230 m, this being the first flight to exceed 15,000 metres. Such precise figures were of course something of a nonsense, but this was recognised in the rules which would not allow a new record unless it exceeded the earlier one by at least 300 metres.

The machine had been designed to fly to 54,000 ft, however, and a number of modifications were carried out, mainly to the propeller and wheels, the latter being reduced in size and the brakes removed to save weight. Following further test flights to 50,000 ft, the machine was flown from Farnborough by Flt Lt M.J. Adam to a new record height of 53,967 ft on 30 June 1937, thus wresting the prize back from the Italians, whose Caproni 161 had reached 51,362 ft on 8 May 1937.

The Air Ministry wished to continue with this line of research, and in the meantime had placed an order for a second machine, designated Type 138B. Given serial number L7037 (sequence number 8136), this was delivered as a bare two-seat airframe to Farnborough where it was to have been fitted with a 500 hp supercharged Rolls-Royce Kestrel S liquid-cooled in-line engine for further high-flying experiments, but the installation was never completed. Both machines ended their days as ground instructional machines, going in 1940 to the recently-opened No.10 School of Technical Training at Kirkham, Lancs., L7037 being renumbered 2339M, and K4879 becoming successively 1951M, 2393M and 2739M.

The pilot of the Bristol 138A being incarcerated in his experimental pressure suit. (via J.D. Oughton)

Chapter 10
THE QUEST FOR DISTANCE

Another aspect of aeronautical endeavour gaining attention between the wars was that of producing aircraft which could fly long distances. This was mainly achieved under the aircraft's own power, it being designed specially for the purpose, and loaded with as much fuel as it could carry on take-off. However, other methods were also tried, in which the aircraft received some form of assistance, either on take-off or during flight.

FAIREY LONG RANGE MONOPLANE
Towards the end of 1927 the Air Ministry's Directorate of Technical Development produced Specification 33/27 for what was described as a postal machine with a range of 5,000 miles. The engine was to be a twelve-cylinder liquid-cooled Napier Lion and the all up weight of the order of 16,000 lb. The contract, number 826964/28, was awarded to Faireys, who accepted an airframe price of £15,000.

Officially it was given out by the Air Ministry that the aircraft was intended for the study of practical methods by which range could be increased. In reality it was intended for an attempt on the world long-distance record, which at that time stood at 3,911 miles, set in June 1927 by an American Bellanca. Various biplane and monoplane designs were investigated, but wind-tunnel tests of a model suggested that a high wing monoplane would be the best configuration. This also had the advantage that the main fuel tanks could be housed in the thick wing, with gravity feed to the engine.

Work started in the Hayes factory in May 1928, but the stakes were soon increased when two months later the record was raised to 4,466.6 miles by an Italian Savoia-Marchetti S64. The Long Range Monoplane, as the machine became known, had a well-streamlined fuselage, 48 ft 6 in in length, and was fitted with a large angular-shaped fin and rudder. To provide some measure of comfort for the crew of two, the cockpit was upholstered and there was also a pneumatic bed. The wings were of 82 ft span and 850 sq ft in area, being constructed with specially developed steel pyramid bracing which enabled each section of the wooden spars to carry a good proportion of the overall load. The tanks could carry up to 1,043 gallons, the gravity-fed fuel being collected in a fuselage tank, then pumped mechanically to the engine, a fall-back device consisting of a windmill which could be projected into the slipstream to drive an emergency pump. The engine finally selected was a modified 570 hp Napier Lion XIA which for the record attempt would have a slightly

The first prototype Fairey Long Range Monoplane at Hinaidi on its return from India in June 1929. (Flt Lt E.H. Simpkins).

raised compression ratio, and be fitted with a specially tuned carburettor giving a lowered rate of fuel consumption.

The aircraft, serial number J9479, had its first flight at Northolt on 14 November 1928, piloted by Squadron Leader A.G. Jones-Williams, MC. On 8 December it was flown to Cranwell, to take advantage of what was then the longest available take-off run at any RAF aerodrome, with the intention of flying non-stop to Cairo, then on to Cape Town. Partial-load take-off tests were undertaken, followed on 22-23 February 1929 by a 24-hour endurance flight which covered about 1,950 miles. The trials were not without problems, mostly relating to the engine which had to be changed twice, but nevertheless a still-air range of 5,200 – 5,500 miles seemed possible.

With these and other delays, the possibility of a flight to South Africa receded, the chance having been lost of favourable wind and weather conditions early in the year, and the destination was therefore changed to India. Tests at the end of March also established that there was little possibility of starting with a full fuel load, particularly as the westerly wind had necessitated an uphill take-off. Finally, at 09.37 hrs on 24 April 1929, J9479 took off with a reduced load, piloted by Squadron Leader Jones-Williams accompanied by Flight Lieutenant N.H. Jenkins, OBE, DFC, DSM, with a Felixstowe-based Supermarine Southampton in company until they reached the Dutch coast. Their original destination was Bangalore in southern India, but strong head winds after overflying Baghdad meant that by the time they reached Karachi two days later they had only six hours' fuel left. If they had continued they would have needed to fly a further 650 miles to beat the existing record, and with no choice but to crash land in the dark once their tanks were empty. With reluctance, therefore, they returned to land safely at Karachi, with only 83 gallons of fuel remaining in the tanks, having flown a Great Circle distance of 4,130 miles in 50 hrs 37 min.

The aircraft was flown back to Cranwell in stages, arriving there on 15 June, and a further attempt was then planned, reverting to the South African target. In the meantime, however, the record had again been broken, this time with a flight of 4,912 miles by a French Breguet XIX in September 1929 . After some modification, and with take-off weight increased to 17,000 lb, J9479 again left Cranwell at 08.00 hrs on 16 December with the same crew, but this time disaster struck. For reasons never satisfactorily explained, they descended steadily after passing Sardinia, until at 18.45 hrs they struck high ground in poor weather some 30 miles south of Tunis, both crew members being killed and the aircraft being a complete write-off.

After some deliberation a second machine was ordered, to new Specification 14/30, this becoming known as the Long Range Monoplane MkII. It was of basically the same design as the MkI, but the wheels were spatted, an early automatic pilot was fitted, and the fuel system was completely redesigned. The new aircraft, serial number K1991, flew on 30 June 1931, but a further record of 5,011 miles was set the following month by an American Bellanca.

A proving flight was made to Egypt in October 1931, a distance of 2,857 miles being covered from Cranwell to Abu Sueir in around 31 hours, but the aircraft was damaged when it eventually returned, having to make a forced landing in a ploughed field near Saffron Walden, Essex when it met fog on 15 December. Weather conditions largely dictated the date of the next attempt, which was not to be until early 1933, the destination now being the original one of South Africa. On 6 February, K1991 took off loaded up to 17,500 lb, crewed by Squadron Leader

The second Fairey Long Range Monoplane, K1991, in October 1931. (RAF Museum P.101027)

O.R. Gayford, DFC and Flight Lieutenant G.E. Nicholetts, AFC. The automatic pilot failed the following evening, and poor weather caused diversions from the originally intended route, making an attempt to reach Cape Town impossible. A landing was therefore made some 781 miles north at Walvis Bay, but this was sufficient to gain the record. When the aircraft landed at 16.40 hrs GMT it had covered a Great Circle distance of 5,341 miles, giving Britain a hat trick as it already held both the speed and altitude records.

The new distance did not stand long, however, being raised to 5,657 miles three months later by a French Bleriot-Zappata 110. Later that year Specification 27/33 was issued for a proposed revised version of K1991, fitted with a retractable undercarriage and powered by a 600 hp Junkers Jumo IV, a German diesel engine which it was planned to build under licence as the Napier Culverin. It was estimated that this might achieve a range of 7,500 miles, stretching to 8,300 miles if the later Jumo V was used, an alternative being to use a 470 hp Bristol Phoenix radial engine fitted with a variable-pitch propeller to offset the comparatively low power it gave at take-off.

It became apparent that redesign, conversion and test flying could not be completed before early 1936, and might well take longer in view of the work involved in fitting a retractable undercarriage and possibly leading-edge radiators. The Bleriot machine, on the other hand, already had a claimed still-air range of 7,825 miles, which might therefore be capable of being increased to around 10,000 miles. Farnborough suggested that in order to beat the existing machine by a substantial margin a completely new design would be needed. By this time, however, rearmament was taking increasing priority of the industry's limited resources, and the Fairey design staff were working hard to submit designs to many of the new military specifications then coming out of the Air Ministry. In the event the distance record next went to a Russian ANT-25 with a flight of 6,306 miles in July 1937, the only other pre-war record being established by Vickers Wellesleys of the RAF's Long Range Development Flight, which in November 1938 pushed the distance up to 7,158.4 miles with a flight from Ismailia to Darwin. The magic figure of 10,000 miles was not exceeded until late 1946, when an American Lockheed P2V Neptune flew 11,235.6 miles. With Shuttle space craft having now flown in continuous orbit, and manned space craft having flown to the moon, the quest for distance with conventional aircraft has now virtually lapsed.

SHORT-MAYO COMPOSITE
Early in the 1930s, Major Robert Mayo, then Technical General Manager of Imperial Airways, devised what he

The Short Mayo Composite on the Medway at Rochester late in 1938.

saw as a practical way of extending the range of a fast fully-laden medium sized commercial aircraft. He proposed that such a machine be lifted off in a piggy-back arrangement by a larger and more powerful but lightly laden aircraft, from which it would be launched once sufficient height had been gained.

Such an idea was not entirely new, experiments having been carried out during the First World War with the object in that case of getting small aircraft aloft ready to be sent after a Zeppelin. In August 1915 one trial involved a B.E.2c carried under an SS-type airship from Kingsnorth, the aircraft's pilot being unfortunately killed when it crashed after launch. A more successful launch was that of a Bristol Scout from a Porte Baby flying boat over Harwich on 17 May 1916.

It was apparent to Mayo that a land-plane carrier aircraft was not a practical proposition, since it was estimated that a take-off run of about three miles would be required for the fully-loaded combination. Thoughts therefore turned to a flying boat, which would solve the problems of both take-off and weight, and therefore to Short Brothers who were then in the business of designing successful flying boats and seaplanes.

During 1932 the proposed scheme was worked out in some detail, and Mayo then used his powers of persuasion to such good effect that late the following year joint Air Ministry/Imperial Airways Specification No.13/33 was issued, and a contract placed with Shorts. From the start it was intended that the Short-Mayo Composite, as it became known, should be a commercial proposition, and not simply a means of testing and proving the concept. In 1935, therefore, the Mayo Composite Aircraft Co. Ltd was formed with the object of acquiring and handling the world rights in composite aircraft.

Shorts were at that time working on other new flying boat and seaplane designs, and similarities with the two composite aircraft were therefore not surprising. The upper part of the combination was to be a four-engine seaplane with a high cruising speed, somewhat on the lines of the new Scion Senior, though larger and more powerful. It was given the constructor's number S.796 and designated Type S.20, being later named Mercury. The designed wing span was 73 ft, length 50 ft 11 in, height 20 ft 3 in and wing area 611 sq ft. Power was to be provided by four Napier Rapier V H-configured in-line engines, and the 1,200 gallons of fuel to be carried within the main spar was expected to provide a range of 3,750 miles at a cruising speed of around 170-180 mph.

The lower aircraft, designated the S.21 Maia and given constructor's number S.797, was even more akin to another new design, in this case the S.23 Empire Flying Boat, later to emerge as the C-Class for service with Imperial Airways. The design of the S.21 followed that of the S.23 very closely, the wing span, for instance being identical at 114 ft, and like its contemporary it was powered by four 915 hp Bristol Pegasus Xc engines, though these were placed somewhat further out on the wings so as to clear the seaplane's floats when released. Other dimensions were

length 84 ft $10\frac{3}{4}$ in, height 32 ft $7\frac{1}{2}$ in and wing area 1,750 sq ft, the latter representing an increase of 250 sq ft over the S.23.

To offset any disturbance caused by the superstructure or by the floats and fuselage of the seaplane, Maia was fitted with a taller fin and rudder of greater area than that of the S.23. The control surfaces had to be particularly effective, as they had to perform the work of manoeuvring both aircraft right through from taxiing and take-off until the actual moment of separation. This aircraft also had a flared beam to provide sufficient lateral stability when the combination was on the water, this being in the form of an out-turned chine where the sides of the hull joined the bottom of the aircraft.

Both machines were completed by the late summer of 1937, the first to take to the air being Maia, with the civil registration G-ADHK, which flew on 27 July 1937 with Shorts Chief Test Pilot, J. Lankester-Parker, at the controls. Mercury (G-ADHJ) was flown by Parker 5 September. Maia initially had four-bladed propellers, but these were soon replaced by de Havilland three-bladed metal ones with controllable pitch, providing improved performance on take-off. On top of its fuselage were two seven foot high steel pylons connected by a cross beam, to provide the main support for the seaplane, whose floats were given additional support by two smaller structures fitted on top of the inner wing sections of the flying boat. The release mechanism was located in the central hull of the seaplane.

The first full take-off and separation took place at Rochester on 20 January 1938, with Parker in Maia and H.L. Piper in Mercury, this exercise being repeated on 5 February. The two aircraft then went to the Marine Aircraft Experimental Establishment, where they were tested both separately and in combination. Maia was the first to receive its Certificate of Airworthiness, on 1 June 1938, but Mercury had to be refitted with uprated Rapier VIs giving 370 hp before it too received its C. of A., on 7 July 1938.

The combination could take off in only 1,350 ft and had an initial rate of climb of 800 ft/min, the cruising speed being 167 mph at 7,500 ft. Maia weighed 24,755 lb unloaded, and 27,700 lb when fully fuelled for an Atlantic trip, whilst Mercury had an empty weight of 10,163 lb, rising to 20,800 lb for transatlantic flight.

Commercial flying began on 21 July 1938 when the combination took off from Foynes in Ireland, Mercury separating at 20.00 hrs BST in the hands of Captain (later Air Vice-Marshall) D.C.T. Bennett, later of Pathfinder fame. At 16.20 hrs (BST) next day it landed at Montreal after a flight of 2,930 miles, the fastest non-stop Atlantic crossing ever at that time by a commercial aircraft, the aircraft then going on to New York. The return journey was more leisurely, in the absence of a carrier aircraft, being made a few days later by way of Montreal, Botwood, the Azores and Lisbon.

The twelfth recorded separation, over Dundee on 6 October after taking off from the River Tay, was followed by a flight of 6,045 miles to Orange River, South West Africa, again piloted by Bennett, setting up a new world

long distance record for seaplanes. Provision of additional fuel for this great distance was achieved by turning the twin floats into fuel tanks, producing an all-up weight of 26,800 lb.

The concept fell into disuse with the outbreak of war, the aircraft then being used for other purposes, though both retained their civil registrations. Maia was eventually converted to C-Class standard and fitted with Pegasus XXII engines, only to fall victim to a German raid on Poole Harbour during the night of 11 May 1941. Mercury flew for a time during 1940 as a crew trainer with No.320 Squadron, a Dutch-manned seaplane unit flying Fokker T.8Ws out of Pembroke Dock, before being broken up in 1941.

The experiment was a complete success, but was not pursued further during the war on the Allied side, though a number of similar experiments were carried out by the Germans with the object of extending the range of pilotless bombs. Post-war improvements in aircraft design and the advent of economical jet engines rendered the concept unnecessary, however, for civil use in the postwar period.

FLIGHT REFUELLING

In early 1939, Flight Refuelling Ltd took delivery at Ford of three converted ex-RAF Handley Page Harrows (K6933, K7029 and K7027) for the experimental refuelling of transatlantic Short C-Class Empire flying boats. By chance, the British civil aircraft register had reached a stage at which Sir Alan Cobham, the founder of the company, saw an opportunity to have registrations issued which incorporated his firm's initials, and they accordingly became respectively G-AFRG, G-AFRH and G-AFRL. Each was fitted with fuel tanks giving a total capacity of 1,000 gallons, these being connected to long hoses which could be reeled out and back in the air by powered winches, valves being fitted to control the flow of fuel.

A regular mail run across the Atlantic was scheduled to start in August 1939, and the first two Harrows were

A dramatic air-to-air shot of Handley Page Harrow refuelling Short C-Class flying boat Cabot (G-AFCU) over Southampton Water. (RAF Museum P.105364)

shipped to Montreal, then reassembled by Fairchild before being based at Gander Airport, then known as Hattie's Camp. The third machine, G-AFRL, was based at Shannon Airport (then Rineanna). On 5 August, Empire Boat *Caribou* (G-AFCV), piloted by Captain J.C. Kelly-Rogers, alighted at Foynes after the first leg of its journey from Southampton, and after normal refuelling took off again. It then topped-up with further fuel from tanker G-AFRL based at Rineanna, a process which was completed only 16 minutes after take-off. On this occasion the two aircraft circled for the benefit of onlookers, though they would normally have flown straight out to sea. Poor weather conditions delayed the crossing, which took over 19 hours instead of the expected 16 hours, *Caribou* arriving at Botwood, Newfoundland at 13.30 the next day before continuing to Montreal and Port Washington, New York, most of the 70,000 letters it carried on this occasion being, of course, souvenirs. It started the return journey on 10 August, but fast westerly winds obviated the need for flight refuelling in Canada.

The following week the feat was repeated when *Cabot* (G-AFCU), piloted by Captain D.C.T. Bennett, was refuelled at Foynes on 12 August – taking as a gift to President Roosevelt a brace of grouse shot on the Yorkshire moors that morning! For the return journey the flying boat left New York on 17 August, and on this occasion tanker refuelling took place at Botwood. *Caribou* later made another trip, and a total of eight round trips were made by the two machines before the outbreak of war intervened. G-AFRG and G-AFRH were later taken over by the RCAF, whilst G-AFRL was destroyed in an air raid on Ford in August 1940.

These experiments were continued after the war, and today a developed form of flight refuelling is accepted practice for military air arms.

Chapter 11

MILITARY EXPERIMENTS

With the formation of the Royal Air Force on 1 April 1918, and the consequent disbandment of the Royal Flying Corps, the Army became completely dependent on the RAF for its aviation needs. Between the wars this mainly took the form of RAF-manned army co-operation squadrons, which under the impetus of war were later developed to become tactical reconnaissance squadrons, though these remained RAF-operated.

Wartime needs were to change this situation, however. Airborne forces came into existence, involving both parachute dropping and military gliders, and in mid-1941 was formed the first of the Auster-equipped Air Observation Post squadrons. The Army was heavily involved in all of these aspects, and for the first time since 1918 it had its own pilots. These developments were to lead in 1957 to the formation of the present Army Air Corps, by then largely changing over to small helicopters.

In the early days of this resurrected Army aviation, much research went into trying to meet its expanding needs. Apart from the main stream of such developments, some less likely experiments were carried out, including three of a somewhat diverse nature, detailed here.

HAFNER ROTACHUTE

A leading light in this field was Raoul Hafner (see Chapter 5), whose rotary-wing designing talents were, after a period of internment, diverted for this purpose early in the second World War. In 1940, under the auspices of the Ministry of Aircraft Production, he began work at the Central Landing Establishment, Ringway, on a proposed small man-carrying machine to be named the Rotachute.

Silk being then in short supply, with a consequent need to conserve stocks for use in parachutes, Hafner designed as a substitute a two-bladed rotor which could be strapped to a soldier's back. The idea was that the blades would be kept folded whilst he was in the aircraft, but as soon as he jumped out they would extend and act like autogiro blades, allowing him to descend at a sufficiently slow rate to make a soft landing, his direction being controlled by the angle of the rotor blades, which he could tilt simply by inclining his body.

The first launch, with a model having a 3-ft diameter rotor, from a Whitley on 16 October 1940, was a failure, but another attempt on 7 November from between the wings of a Tiger Moth was successful. Various launching methods were tried, a 10-ft diameter model known as the M-10 being successfully launched from an Overstrand on 14 March 1941.

These tests had resulted in the original harness concept being dropped, and instead, under the designation H-8, a full-scale machine was built consisting of a rotor on a tubular metal frame in which the soldier would sit. A fin was fitted to give directional stability, and the soldier could now tilt the rotor by means of a control column fastened directly to the rotor hub. He was armed with a detachable .303 inch Bren gun, which he could take with him after landing.

The original concept was that several Rotachutes would be dropped from a Whitley, but stowage problems led to this idea being abandoned. Instead the design progressed as a rotary-wing glider, prototypes being ordered from both Airwork General Trading at Hounslow and F. Hills & Sons Ltd at Manchester. Initial tests were made at Ringway using a rig mounted on a lorry, which sped along the runway at up to 60 mph. Then on 12 February 1942 the Rotachute MkI, as it became known, made its first attempt at free flight. Towed by a Humber car, it

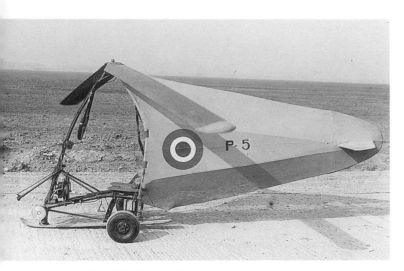

The fifth Hafner Rotachute.

rose to 6 ft after release, but the 15-ft diameter blades were broken when it overturned on touch down.

Two further flights, at Ringway on 16 February and at Snaith on 24 February, also resulted in damage on landing, and to help solve the problem a Rotachute MkII appeared, fitted with wheels instead of the original skid undercarriage. This model proved satisfactory, making a number of successful flights, and it was then succeeded by the Rotachute MkIII, which was to become the standard model. This version had an enlarged tail fairing and a rigid tailplane fitted later with trimming tabs. A number of successful tests were made at Ringway commencing in June. The first ground tow was made by Flg Off. Blaicher on 16 June, and the first air tow by Flt Lt Little on 27 June, the machine being towed by a Tiger Moth. Later tests were conducted on the longer runways at Chelveston and Snaith, the maximum permissible speed under tow being 93 mph, a height of 400 ft being reached. The programme came to an end on 18 October 1943 after a total of 54 flights had been made, Specification 11/42 having been issued in the meantime to cover the MkIV version, which first flew on 29 April 1943. This version had twin endplate fins on the tailplane, and five of the earlier machines were modified to this standard. Over twenty Rotachutes were produced, bearing markings P1 onwards, of which P5, a MkIII, still survives in the Museum of Army Flying at Middle Wallop.

HAFNER ROTAPLANE

The good progress then being shown by the Rotachute project led in 1942 to the issue of another Specification, 10/42, for a machine of somewhat similar concept but sufficiently large to be capable of being attached to a standard wartime 4-seat Jeep, otherwise the Willys 4x4 model MB. Such a concept would produce a rotary-wing glider with the advantages of being both cheap and lightweight. Construction was entrusted under contract SB.24944/C.20a

to R. Malcolm Ltd of White Waltham, who built the machine at Slough. The design was given the name Rotabuggy or 'Flying Jeep', and the designation Experimental Aeroplane No.207 was allotted under the wartime system.

First it had to be established that a Jeep could withstand such treatment, particularly that likely to be meted out to it on landing, and one was therefore subjected to being dropped from heights of up to 7 ft 8 in on to concrete, loaded with weights simulating that of a driver and the glider. No damage was sustained by either the vehicle or its tyres in these tests, which says much for their robust construction.

With the help of H. Morris & Sons, a 46 ft 8 in diameter rotor was built with a tip speed of 860 ft/sec, this being probably the largest rotor with the greatest tip speed produced anywhere at that time. The tail unit consisted of a twin-finned fairing attached to the rear of the vehicle. No rudders were fitted, but a large tailskid was provided to reduce the risk of damage to the rotor on landing. There was no special undercarriage, the normal wheels and suspension proving adequate during trials.

The rotor was fitted on a pylon above the front seats so that the thrust vector was close to the centre of gravity, but so as to keep the C of G low for landing stability its hub was placed only just above the roof, elastic suspension being provided to reduce vibration. Initial rotation was from a starting cable pulled by another vehicle, after which it operated as an autogyro. A standard towing release gear was fitted so that it could be towed like an ordinary glider. The combination had a height to the hub top of 6 ft 9 in, the length was 21 ft, and the width was 9 ft 6 in excluding the rotors. The attachment weighed 550 lb, bringing the loaded weight up to 3,110 lb.

Transported on 26 October 1943 by road from Slough to the Airborne Forces Experimental Establishment at Sherburn-in-Elmet, grounds runs were made on 16 November towed by a lorry, and again six days later towed this time by a 4½ litre Bentley car. Then on 27 November the Bentley pulled it successfully into the air and back down again. To achieve higher speeds than the 65 mph it could manage using the car, tests were made behind a Whitley commencing on 30 January 1944. At a towing speed of 82 mph the optimum gliding angle was 1 in 5.7, 118 bhp being required for towing at that speed, increasing to 320 bhp for towing at 150 mph. Minimum take-off and landing speed was 36 mph, and the minimum rate of descent was 16 ft/sec.

There was a minor mishap on 23 February 1944, but by 11 September 1944 it was ready for the first attempt at free flight, with Sqn Ldr I.M. Little as pilot and Flt Lt R. Packman as observer. The intention had been to release the Rotabuggy at a height of 7,000 ft, but rotor vibration problems caused the plan to be aborted at 1,500 ft, and the pilot was able to land safely only after a strength-draining struggle to maintain control.

For all practical purposes, this was the end of the Rotabuggy, for which there was in any case now no real need. The D-day landings had proved the practicability

The seventh Hafner Rotachute. (Air-Britain Lincoln Branch)

The Hafner Rotabuggy with its original tails. (via F.G. Swanborough/P.H.T. Green)

of transporting Jeeps safely by gliders, and tests were showing that they could also be dropped by parachute. Proposals to transport tanks in this manner were made equally unnecessary by the advent of the Hamilcar tank-carrying glider. Nevertheless, although nothing of practical use stemmed directly from Hafner's wartime efforts, the experience he gained was to prove invaluable in post-war British helicopter development. His machine was officially struck off charge on 1 December 1947 for reduction to scrap.

BAYNES CARRIER WING

Another quite different machine for Army support was the brainchild of L.E. Baynes, who just before the war was responsible for the Baynes Bee light aircraft and had produced designs for other machines. In 1941 he put forward a proposal for a 100 ft wing which could be attached to a medium-sized tank or other armoured fighting vehicle, to enable it to be towed to battle behind a glider-tug.

Baynes was by no means the only designer to consider such an approach to the problem. The project which ended up as the General Aircraft Hamilcar was in the early stages considered in the form of a wing and tail to be fitted to a tank. The Baynes concept was even more original,

Three-view of the Hafner Rotorbuggy.

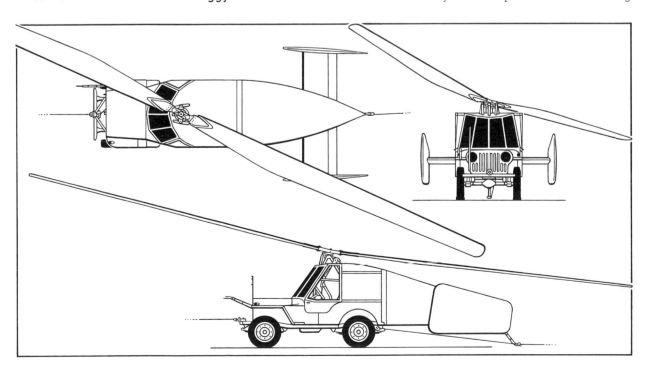

Cine stills of the Hafner Rotabuggy in flight at the Airborne Forces Experimental Establishment at Sherburn-in-Elmet. (via J.D. Oughton).

however, in that there would be no need for a tail, as the vertical control surfaces would be incorporated in the wing tips to form in effect a flying wing. There would, moreover, be no need for a separate fuselage or undercarriage, since the vehicle's own body and wheels or tracks would suffice. The wing would be detachable immediately on touch-down, being carried away by residual lift on operating a quick-release device, and as the tank's engine would have been started on cast-off, it would be ready to go straight into action.

Approval was given by the Air Staff to pursue the project, which became known officially as the Baynes Carrier Wing and unofficially as the Bat. Little was known at that time, however, about the aerodynamic properties of flying wings, and therefore a contract was placed for a one-third piloted scale model. Baynes was then with the Aircraft Section of Alan Muntz Ltd of Heston, but construction was entrusted to the leading British glider manufacturer, Slingsby Sailplanes Ltd at Kirkbymoorside.

The model, which was constructed under contract SB.25046, was designed with a span of 33 ft 4 in, a length of 11 ft 4 in, and a wing area of 160 sq ft. Empty weight was 763 lb, and with ballast its loaded weight was 963 lb. Of necessity it had to be fitted with a fuselage and under-carriage, therefore it was not a true flying wing. The fuselage comprised a lower section below the wing in which was the pilot's seat, whilst his head was in an upper transparent cupola. The undercarriage took the form of a skid, a removable two-wheel trolley being attached for take-off.

On completion the aircraft was transported to nearby Sherburn-in-Elmet, then the home of the Airborne Forces Experimental Establishment, and it was only at this stage that a serial number was allotted, this being RA809. Following taxiing trials behind a Jeep, it had its flight trials from 10 August 1943 at the hands of an experienced pre-war glider designer and pilot, Flt Lt R. Kronfeld, AFC. The tug for these tests was an Avro Tutor and they soon established the glider's stability and ease of control in both towed and free flight. In his report Kronfeld concluded that, in spite of its unorthodox design, the aircraft handled similarly to other light gliders, its controls being light and responsive, and that it was safe to be flown by service test

The third scale Baynes Carrier Wing. (via P. Jarret)

pilots in all normal attitudes of flight. The flaps were found to be very effective in controlling the glide-path during approach and landing, which were easy and normal, with little tendency to float. Wing-tip slots were to have been fitted, due to wind-tunnel test at Farnborough having indicated the likelihood of premature wing-tip stalling, but these were not available in time, and in fact proved super-fluous.

Despite the success of the trials, the project went no further. There was no entirely suitable tank then available, and the success of the Hamilcar in transporting tanks made the concept unnecessary. Nevertheless, RA809 had proved that a tailless monoplane with flaps was a practical proposition, and it continued to do good work for some time at Farnborough, where it was used to provide invaluable data on the stability and control of tailless aircraft.

M.L. UTILITY

An unconventional post-war aircraft resulted from an order placed in 1954 by the Ministry of Supply on behalf of the War Office. M.L. Aviation Ltd at White Waltham, which until 1946 had been R. Malcolm Ltd, was asked to build three inflatable-winged machines, to be serialled XK776, XK781 and XK784, the design being produced by Marcelle Lobelle. To be built under contract 6/Acft/11887/CB.9(d), they were officially to be known as the Inflatable Wing Mk.I, sometimes being also referred to as the Air Jeep. It was seen as a possible communications and reconnaissance aircraft for company commanders, but might also interest the Royal Navy and the RAF, and have potential civil applications, such as for farmers or in areas with poor road communications.

The first aircraft, which initially carried no markings, but later became XK784, was flying by August 1955 and arrived at the Aero Department at Farnborough on 26 January 1956, being strictly a trials machine for restricted flying to test the principle, having a fairly crude box-like chassis seating a pilot and passenger in tandem. A 65 hp McCulloch engine driving a pusher propeller was mounted aft on a framework from which extended the axles for the

ML Utility Mk1 XK776 ready for flight at Middle Wallop. (M.J. Hooks)

two main wheels, a small nosewheel being fitted immediately under the front of the chassis. These were all fitted with Palmer lightweight wheels equipped with brakes, the nosewheel being steerable by foot control.

Above each corner of the chassis extended wing supports, giving it a superficial resemblance to a four-poster bed. These held up the inflatable thick delta-shaped wing, which had a ribbed structure and incorporated a fin at the rear. This wing, which had 45 degrees of sweep on the leading edge, was constructed of top quality dinghy-type fabric, being fastened to the tops of the uprights by lacing, and given additional bracing by wires stretched to lugs on the wheel hubs. It was fitted with separately inflatable trailing edge surfaces to act as elevons, that is to say that used in unison they were effective as elevators, but used differentially they became ailerons. The contours of the wing were maintained by spanwise porous fabric diaphragms to maintain a symmetrical aerofoil.

The wing, which had a maximum thickness of 4 ft 6 in, had a span of 40 ft and length was 17 ft 6 in, the height being 10 ft 1 in. Empty weight was only 550 lb, but a useful load of some 400 lb could be carried. It carried sufficient fuel for 100 miles of flying, and cruised at 45 mph. XK784 had a major accident at Farnborough on 26 March 1956,

when it struck trees during a spiral turn to starboard. It was repaired, however, going to Boscombe Down on 27 January 1958 for assessment trials.

The second machine to appear was XK776, sometimes referred to as the Utility Mk1. The chassis was now gondola-shaped, with a rounded nose and a 38.5 hp derated Walter Mikron III engine faired into the rear end. A new unribbed wing with an area of 400 sq ft had a span of 35 ft, and the length was now 23 ft 3 in. Empty weight was 515 lb and all-up weight with pilot, passenger and 40 lb baggage was of the order of 1,000 lb. A maximum speed of 58 mph was claimed, with a cruising speed of 50 mph. Initial climb was 690 ft/min and ceiling 5,000 ft.

At a demonstration at White Waltham in May 1957, by which time it had accumulated about 40 hr flying time, the wing of XK776 was inflated in only 15 minutes, and it then flew round very purposefully despite bumpy wind conditions. It demonstrated good directional and lateral stability, making several turns near the ground in the course of a number of take-offs and landings, the only slight criticism being a tendency to yaw on occasions. This machine was delivered to Boscombe Down on 6 September 1957 for assessment on behalf of the War Office, but suffered some damage to the struts and propeller in an accident on 25 October. Following repair by the manufacturers it returned to Boscombe Down on 18 November 1957 to continue the trials, until being despatched to the Army Air Corps at Middle Wallop on 22 August 1960.

The final machine, XK781 had further improvements, and was designated the Utility Mk2, being fitted with a J.A.P. engine when it went to Boscombe Down on 14 March 1958 to help with the assessment trials. It was also fitted later with a Wooller engine of around 60 hp. Tests ended in 1960, the sole survivor being XK776 which is now held on loan at Middle Wallop by the Museum of Army Flying, having been received there from Cardington in July 1982.

ML Utility Mk1 XK781. (MAP)

Chapter 12

WARTIME WING EXPERIMENTS

Wing design has always been a fruitful field for research, and during the Second World War several interesting experiments were carried out on unusual wing configurations. Among these were slip-wings to assist take-off, and two quite different wing layouts from the imaginative Miles fold, though none of these led to anything of practicable use.

HILLSON BI-MONO

The increasing weight of aircraft was leading to problems of weight limitation during take-off. The Short Mayo Composite had attempted to get around this difficulty by having a lightly loaded mother aircraft undertake the piggy-back take-off of a smaller aircraft which was fully fuelled as well as having a full payload. Another possible solution being tried was that of in-flight refuelling.

An alternative approach was to increase wing area for take-off by fitting an upper slip-wing which could be jettisoned when the aircraft was airborne. An idea for such a device fitted to a bomber had been submitted to the Air Ministry in the late 1920s by W.S. Gray, but he had been given no encouragement. Then around 1937/38 H.J. Stieger, chief designer of Blackburn Aircraft, who earlier was the originator of the monospar wing developed by General Aircraft, drew up a design for a large transatlantic flying boat using the slip-wing principle. He followed this up with a proposal for an unarmed bomber with high wing-loading in flight, but which took off as a biplane with an additional wing cast off when a safe height had been reached. He claimed that a very high speed could be obtained with a large bomb and fuel load, but when his design was examined in detail it was found that the drag estimates were optimistic and that the fuselage cross-section and space available in the wing was insufficient to permit a standard bomb load and fuel to be stored. In practice the only gain would be in shortening the take-off distance and increasing safety during climb. Receiving no encouragement Blackburn then dropped the idea, being more anxious to design an aeroplane to an Air Staff Requirement rather than a purely experimental aeroplane.

The idea re-emerged in 1940, when W.R. Chown, Managing Director of F. Hills & Sons Ltd, which manufactured light aircraft at Trafford Park, Manchester, put to the Air Ministry the idea of a cheap fighter which could take off from grass fields and roads using a detachable wing. Official support was not forthcoming, but work nevertheless commenced as a private venture on a scale model, this being a small low-wing monoplane with a detachable upper wing, completed and constructed in just over seven weeks from inception. Fitted with 200 hp de Havilland Gipsy Six engine the Bi-Mono, as it was known, had a wing span of 20 ft and a length of 19 ft 6 in, the two equal-span wings each having an area of 66 sq ft. It was never given any form of registration or serial number, but was allotted the appellation Experimental Aeroplane No.133 in the wartime series.

When the aircraft was complete, Chown went to see the Ministry, but a subsequent official internal memorandum dated 28 November 1940 laid emphasis on the fact that the Directorate of Technical Development had no connection at any stage with the scheme, and that they thought it unlikely to come to anything. Chown was nevertheless still keen to go ahead, so it was agreed that someone from Farnborough should look at the machine so as to be satisfied it was reasonably safe in its existing form, and then help him to test it, though reservations were expressed as to whether it would turn out to be safe to try throwing

The Hillson Bi-Mono in biplane configuration.

The Hillson Bi-Mono in monoplane configuration.

away the top wing.

Some modifications were made, and numerous tests were then carried with the completed form, both in monoplane and biplane configuration, and also ground tests using bungees attached to the upper wing. On 16 July 1941, following a conference at Farnborough, the machine took off as a biplane from Squires Gate. Escort

HILLSON BI-MONO
GIPSY VI
ARRANGED AS MONOPLANE
NOV 1941

was provided by a Lockheed Hudson equipped with cine-camera recorders, and carrying Chown and his chief designer in addition to scientific research staff from Farnborough. After climbing to 4,500 ft, about five miles west of Blackpool Tower, the upper mainplane was jettisoned. It sailed away safely above the aircraft before being lost in the sea, and the pilot had no difficulty in keeping control. He experienced no alteration of trim during the transition, which was only followed by a gentle and controlled loss of height of a few hundred feet.

SLIP-WING HURRICANE

Having proved the feasibility of the idea, Hillsons then went on to carry out a full-scale trial using an adapted Hawker Hurricane. This was a British-built machine (originally L1884), fitted with a standard Rolls-Royce Merlin II, but which by the time of its allotment was carrying the RCAF serial number 321, which it retained. It was known as Experimental Aeroplane No.205 in the wartime series, and Hillsons designed a supplementary wing of the same outline as the normal Hurricane wing, of plywood-covered two-spar wooden construction. With an area of 328 sq ft and root chord of 7 ft, it weighed 693 lb including the release gear, and was attached to the lower wing by N-struts, as well as having smaller struts attached diagonally to the fuselage below the cockpit in order to prevent lateral movement. The only modification to the basic machine was an extra ten per cent elevator area to give supplementary control. The wing was released by means of an electric solenoid, but as a precaution a mechanical release

Hawker Hurricane RCAF321 fitted with the Hillson slip-wing.

device was also provided. A number of tests were carried out from 1942 at Sealand and later Farnborough on the F.H.40 Mk.I, as the combination was called, but development of the idea eventually ceased, the company concentrating on producing Percival Proctors under sub-contract.

MILES X-MINOR

In 1936, the prolific brain of F.G. Miles had come up with the notion of a proposal for a revolutionary design of commercial transport aircraft. Designated the 'X', the machine would have had a broad, shallow fuselage of aerofoil section, the wings merging gradually into the fuselage sides. Power was to be by four 750 hp Rolls-Royce Kestrel VI engines buried in the wings, their propellers being driven through gearboxes and extension shafts, a top speed of 275 mph being envisaged. The fuselage design would provide space for a greater amount of fuel and either passengers or freight, than would have been possible with an equivalent sized orthodox machine.

A revised version in 1938 was designated the X.2, and this time 800 hp Kestrel IX engines were proposed, giving an estimated top speed of 295 mph and a range of 4,200 miles. Wingspan was limited to 99 ft as this was the most which could be fitted with adequate clearance in a standard hangar. The Air Ministry was sufficiently interested to offer a £25,000 development contract under Specification 42/37, but this was declined.

The advent of war put the project in abeyance for a time, but by 1941 further design studies were in progress with projects ranging up to the X.15 in 1943. Sizes increased up to a span of 150 ft in some instances, and various configurations of 4, 6 and 8 engines were considered, power

The Miles X-Minor U-0233 scale-model for the X-series of projected aircraft. (MAP)

being supplied it was proposed variously by such engines as the Merlin, Griffon, Centaurus and Sabre, as well as the abortive Rolls-Royce Crecy.

In 1941, Miles decided to build a flying scale model to test out his theories. Given the company designation M.30, it was known as the X-Minor, and received the wartime Class B registration U-0233. In practice this design did not prove easy, due to problems of scale, but the project went ahead nevertheless. There could be no question of housing the engines within the wings, and instead these were fitted with two underslung 130 hp de Havilland Gipsy Major Is. The fuselage had to be of sufficient depth to accommodate the crew of two, and even with them sitting on the floor it was not possible to produce full merging of the lower fuselage with the wings. A tricycle undercarriage was fitted, and the cockpit was situated in the nose, having a large Perspex moulding.

The machine was given its first flight test at Woodley in February 1942 by Tommy Rose, and a number of subsequent flights were made, producing much useful data. In 1944 the company put forward its six Sabre-engined X.15 design as a competitor for Specification 2/44, based on the Brabazon Committee's Specification No.1 for a large post-war civil airliner, but the contract for this was won by the Bristol company, which produced its Type 167, later named the Brabazon. The X-Minor had meanwhile finished its flight trials, and ended its days as part of the technical equipment of the Miles Aeronautical Technical School.

MILES LIBELLULA

Yet another unusual concept from the Miles stable was the unorthodox tandem wing design known as the Libellula, its name being derived from the entomological title of the dragonfly family. It was first envisaged by George Miles

in late 1941 as a carrier-borne aircraft, for which he saw several advantages over the modified Spitfires and Hurricanes then being hastily produced for this purpose. Its narrow span would obviate the need for wingfolding, simplifying handling aboard ship, and making less demands on hangar space. An additional advantage would be the excellent field of view from the nose-mounted cockpit, reducing the hazards of deck landing.

To prove his theories, Miles had a wooden flying scale model constructed, designated the M.35. Fitted with a 130 hp de Havilland Gipsy Major I engine and having a tricycle undercarriage it used surplus spare parts around the factory, and took only six weeks to complete. Given the Class B registration U-0235, it took to the air at Woodley in the hands of its designer on 1 May 1942, only to prove longitudinally unstable, a fact which could have been deduced beforehand had wind tunnel tests been carried out.

Undeterred, Miles made a number of modifications, and was able to continue trials with some success. The aircraft had its limitations, however, as due to lack of proper cooling the engine soon reached its maximum temperature, and the machine could therefore never be taken higher than a few hundred feet. No official support was forthcoming, and in fact the design team met with disapproval for having built the prototype without sanction. Needless to say, this did not deter Miles from continuing with the concept.

Turning his attention to a larger machine on the same lines, the M.39 design was submitted to meet Specification B.11/41 for a high speed unarmed day bomber, which also attracted interest from Armstrong Whitworth, de Havilland and Hawker. The specification required a machine capable of 350 mph at 30,000 ft, with a still-air range of 1,600 miles carrying a bomb load of 4,000 lb. The Miles submission would have had a swept rear wing with a span of 55 ft 9 in, and a straight front wing of 40 ft span, giving

Miles M.35 Libellula in flight (MAP)

Ground view of Miles Libellula M.39B UO244. (via R.C.B. Ashworth)

a combined wing area of 556 sq ft. Estimated all-up weight was 26,750 lb, and power would have been provided by two 1,600 hp Merlin 61 engines. Looking ahead, three Whittle W.2/500 jet engines were envisaged, giving an outstanding performance and bomb load, but these were unavailable at that stage.

Sufficient interest was shown in the Miles design for

3169.

Flying view of the Miles Libellula with new serial number SR392. (MAP)

a five-eighths scale model to be ordered, to Specification B.11/41/2, and this received the wartime designation Experimental Aeroplane No.217. Known by the company as the M.39B, it had the Class B registration U-0244, and was powered by two wing-mounted 130 hp de Havilland Gipsy Major Is. George Miles again undertook the first

flight, on 22 July 1943, and the new aircraft proved much more stable. Despite this, no orders were placed, and in fact the B.11/41 Specification lapsed. U- 0244 was later purchased by the Ministry of Aircraft Production, however, and flown on 12 February 1944 to Farnborough, where it undertook development work with the military serial number SR392. It later returned to Woodley, with the post-war Class B Registration U4, but was scrapped after the firm went into liquidation in 1948.

The third de Havilland Swallow in flight. (RAF Museum)

Armstrong Whitworth AW.52 RG324 at the SBAC Show Farnborough in 1955. (M.J. Hooks)

Handley Page HP.115 XP841 showing its classic 'paper dart' planform (M.J. Hooks)

Avro 707C WZ744 side-by-side trainer preserved at the Cosford Aerospace Museum in 1986. (Stuart Howe)

Handley Page HP.115 XP841 lined up for take-off. (M.J. Hooks)

Boulton Paul P.111 VT935 seen in a static display 1974. (M.J. Hooks) C6 ▲

Fairey FD.2 WG774 first prototype in its original natural finish in 1955. (RAF Museum)

BAC.221 WG774 ready for take-off, 1966. (M.J. Hooks)

BAC.221 WG774 in the landing configuration. (BAC)

The second prototype Fairey FD.2 WG774, and the first machine WG777, after modification to BAC.221 configuration, flying together at RAE Bedford in October 1966. (BAC)

Reid & Sigrist Bobsleigh VZ728 prone-pilot research aircraft painted in an inaccurate wartime colour scheme in 1974. (M.J. Hooks)

Gloster Meteor WK935 prone-pilot research aircraft preserved at the Cosford Aerospace Museum in 1986. (Stuart Howe)

Facing page photographs:
BAC Concorde G-BSST taking off from Filton for its maiden flight at the hands of Brian Trubshaw, 9 April 1969. (BAC)

BAC Concorde G-BSST shows off its planform. (BAC)

Short SC.1 XG900 in hover above a special platform at Belfast. (via Mike Stroud)

Hawker P.1127 XP831 in a static display at Upavon, 6 June 1962. (M.J. Hooks)

Hawker P.1127 XP972 in the colours of the Tripartite Evaluation Squadron, September 1962. (RAF Museum P.100446)

Hunting H.126 XN714 preserved in its original bright yellow colour scheme, at the Cosford Aerospace Museum in 1986. (Stuart Howe)

Hawker P.1052 VX279 in its original form before conversion to become the Hawker P.1081, seen above the clouds on 22 April 1949, a few days after its first flight. (RAF Museum)

Supermarine 510 VV106 preserved at the Cosford
Aerospace Museum in 1986. (Stuart Howe)

Cierva Air Horse VZ724 in September 1949. (RAF
Museum P.100131)

Fairey Rotodyne XE521 in its original natural
finish, May 1958. (RAF Museum)

Fairey Rotodyne XE521 in its later colour scheme, 1959. (M.J. Hooks)

Bristol 173 XH379 in natural aluminium finish. (M.J. Hooks)

Bristol 173 G-ALBN flying low over the Severn Estuary, 19 September 1952. (RAF Museum)

Fairey Jet Gyrodyne XJ389. (M.J. Hooks)

Fairey Gyrodyne G-AIKF taking off from White Waltham, June 1948. (RAF Museum)

Facing page, top:
Saro SR.A1 G-12-1 at the Skyfame Museum, Staverton in 1966. (M.J. Hooks)

Facing page, bottom:
EEC P.1 prototype WG760 bearing ground instructional serial 7755M and a spurious Lightning colour scheme, Henlow 1967. (M.J. Hooks)

BAC TSR.2 XR219 takes off on a test flight. (BAe)

A superb air-to-air of BAC TSR.2 XR219, showing off its angular lines. (BAe)

Saro SR.53 XD145 jet/rocket fighter. (Michael Stroud)

Saro SR.53 XD145 close-up showing the wingtip fitting of the de Havilland Firestreak air-to-air missile. (M.J. Hooks)

Bristol 188 XF926 in company with a Hunter chase aircraft at Filton. (BAe)

BAe EAP ZF534 demonstrates future thinking for fighter aircraft. (BAe)

Chapter 13
BIRTH OF THE JET

During the early part of 1938 the Air Ministry decided to place an order for one of the new Whittle jet engines, for practical flying trials. The question of an aircraft constructor then arose, and as luck would have it, Sqn Ldr J.McC. Reynolds, a friend of Frank Whittle from his cadet days at Cranwell was then Ministry overseer at Glosters. In the period immediately before the war that experienced company had little work of its own in hand and the design staff were only engaged in abortive studies, so rather fortuitously there were both technical skill and construction facilities readily available.

Accordingly, on 21 January 1940, the Directorate of Technical Development issued Specification E.28/39 to cover the design and construction of a high speed single-engined single-seater research aeroplane powered by the Whittle jet engine, and this was received by Gloster on 3 February. Maximum speed at sea level was to be not less than 380 mph, and the sea level rate of climb was to be at least 4,000 ft/min, though these were both contingent on the engine producing a maximum static thrust of 1,200 lb. Some consideration was given to the comfort of the pilot, an efficient heating system being specified as well as precautions to exclude draughts. He was also to have adequate escape hatches in case he needed either to parachute from the aircraft in flight, or to exit in the event of the machine overturning on the ground.

The design was to be kept as simple as possible so as to reduce costs and facilitate manufacture, and a mock-up was required within three months. The engine installation and related equipment had to be carried out to the satisfaction of Power Jets Ltd, its manufacturers, and the engine had to be suitably protected against the ingress of solid bodies to the compressor. A reliable method would be necessary for starting the engine on the ground, and

there would have to be some means of re-lighting the burners in the air. A tail parachute was also to be fitted.

Interestingly, although it was to be primarily a research machine, the design was also to be based on the requirements for a fixed gun interceptor fighter, as far as the limitations of size and weight imposed by the available power unit would permit. Armament was to comprise four .303 in Browning guns and 2,000 rounds of ammunition, although in practice this was never installed.

At a meeting held on 10 April 1940 it was stressed that the primary purpose of this aircraft was to get the engine in flight and to give experience in jet propulsion. Two machines were to be ordered under contract SB.3229, serialled W4041 and W4046, of which W4041 was to be tested with the W.1 and W.2, and the W4046 with the W.1A and W.2., though in the event things turned out differently.

Glosters already had design experience of a single-engined monoplane fighter, the unsuccessful F.5/34, and the new machine followed roughly similar lines. George Carter, the chief designer, and Frank Whittle worked closely together on the project, which emerged as a low wing monoplane fitted with a tricycle undercarriage and a single fin and rudder mounted forward of the tailplane. The large cockpit was sited well forward on the fuselage, which had a circular cross-section, the nose intake being also circular, whilst the engine was installed above the centre section, with a small-diameter jet-pipe in the lower tail. In addition to alternative engines, three sets of wings were to be built, two having a normal NACA 23012 section and the other a high-speed EC1240 section.

Due to the danger from enemy bombing, construction of W4041 was dispersed to Regent Motors at Cheltenham, and from there it was transported by road to Hucclecote for taxiing trials. Fitted initially with a Whittle

An early shot of Gloster E.28/39 prototype W4041 bearing heat-sensitive paint strips on each side of the rear fuselage. (via M.J. Hooks)

W.1X engine and the NACA-section wing, it undertook three taxiing runs on 7 and 8 April 1941 at the hands of the firm's chief test pilot, P.E.G. Sayer. He reported that the engine ran very well, being very smooth indeed with no vibration being observed in the pilot's cockpit. In each of the three runs, the aircraft had left the ground and risen to a height of about 6 ft for between 100 and 200 yards. The undercarriage rode very well, particularly taking into account the rough surface of the aerodrome.

Lateral stability was good, and there was no tendency to drop a wing after leaving the ground at a fairly high angle of incidence. Nor was there any tendency for the nose wheel to shimmy. His only real criticism related to the throttle, which he found too coarse, a large increase in engine revolutions being obtained with little forward movement of the throttle lever. It was then decided that further tests could be undertaken with greater security in the more sparsely populated Lincolnshire area, so the prototype was transported by road to RAF Cranwell in great secrecy and under armed guard. Its serial was painted as W4041/G – the 'G' indicating that it had to be guarded at all times whilst on the ground – and given the wartime designation Experimental Aeroplane No.137.

Sayer carried out a preliminary taxiing run on 14 May, then the following day became the pilot of the first British turbo-jet to fly, powered this time by a Whittle W.1 engine providing 855 lb static thrust and fitted with one of the NACA-sectioned wings. To give himself the longest run available on the aerodrome he taxied down to the most easterly end of the Cranwell runway, though in the event his aircraft left the ground after only 500-600 yards. He then climbed slowly, finding the aircraft rather unstable fore and aft, which he thought might have been due to the elevators being oversensitive. After a few gentle turns he came in for a landing which he found to be straightforward, having been aloft for just 17 minutes.

By the end of the month 15 flights had been made without any real problems, a full load of fuel being carried on each occasion to allow flights of up to 56 minutes. A level speed of 317 mph had been attained at heights up to 20,000 ft at 16,500 rpm, and 350 mph at 25,000 ft at 17,000 rpm. A height of 24,000 ft had been reached in 25.5. min at 16,000 rpm. Stability had been found satisfactory, and elevator control had been improved by fitting trimmer cord above and below the trailing edge. The rudder was fairly light and the ailerons reasonably light and responsive at a small angle. Nose wheel unlocking was unsatisfactory, however.

On 28 July three Americans visited the Gloster factory on behalf of the US Government, Col. Lyon, Major Brandt and Mr Schoultz being accompanied by Dr. Roxbee Cox and Mr Allright of the Ministry of Aircraft Production. They asked for specifications and drawings of both the E.28/39 and F.9/40 to be released to the American Government, and eleven days later the Minister agreed to this.

Around the same time a target date of 15 September was set for W4041 to resume flight trials, with W4046 having its first flight soon afterwards, powered by a W.2B, the latter due for delivery from Power Jets by about the

Second prototype Gloster E.28/39 W4046/G in flight. (Rolls-Royce Ltd)

end of October. All this turned out to be very optimistic, and it was not until 4 February 1942 that W4041 was ready for further taxiing trials, this time at Edgehill in Warwickshire, now powered by an 860 lb thrust W.1A(1) and fitted with the high speed wing. The new engine soon caused trouble, various problems being encountered, including a complete failure on 6 June resulting in a forced landing, fortunately without damage to the aircraft. Oil feed problems at high altitude turned out to be the cause, and at the end of May another trial was carried out with modification to prevent freezing at height. Very low oil pressure, however, caused another forced landing in front of an audience of distinguished American visitors, the skin of the port wing being damaged when it scraped the ground on touchdown.

W4041 was again out of action for a time, and this turned out to be Sayer's last flight in her, for in October he was killed when his Typhoon crashed into the sea after a collision during a visit to RAF Acklington. His place was taken by his assistant, Michael Daunt, who made the next flight from Farnborough later in the year, to complete tests of the new oil system before handing her over to the RAE test pilots.

In the meantime W4046/G was at last nearing completion, and made its first flight on 1 March 1943, fitted with a 1,200 lb thrust Rover-built W.2B and piloted by John Grierson, the firm's development test pilot. On 16 April it flew with a 1,526 lb thrust Rolls-Royce W.2B/23 (later known as the Welland), and the following day made a cross-country trip to Hatfield to be demonstrated before Win-

ston Churchill. This machine, which was sometimes referred to there as the 'Weaver' but codenamed 'Tourist' at Farnborough, met its end on 30 July 1943 when the ailerons froze up at 37,000 ft during a ceiling climb and went into an inverted spin, Sqn Ldr Douglas Davie becoming the first pilot to bale out from a British jet aircraft.

This was a setback, but jet engine power was now an established fact, and the trials continued with W4041/G, which flew again on 23 May 1943 fitted with a 1,620 lb thrust Whittle W2/500 and incorporating other modifications. After an initial flight by Daunt at Hucclecote, engine development trials were continued at Barford St.John by Grierson, who reached a height of 42,170 ft on 24 June during an oxygen climb thus becoming the first jet pilot to climb above 40,000 ft. The high-speed wing was fitted afterwards, resulting in an increase of 4 mph in the stalling speed. W4041/G was then sent to Farnborough, being fitted with end-plate fins to counteract some instability.

On 4 June the aircraft had been flown by a service pilot, Group Captain A.H. Wheeler, who carried out various manoeuvres, and attained a speed of 360 mph at the bottom of a dive. He reported that he considered it an excellent aircraft and engine with which to do aerobatics, and did not contemplate any trouble at all in executing any manoeuvres. Delays in delivery of a new W.2/500 producing 1,760 lb thrust delayed further trials until April 1944, following which a ten-hour flying programme was completed to provide aerodynamic data of various kinds.

This historic aircraft, which has been referred to as the 'Pioneer', is now preserved in the Science Museum in South Kensington, where it was sent on 28 April 1946 for permanent exhibition.

Chapter 14
SECOND GENERATION JETS

With the appearance of the jet engine, and its successful first flight in the Gloster E.28/39, ways of utilising its potentially great power were sought, and the evolution of British jet propelled aircraft then branched off in several directions. Glosters themselves developed their F.9/40 design into the highly successful Meteor fighter. Three other wartime projects stemming from official Specifications classified as Experimental are the subject of this chapter, one of them also by Gloster.

DE HAVILLAND SPIDER CRAB

An early example of this development phase was Air Staff Requirement OR.107, leading to Specification E.6/41 for a high-speed single-seat fighter utilising Major F.B. Halford's jet engine design, and suitable for operation at great heights, and anywhere in the world. Minimum requirements included a service ceiling of 48,000 ft and a maximum speed of 490 mph at 35,000 ft. It was to be fitted with a pressure cabin which was to be automatic, and sufficient to maintain conditions appropriate to 25,000 ft when flying at 40,000 ft. The aircraft had to provide a steady gun platform and be kept as small as possible consistent with the use of a pressure cabin. The design of the latter, with its associated equipment, was to be carried forward in full co-operation with the Royal Aircraft Establishment. Whoever won the contract must pool all ideas on this aspect not only with the RAE, but also with other firms designing pressure cabins for the Ministry of Aircraft Production.

The task was eventually entrusted to de Havilland who were initially awarded a contract, number SB.24539/C.23(a), in May 1942 for two aircraft, to be given serial numbers LZ548 and LZ551, this being extended a month later by an additional prototype to be MP838. The Specification was not finalised until 8 December 1942, but the firm lost little time on this exciting venture, and by 24 August 1943 LZ548/G was ready for taxiing trials at Hatfield.

The fitting of a jet engine, the Halford-designed 2,700 lb thrust de Havilland Goblin D.Gn.1, had allowed the design of a completely new concept, bearing little resemblance to previous practical aircraft. The main fuselage consisted of a relatively short streamlined nacelle with the pilot's cockpit situated well forward, giving him an excellent view. The engine was fitted immediately behind him, with a round exhaust at the rear of the nacelle and the intakes built into the roots of the unswept wings which were sited towards the rear of the nacelle. This method of installation had the advantage of needing minimal ducting and tailpipe lengths, thus avoiding undue frictional losses. Twin tail booms extended from the wings, aligned just outside the intakes, twin pointed fins being joined by a tailplane set fairly high to avoid compressibility problems. With no propeller to worry about, the tricycle undercarriage was quite short, so that the machine sat low on the ground. Overall length was 30 ft 9 in, span 40 ft and wing area 250.7 sq ft.

Five taxiing runs were made that first day, in each of which the aircraft left the ground for approximately 100 yards, the only problem noted being that due to the short undercarriage legs the rear end of the tail booms were very near the ground, and on one occasion touched it. This was easily corrected by altering the ground angle in relation to the longitudinal datum, in order to increase ground clearance.

By 20 September, now bearing the unlikely code name of Spider Crab, it was ready for proper flight, taking off for a trip which lasted thirty minutes. This was largely

The first prototype de Havilland Spider Crab LZ548/G at Hatfield on 16 August 1943, prior to the first taxiing trials.

satisfactory, though several criticisms were made by the pilot, Geoffrey de Havilland, junior. The ailerons proved to be overbalanced at speeds exceeding 400 mph ISA, and with the overbalance came an out-of-true, left wing down attitude. Both longitudinal and directional stability were generally satisfactory, except for a slight residual oscillation after the aircraft was yawed by rudder movement.

On 12 November 1943 the aircraft was given an official test by Wing Cdr H.J.Wilson, who was quite impressed. He reported that the cockpit layout was simple and satisfactory. The taxiing characteristics and view were also satisfactory, the aircraft was easily controlled on take-off, the undercarriage retracted quickly and the initial rate of climb was very good. He found the controls light and responsive, and both longitudinal and latitudinal stability were very good apart from snaking, especially in bumps. Rather disconcerting, however, was the absence of any warning of the stall, which occurred at 86 mph with flaps down and 95 mph with them up. His overall conclusion was that it was an extremely pleasant and easy aircraft to fly, though directional hunting required some correction and the stall characteristics ought to be improved if possible. Having said that though, he commented that there were aircraft already in service with stalling qualities which were just as bad.

In an attempt to improve directional stability, LZ548 was tested on 3 January 1944 with fin modifications, and five days later it flew with a sharper lip to the air intakes in a successful attempt to improve the stalling characteristics. On 10 February, Wilson carried out a further test, again commenting that he found it a very nice aircraft to fly, all the controls being correctly light and well harmonised, and the response exceptionally good. The view out and the freedom from noise and vibration inspired him with great confidence and, he reported, he had never flown a nicer aircraft.

On 21 January 1944, MP838/G became the second aircraft to fly, this being fitted with what became a standard armament of four 20 mm Hispano cannon in the nose, and being used for development and armament trials. It was followed on 17 March by the unarmed LZ551/G, the name Spider Crab being still in use at that time.

Machine MP838/G, the third prototype, was sent to Boscombe Down for evaluation as to its suitability for possible use as an RAF fighter. Powered by a single Halford H.1A engine it was flown from Hatfield on 21 May 1944, and tested until 23 August when it left by road for the English Electric works at Preston. Performance tests were limited, due to the needs of other trials then being carried out, but the provisional assessment was that the machine compared very favourably with fighter aircraft of that time. It proved to have excellent aileron control, it was easy to manoeuvre in a loop, and it could attain high speeds at low altitudes. The cockpit was described as being well laid out, and there was an extremely low noise level.

On the debit side, however, both front and rear view from the cockpit were poor, and the control grip came

The second prototype de Havilland Spider Crab taking off from HMS *Ocean* in December 1945. (RAF Museum 6089-9)

in for some criticism. The pilot was likely to experience difficulty in jettisoning the hood in an emergency, and it was therefore advised that the locking pin be replaced by a locking wire which could be easily sheared. With regard to performance, acceleration in level flight was inferior to that of contemporary fighters, and a marked directional steadiness would seriously impair its suitability for this role. Endurance was limited, the rate of climb was poor, and it was thought there could be difficulties in formation flying.

LZ548/G was eventually lost when it crashed through engine failure on 23 July 1945, but LZ551/G was converted to become the prototype for a navalised version of the Vampire, being known as the Sea Vampire F.10. Fitted with an arrester hook, it flew from Hatfield to Farnborough on 26 September 1945, making the first ever deck landing of a jet aircraft, aboard HMS *Ocean* on 3 December at the hands of Lt Cdr Eric 'Winkle' Brown, though he was not happy about the prospects for using jet aircraft aboard carriers. This aircraft was later used for rubber deck landing trials at Farnborough, and in 1972 finally went to the FAA Museum at Yeovilton.

The design went on to be a considerable success, renamed more sensibly as the Vampire. It was used extensively by many air forces in addition to the Royal Air Force. Despite Lt Cdr Brown's misgivings, it went into service with both the Royal Navy and the Royal Australian Navy as the Sea Vampire, and total production of land and sea vari-

ants was well into four figures. Although trials were carried out with de Havilland Ghost and Rolls-Royce Nene engines, the Goblin remained the standard power plant on British aircraft.

The success of this and other contemporary de Havilland designs led to much of the early Vampire production being undertaken by English Electric at Preston, and substantial numbers were also produced in France as the Mistral. Both the French and RAN versions used the Rolls-Royce Nene engine, manufactured by Hispano-Suiza and the Commonwealth Aircraft Corporation respectively. Side-by-side two seat variants included both night fighters and trainers, and a development also went into full production as the Venom.

The third prototype de Havilland Spider Crab fitted with an extended fin and rudder.

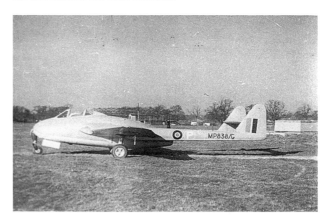

GLOSTER E.1/44

On 31 January 1942 Glosters wrote to the Ministry of Aircraft Production putting forward their own proposal for a single-engined jet propelled fighter taking advantage of their experience with the E.28/39 and F.9/40. This fell on receptive ears, as the Ministry were at that time concerned about delivery delays with both the de Havilland-built Halford engines and the Rover-built Whittle W.2Bs required for the F.9/40 prototypes. As a contingency plan, therefore, Air Staff Requirement OR.116 was drawn up for such a single-engined machine, leading to Specification E.5/42. In fact the problems with the F.9/40 were eventually overcome, and the machine went on to become famous as the highly successful Meteor, but that could not have been foreseen at the time.

Ministerial approval for the project was given in a letter dated 3 July 1942, which also bestowed the name Ace. Although the project had originated with Gloster, it was no means automatic, however, that they would gain the contract. The Ministry thought the task should be entrusted to Armstrong Whitworth to be worked out in detail, on the assumption that they would be able to devote much attention to the design straight away, rather than Gloster who had a heavy design commitment on the F.9/40. Gloster were having none of this, pointing out in a letter to the Ministry on 11 July that they saw the Ace proposal as merging into one aircraft all the knowledge and experience they had acquired as a result of the specialised work they had done during the past few years. The project was at a somewhat critical stage of development, and they regarded the proposal as impracticable and certain to involve the very great risk of more serious delay and confusion. Nine days later Sir Frank Spriggs wrote to the Ministry from Hawker Siddeley Aviation, the controlling company, to say that of his two constituent companies he would prefer to leave the project with Gloster. On 14 August the Ministry backed down and finally agreed to the commitment remaining with Gloster.

Jet aircraft were then still in their infancy, and although the design was intended from the start to become a fighter, it was to be regarded initially as an experimental project, hence the E-prefix to the specification. Nevertheless, future requirements would have to be borne in mind, and particularly the need for possible mass production under the limitations of wartime conditions.

The Specification called for an aircraft fitted with a pressure cabin and capable of at least 485 mph in level flight at 30,000 feet as well as a maximum diving speed of 550 mph. Service ceiling had to be not less than 47,000 feet, and preferably much greater. Armament was specified as two fixed 20mm Hispano MkIV or MkV guns, with provision for two further such guns. The aircraft must be as small as possible, but would have to be capable of operation at great height and in any part of the world. The firm received a contract (SB.26236) on 29 January 1943 for three prototypes, to carry serial numbers NN648, NN651 and NN655 and be powered by a 2,300 Halford H.1 or H.2 engine. The specification was in the meantime still being

An unpainted Gloster E.1/44 with a low tailplane, almost certainly SM809. (via R.C.B. Ashworth)

developed, not being finalised until 26 March 1943. Between April and August a 1:4.5 scale model of the design was tested in the low-speed wind-tunnel at Farnborough, and in November construction work began at the Gloster experimental factory at Bentham, not far from its main base at Hucclecote.

By early 1944 a substantial number of further modifications had been made to the original specification, and on 7 February 1944 Glosters received a revised contract, the machines losing their originally intended identities to become SM801, SM805 and SM809. A new Specification was also drawn up, and this was issued on 29 May 1944 as E.1/44 and the engine was now to be a 5,000 lb thrust Rolls-Royce Nene.

Around this time the three machines were brought into the standardised SBAC type numbering system in which each firm used an identifying company letter, followed by a letter/number combination commencing at A1. Glosters made comparatively little use of the system, but GA.1 was allotted to the Ace, and the wartime designation Experimental Aeroplane No.248 was also applied.

Of the three machines, SM801 was intended purely as a flying shell and SM805 as an operational prototype. The changing demands of the Specification, however, led to extensive reworking of the design, and the consequent abandonment of work on these two. In their place, construction of SM809 began during the latter half of 1944 under the designation GA.2. In its new form it was designed specifically with sub-contracted production in mind, the fuselage comprising five sub-assemblies, and the wings being divided into four parts.

On 26 January 1945 three further prototypes were ordered under contract SB.27324/C.23(a), still under the GA.2 designation, to have serial numbers TX145, TX148 and TX150 and be fitted with 5,000 lb thrust Nene 2 engines.

During that year tests were carried out in the Farnborough wind-tunnel of a 1:4.5 scale model of the latest design, as well as tests of a 1:2.5 scale model of an engine intake duct.

By 29 April 1946 the design was considered sufficiently encouraging for a pre-production contract, number 6/Acft/117/CB.2(a), to be issued for 20 machines, serial numbers VP601 to VP620. This was followed on 2 July 1946 by a similar order for 20 more, VR164 to VR183, only for this order to be cancelled a few days later. Specification 23/46P was issued on 29 November 1946 to cover proposed full Nene-engined production, under the designation GA.4, but meanwhile work on the prototypes continued and in July 1947 SM809 was despatched to Boscombe Down for its initial flight. This was not to be, however, as during the road journey the transporter jack-knifed while going downhill, and the resultant damage to the aircraft was too much for repair to be contemplated.

To counter this disaster, work on TX145 was speeded up, and this time the journey to Boscombe Down was accomplished in safety, the maiden flight taking place on

The clean lines of the Gloster E.1/44 are seen in this photograph of TX148, fitted with a raised tailplane. (Russell Adams)

9 March 1948 at the hands of Bill Waterton, the firm's Chief Test Pilot. The subsequent test report looked favourably on the climb rate, and also the maximum achieved speed of 620 mph, but was critical of overall handling. As a consequence, a number of modifications were made to the next prototype, TX148, including a raised tailplane, and when it flew at Boscombe Down early in 1949 it proved to have an improved handling ability over its predecessor. A spin-off from the modification work was that the new tail was to provide the basis for a revised Meteor tail unit, fitted as standard on production F.8s.

Time was now running out for the E.1/44, however. Its role as a possible substitute for the Meteor was proving unnecessary, and the latter machine was seen as having more potential for development. TX150 was nearing completion, re-engined with a 5,000 lb thrust de Havilland Ghost engine, under the designation GA.3, but work was finally stopped before it could be completed, it being accepted on 8 November 1949 only for structural tests before being sold on 14 April 1950 to the College of Aeronautics.

TX145 and TX148 were retained for some time at Farnborough, where they arrived on 2 December 1949 and 14 February 1950 respectively. They were used for a time

in trials on parachute-braking and flying controls systems, but TX145 had its undercarriage damaged on 2 November 1950 when it suffered an engine failure, and on 10 January 1951, following repair, it developed a violent nosewheel shimmy during taxiing. On 24 September 1951 both were finally assigned to the Proof and Experimental Establishment at Shoeburyness.

SUPERMARINE 392

On 4 July 1944 Vickers Armstrong wrote to the Ministry of Aircraft Production putting forward a proposal for a new jet-powered aircraft then referred to as the 'Supermarine Specification 477'. It was suggested that by embodying a Supermarine Spiteful wing with the radiators removed, it would be possible to get into production at an early date, and with the minimum of labour, a jet fighter embodying all operational requirements.

Preliminary design work had in fact started only a fortnight earlier, based on Spiteful laminar-flow wings with extra fuel tanks replacing the wing radiators. Power was to be provided by the newly-designed Rolls-Royce RB.41 engine, the cabin would be pressurised and the four wing cannon retained.

This was immediately seen as an attractive proposition, an internal memorandum dated 21 July referring to it as being worthy of careful consideration. By using the Spiteful wing, it was considered possible to produce a prototype in little more than a year by which time any teething problems with the Spiteful wing or ailerons should have been worked out. Considered to be perhaps of greater importance was the large amount of fuel squeezed in (395 gallons), giving a far better range than any other existing jet fighter except the Lockheed P-80A. Some difficulties were foreseen with the centre of gravity and with retaining the conventional Spiteful undercarriage, but these could be overcome, and on 29 July a reply was sent to Vickers Armstrong requiring three prototypes, the first flight target date being optimistically set at 30 March 1945. More realistically, the Vickers response on 4 August suggested that this timetable was very tight, but nevertheless agreed it was possible.

Air Staff Requirement OR.182 was then formulated, followed in September by Specification E.10/44, which referred to a maximum speed of not less than 550 mph TAS at all heights up to 30,000 ft, and a service ceiling as high as possible, with a minimum of 45,000 ft. The design was to be such that a limited number of aircraft could be converted without difficulty during production for photographic reconnaissance duties. It was also suggested that the armament be transferred from the wings to the fuselage due to shortcomings in the Spiteful wing installation which, though an improvement on that of the Spitfire, was by no means ideal and did not compare with the Tempest for accessibility and maintenance.

On 9 September 1944 the company received a firm contract, number Acft/4562/C.23(c), for three prototypes of the Type 392, to be given serial numbers TS409, TS413

and TS416. Expenditure was initially limited rather sparingly to £150,000, though this was later increased to £500,000.

A mock-up of the aircraft was built, but work proceeded far more slowly than had been hoped, matters not being helped when the first prototype of the Spiteful crashed in September 1944, less than three months after its first flight. The second machine did not fly until 8 January 1945. This was not the company's only problem, however, as two days later they wrote to the Ministry pointing out that nearly six months had elapsed since the go-ahead had been given for three aircraft, during which time the Ministry of Labour had done practically nothing to help regarding skilled men for experimental and pre-production development. As a consequence they could not possibly give reliable delivery estimates. They optimistically said they would try for 10 completed aircraft by the end of that year, but made it plain that this was a pure guess.

In a reply dated 26 January they were told to give priority to the Jet Spiteful, as it was now referred to, and drop other projects not of high military urgency, such as the Seagull reconnaissance amphibian. Specification E.10/44 was finally issued on 6 February 1945 in what might be considered a re-run of the Spitfire's origins, that too having been originally a Supermarine concept, followed by an Air Staff Requirement leading to an official Specification.

On 21 March the Ministry carried out an official visit to Hursley Park, as a result of which a number of criticisms were made of the Type 392 design, centring around the undercarriage and engine. They were particularly unhappy about the lack of a tricycle undercarriage, which could lead to a risk of hot exhaust gases cracking concrete during run-up, destroying grass aerodrome surfaces during taxiing, and causing miniature sandstorms in desert take-offs with a deteriorating effect on the engines of following aircraft. No serious thought appeared to have been given to the need for rapid engine changes, and the firm were told that it would probably not be practical to change parts and therefore they must investigate quicker methods for a complete engine change.

In the meantime the possibility of a naval variant was explored under OR.195, leading to Specification E.1/45 being issued on 26 July 1945, and the second and third machines were now to be completed to this standard. Formal issue of the new Specification had in fact been preceded on 7 July by the award of a contract, number Acft/5530/CB.7(b), for 24 pre-production aircraft. These were to comprise six E.10/44 type, serial numbers VH980-VH985, and eighteen E.1/45 type of which the first four, serial numbers VH987-VH990, would be without folding wings and the remainder, serial numbers VH995-VH999 and VJ110-VJ118, with fully-folding wings, but this order was later cancelled. A naval variant of the Spiteful had been named the Seafang, and the E.1/45, which had the manufacturer's Type number 398, came to be known as the Jet Seafang, this being later changed to the rather clumsy Hooked Jet Spiteful.

The first prototype Supermarine 392. (via J.D.Oughton)

Even at this stage it was envisaged that the first prototype would fly by September 1945, followed within two months by the other two machines. All three were being constructed at the Hursley Park works, and it was planned to transport them to firm's aerodrome at High Post for final assembly, before being test flown at Boscombe Down. However, protracted handling problems with the Spiteful delayed progress on the Type 392, and by February 1946 the Admiralty had become so impatient, with its need to introduce jet aircraft into the Fleet Air Arm, that the whole of the pre-production order was cancelled. Instead, de Havillands received a welcome order for 18 Sea Vampire F.20s.

The first prototype, Type 392, TS409, finally emerged in mid-1946. Its 37 ft 16 in fuselage had of necessity a comparatively large cross-section, due to the diameter of its engine, but its curved lines were exceptionally clean, being broken only by the well-streamlined cockpit, beside which were two large air scoops. By contrast, the 36 ft 11 in span wings of 227.2 sq ft area retained the angular unswept lines of their Spiteful origins, the tail surfaces being of similar concept. The undercarriage was also essentially that of the Spiteful, but the other two machines were to be completed with long-stroke Seafang-type gear for deck landings.

This aircraft was Supermarine's first venture into jet propulsion, and as a consequence numerous modifications had to be incorporated into TS409 before it could undertake its first flight. This eventually occurred at Boscombe Down on 27 July 1946 in the hands of Jeffrey Quill, power being provided at that stage by an R.B.41 Nene engine

restricted to 12,000 rpm, at which it provided 4,300 lb thrust. It soon became apparent that the aircraft was prone to 'snaking', a type of directional instability which affected most early jet aircraft, particularly at higher speeds, and it was decided to reserve the second machine for investigation and development of handling characteristics.

TS409 put in an appearance at the first post-war SBAC display at Radlett, but it was not until 17 June 1947 that Mike Lithgow flew TS413 for the first time, fitted with a Nene 3. This had a Martin-Baker ejection seat in place of TS409's experimental Supermarine design. Other modifications included a larger tailplane and smaller fin, additional fuel tanks and various alterations to the wing accessories and air intakes. Even more prone to 'snaking', this was eventually corrected by adding beading from the top of the rudder to the bottom of the tab. TS413 soon commenced deck trials, its first landing aboard HMS *Illustrious* being made by Lithgow on 28 October 1947, the only problem being a tendency to float on approach, due to the lack of a propeller which normally provided pilots with an inherent braking effect.

On 26 February 1948 Lithgow set off from the firm's flight test base at Chilbolton for an attack on the International 100km Closed Circuit Record, achieving a speed of 560.634 mph, which he bettered the following day with a further flight in which he attained 564.882 mph. Unfortunately TS413 crashed in Bulford village, near Amesbury, on 23 June 1948, during measured take-off and handling trials, Lt T.J.A. King-Joyce, RN losing his life.

The RAF had little interest in the design from the start, and TS409 was now brought up to naval standard under contract 6/Acft/2949/CB.7(b) dated 18 October 1948, being first flown in this guise on 5 March 1949. It had been the intention to call the land-based version the Attacker, and rename the carrier version the Sea Attacker, but the latter title was dropped and instead all production machines were called Attacker. A deteriorating international situation precipitated an order in October 1948 for 63 naval aircraft.

Trials on instability in certain conditions led to the fitting of an extended dorsal fin on TS409, which left Chilbolton for Boscombe Down on 31 August 1949 to carry out handling trials with dive brakes. Two months later it had to make a wheels-up landing at RNAS Culdrose, but by the end of the year it was undergoing handling and jettison trials with drop tanks, these being continued at Boscombe Down from 6 January 1950. The machine was again damaged, however, on 8 February, when the tail oleo collapsed during a deck landing on HMS *Illustrious*. Following further repairs it returned to Boscombe Down, then in October 1951 went to Farnborough for non-flying barrier trials, before being eventually sent in February 1953 to RNAS Arbroath as a ground instructional machine, renumbered A2313.

The final prototype, TS416 had Type number 513 and was fitted with Nene 3, later replaced with a Nene 4, but it had a relatively short life. It flew on 24 January 1950 with improved wing position and various other modifications

The second prototype Supermarine 392. (Via J.D. Oughton)

including wider intakes, but without folding wings. It undertook a number of trials at Farnborough, including arrester gear, RATOG and ground deflection of jet exhaust, before going to RNAS St.Merryn in May 1954 as another ground instructional machine.

Production machines served with several first and second line squadrons of the Fleet Air Arm, and 36 land-based machines were also supplied to the Pakistan Air Force. The design had its limitations, however, and it was in due course superseded in the Royal Navy by the Hawker Sea Hawk.

Chapter 15
TAILLESS AIRCRAFT RESEARCH

On 3 July 1943 the Director of Scientific Research wrote to the Society of British Aircraft Constructors to inform them that a research programme was being inaugurated into tailless and tail-first aircraft. It was proposed to construct full scale aircraft and undertake tests of models.

A Tailless Aircraft Advisory Committee was then set up, and invitations to participate were extended in the first instance to the firms of Hawker, Westland, Saro, Vickers-Armstrong, Handley Page, de Havilland, Phillips & Powis and Fairey. Of these, Hawker wished to be kept informed but not actively involved, and both Saro and de Havilland similarly declined. Their places were taken by General Aircraft and Armstrong Whitworth.

The committee sat at regular intervals, and a series of flying scale models and later full sized aircraft came under their scrutiny. For the model tests, the pilot selected to carry out trials on their behalf was Squadron Leader Robert Kronfeld. His qualifications for this unique task were of the highest order, he not only having tested the tailless Baynes Carrier Wing but commencing in 1929, had experience of flying a series of tailless gliders and powered aircraft designed by Lippisch, Kupper and Henri Mignet – the latter being the infamous 'Flying Flea'.

Wind-tunnel tests with models could provide a certain amount of information, but the handling characteristics of such machines in comparison with conventional aircraft could only be determined by practical tests. It was necessary to establish trim ranges, and data had to be obtained about trim, particularly in relation to large wing incidences and the use of flaps. The best position had to be found for the flaps, and the effectiveness of controls had to be determined over the whole speed range. Stability, and behaviour at the stall, had also to be investigated.

As a yardstick, the General Aircraft Hotspur glider was to be used for evaluation purposes, it being a typical standard cantilever monoplane with pleasant handling characteristics, which could be directly compared with both the tailless glider designs.

HANDLEY PAGE MANX
One powered aircraft was already available. In 1936, Dr Gustav Lachmann, then Experimental Designer with Handley Page, had suggested that the firm undertake development of tailless aircraft. He was particularly concerned to investigate their longitudinal and directional stability and control, as well as landing and taxiing characteristics and the effect of using flaps. A separate research department was set up at Edgware, and a small prototype was planned, fitted with two 140 de Havilland Gipsy Major II engines.

Progress was slow, but two years later construction was entrusted to Dart Aircraft Ltd at Dunstable. By the end of that year financial difficulties had arisen, requiring an influx of funds from Handley Page, and the machine was not delivered to Radlett until just after war had broken out. It had a span of 39 ft 10 in, length of 18 ft 3 in and wing area of 246 sq ft. Its maximum speed was estimated at 146.5 mph and service ceiling 10,500 feet.

At this juncture Lachmann was interned and sent to Canada, being still a German citizen, but he was later brought back and interned in the Isle of Man, where by 1943 it was possible for two members of the firm to visit him for consultation.

His design had emerged with a rather stubby fuselage in the form of a streamlined nacelle with accommodation for pilot and observer. The observer had a semi-circular

The Handley Page Manx pictured in the snow. (via J.D. Oughton)

The Handley Page Manx in close-up. (via A. McMillin)

window above the rear fuselage, and in an emergency he could jettison the hinged tail cone, the pilot being also able to dispose of his own cockpit canopy. The engines were situated between the two crew members, driving pusher propellers on the wing centre sections through flexible extension shafts. Only the outer sections of the wings had sweepback, these being given slight taper and being fitted with both leading edge slots and trailing edge elevons as well as wingtip rudders.

The Handley Page Manx dwarfed by a Halifax from the same stable. (via A. McMillin)

Priorities of work on the Halifax then hampered progress, but engine runs were carried out in November 1939 and weighing the following month, the latter indicating that at 3,300 lb it was above its designed weight. Taxiing runs followed on 29 February and 5 March 1940, but deterioration of the wing structure led to further delays. The nickname 'Manx' was bestowed around this time, allegedly because of its lack of a tail, though not officially adopted until 1945.

After rebuild and modification, the wartime designation Experimental Aeroplane No.186 was allotted and the machine painted with the Class B registration H0222. Taxiing trials were restarted in September 1942 but were beset with problems, including the death of a fitter who stepped backwards into a propeller after starting the engines and removing the chocks. The first real flight took place on 25 June 1943, when the aircraft unexpectedly rose into the air after going over a rise in the Radlett runway at full throttle. The canopy flew off at 100 feet, but the pilot, James Talbot, brought her down safely after a flight of ten minutes.

Various modifications were made, and further test flights carried out intermittently, including one on 30 June 1944 in which an observer was carried for the first time, producing a takeoff weight of 4,103 lb, engine trouble being experienced after half an hour. Then early in November, Robert Kronfeld went to Radlett to report his views for the benefit of the RAE's Tailless Aircraft Committee. He was impressed by the undercarriage arrangement, which was

the best of any tailless aircraft he had experienced, and considered take-off and landing characteristics better than those of conventional aircraft, but made several criticisms of performance.

Around June 1945 the aircraft was belatedly brought into the Handley Page aircraft type numbering system, to become the H.P.75, and three months later it was demonstrated to the Press for the first time. A so-called rider-plane, in the form of an auxiliary aerofoil attached to the nose, for experiments on longitudinal stability in relation to a much larger project was sub-contracted to Percivals, but never fitted before the machine had its last flight at the hands of Kronfeld on 2 April 1946. It was grounded a month later when defects were discovered, being eventually burned as scrap in 1952.

GENERAL AIRCRAFT GAL.56/61

One of the early decisions of the committee was to award General Aircraft a contract, number Acft/3303/CB.10(c), to build four small tailless gliders. Construction of a small wooden glider design would be comparatively cheap and could be expected to provide much quicker results than if a full sized aircraft were to be built. The original intention had been to build six machines, incorporating two differing fuselage designs and three pairs of wing-shapes, but this was curtailed before the contract was finalised. A powered version was also considered but never built.

Serial numbers TS507, TS510, TS513 and TS515 were allotted on 21 October 1944, the first three machines with normal cockpits being given the maker's type number

The first prototype of the General Aircraft GAL.56 with fully swept wings; the sweep angle was 28.4 degrees. (MAP)

GAL.56, whilst TS515 became the GAL.61 with a submerged cockpit. The GAL.56 had a central nacelle to house the pilot and engineer, and an automatic observer was installed aft to provide quantitative data. End-plate fins and rudders were fitted to each end of the swept wings which were attached to the bottom of the fuselage. To save time and expense the undercarriage comprised two Lysander wheels under the wings and a Bisley tail-wheel on a lengthy stalk under the rear fuselage. Electrically operated anti-spin parachutes were later fitted for spinning trials.

Each GAL.56 was to a different configuration, the first (TS507) having the wings swept at an angle of 28.4 degrees, measured at the quarter line, being consequently designated the GAL.56/V28.4° or Medium V. The wings were fully swept and dihedral was adjustable between – 1½ degrees and + 4½ degrees. Its overall length was 18 ft 8 in, height 11 ft 6 in, span 45 ft 4 in and wing area 350 sq ft. With an empty weight of 3,405 lb and all-up weight of 4,200 lb, this aircraft flew for the first time at Farnborough on 13 November 1944 behind an Armstrong Whitworth Whitley, its serial being later painted on as TS507A. Kronfeld reported that the undercarriage was too far forward and that the aircraft yawed and bounced on take-off under tow. Handley Page Halifaxes were later used, and by the following Spring the aircraft was being tested at Wittering, towed behind a Spitfire IX EN498 which took it up to 20,000 ft before release, oxygen being used at this altitude. Spitfire IX NH403 also became a GAL.56 tug, both this and EN498 later being used for towing the Messerschmitt Me 163 Komet rocket fighter.

Kronfeld spoke well of TS507's flying characteristics in a contemporary article, describing it as a pleasant aircraft to fly except at extreme aft Centre of Gravity positions in rough conditions. Farnborough were rather more critical, however, criticising the complete loss of control if the glider happened to enter the slipstream of the towing

The second prototype of the General Aircraft GAL.56 in which only the outer sections of the wing were swept.

aircraft, and also instability at low and high speeds, the former causing difficulties when landing. 'Winkle' Brown has referred to it as the worst aircraft he has ever flown.

Returning to the makers at Feltham after the initial trials, TS507 went back to Farnborough on 22 June 1945, but was damaged when it tipped on its nose while landing on 24 July 1946; it was transported back to the makers three weeks later for repair. It was air-towed back to Farnborough on 10 October 1946, after which it returned again to the makers for them to make a comparison of stalling characteristics with the other GAL.56s, going this time to Lasham on 28 August 1947, but it was not long after this that Kronfeld lost his life in it. On 12 February 1948 it was towed up to 10,000 ft by a Halifax for routine stalling trials, but after release and a short level glide it went into a spin. Kronfeld managed to get out of this, but then it went into a further spin and dived in on its back. The observer, Barry McGowan, managed to bale out safely, but Kronfeld was still in the machine when it crashed at Lower Foyle, five miles from the aerodrome. In 1952 the remains of TS507 were still to be seen on a dump at RAF Colerne.

The second GAL.56 (TS510) had identical sweep to the first, but only on the outer sections of the wings, the centre section being straight, leading to its being described as the Medium U. The dihedral was still adjust-

able. The main undercarriage was set further back under the fuselage, but the legs now protruded forward instead of backward and were provided with a streamlined fairing. Known as the GAL.56/U28.4°, overall length was now 20 ft 6 in, height 13 ft, span 51 ft and wing area 450 sq ft. In this form the GAL.56 had the wartime appellation Experimental Aeroplane No.243, the serial being applied as TS510D. Its maiden flight did not take place until 27 February 1946, at Aldermaston, again by Kronfeld, who soon followed this with two more flights. It had an empty weight of 4,543 lb and a loaded weight of 5,600 lb. It was displayed at the SBAC Show at Radlett in September 1947, then continued trials at Lasham, suffering minor damage when it nosed over during take-off on 19 August 1948. On 14 November 1949 it went to the Airborne Forces Experimental Establishment at Beaulieu for general research on tailless gliders, but suffered a very similar take-off accident on 20 December 1949. This time it was not repaired, its disposal being authorised three months later.

The third machine reverted to the fully swept wing configuration, but had increased sweep and was consequentially designated GAL.56/V36.4° or Maximum V-shaped, the serial being painted as TS513B. It was also known as Experimental Aeroplane No.229. Wing area was again 450 sq ft, but the increased sweep gave an overall length of 21 ft, the span reverting to 45 ft 4 in. Empty weight in this case was 3,484 lb and loaded weight 5,000 lb. This also attended the 1949 SBAC Show at Radlett, eventually joining TS513 at Beaulieu on 8 December 1949, only to be similarly disposed of in March 1950.

The third prototype General Aircraft GAL.56 with fully swept wings of an increased sweep of 36.4 degrees. (via J.D. Oughton)

The only example built of the General Aircraft GAL.61 at Farnborough in 1948.

Finally, TS515, the sole example of the GAL.61 was exhibited at the 1948 Farnborough Show, but all test work with it was cancelled in June 1949.

D.H.108 SWALLOW

By the end of the war it was becoming apparent that, with the rapidly increasing speeds of aircraft, research was required into the characteristics of swept-back wings. De Havillands were particularly interested as they were in the early stage of their D.H.106 project, which was to culminate in the Comet.

With their Vampire in an advanced stage of production, it was decided to use its fuselage as the basis for a tailless pure research aircraft with swept-back wings. Two standard production Vampire F.I fuselages (TG283 and TG306) were selected from the English Electric line at Preston and allocated the fresh serials VN856 and VN860 on 13 December 1945 under contract SB.66562, though in the event these were cancelled on 8 February 1946 and the original serials retained.

TG283 was transported from Preston to Hatfield on 25 September, then to Farnborough on 3 October, returning to Hatfield seven days later. Work started in October 1945, and this was formalised in Specification E.18/45 issued in January 1946 to meet Air Staff Requirement OR.207.

The D.H.108 was generally, though unofficially, known as the 'Swallow'. The design team, led by R.E. Bishop were warned by RAE of the possibility of the new configuration being subject to dutch roll, or severe wing-drop at the stall with poor spin-recovery. The first prototype was therefore fitted with large Handley Page fixed slots and cylindrical wingtip containers holding anti-spin parachutes. Its engine was a 3,000 lb thrust D.H. Goblin 2, and after completion it was partially broken down to be taken by road to Woodbridge in Suffolk, where it was reassembled. It took to the air from the 3,500 yard long runway on 15 May 1946 in the experienced hands of Geoffrey de Havilland. None of the fears appeared to be justified, and he reported that the aircraft handled quite well at even comparatively slow speeds. Trials on this machine were limited to about 280 mph by virtue of the fixed slots, and after the firm had carried out its tests on its swept wing characteristics the aircraft was flown to Farnborough on October 5 1948 for stability, control and landing trials by Captain Eric 'Winkle' Brown, CO of the RAE Aerodynamics Flight.

From 8 December 1948 until the following June the aircraft was used for low speed tests. A report from the RAE Aero Department predicted, as a result of tests on a model, that recovery from an unintentional spin would only be possible if the pilot took immediate action, streaming his anti-spin parachutes from the wingtips. Brown found in stalling trials that below 105 mph the aircraft would oscillate, and except in very still air would develop dutch roll. He therefore made a practice of never attempting such

The de Havilland Swallow prototype TG283 shows off its planform. Note the Handley Page slots and the wingtip-mounted anti-spin 'chute containers.

trials lower than 10,000 feet so that he had adequate height in which to recover. In his log book entry relating to the aircraft, Brown included the comment that it was a 'killer'; this turned out to be only too prophetic.

Meanwhile the second aircraft was completed soon after the first prototype, TG306 having a 3,300 lb Goblin 3 and incorporating a number of improvements. Powered controls were fitted, wing sweep was slightly increased, from 43 degrees to 45 degrees, and it had lockable automatic Handley Page slots. It was flying by June 1946 and it was not long before it was showing itself capable of exceeding the existing world air speed record, which then stood at 616 mph. The machine appeared at the SBAC Show at Radlett in September 1946, Geoffrey de Havilland giving an impressive display, after which it was prepared for him to make an attempt on the record.

The official course was to be near Tangmere in Sussex, and a number of preliminary practice flights were made. Then on 27 September he took off from Hatfield for another such trip, over the Thames Estuary, with the intention of climbing to 10,000 feet before diving down to make a high speed run over the estuary. He was down to 7,000 feet and all appeared to be well, when the aircraft suddenly disintegrated, killing the pilot. The wreckage fell in the mudflats of Egypt Bay, near Gravesend, and subsequent examination showed the cause to have been structural failure at 0.875 Mach.

This meant the end of the high speed research programme, but sufficient had been learnt from the trials with TG306 for a replacement to be ordered. A third Vampire fuselage was diverted and, benefiting from experience gained with TG306, this had a longer and more pointed nose, a redesigned canopy and a lowered pilot's seat. The

The third de Havilland Swallow being moved into a hangar. (BAe)

A unique double. John Derry flying the third de Havilland Swallow in which he had broken the International Closed-circuit Record on 12 April 1948. In company is John Cunningham in extended-wing Vampire TG278, in which he had broken the International Altitude Record on 23 March 1948. (RAF Museum 6235-7)

new nose had previously been tried out on Vampire TG281. The engine this time was the 3,750 lb Goblin 4, and the machine was first flown from Hatfield on 24 July 1947 by John Cunningham, its serial number VW120 evidently having been allocated only two weeks earlier, to meet contract 6/Acft/1067/CB.7(a).

In the light of past experience, further research was undertaken rather cautiously, but by the following Spring it was considered that sufficient data had been gained to make another record attempt. This time the International 100-km Closed-circuit Record was to be the target, the aircraft being entered jointly by the manufacturers and the Ministry of Supply. A special pentagonal course near Hatfield was used, and in the evening of 12 April 1948, VW120 established a record of 605.23 mph at the hands of John Derry, the firm's new Chief Test Pilot. Trials continued, and on 9 September during a flight which lasted 41 minutes, Derry exceed Mach 1 in a dive from 30,000 feet the first British pilot to do so. Two days later he was demonstrating the aircraft at the SBAC Show at Farnborough.

Test flying continued at Farnborough, but tragically a second death occurred when, on 15 February 1950, VW120 crashed near Birkhill, Bucks, in circumstances which were very similar to the loss of TG306, the unfortunate pilot on this occasion being Sqn Ldr J.S.R. Muller-Rowland. Unhappily, while undertaking a stalling test, TG283 was also lost when it spun into the ground near Hartley Witney, Hants on 1 May 1950, killing the pilot, Sqn Ldr George Genders, Brown's successor as head of the Aerodynamics Flight.

In retrospect, the D.H.108 certainly produced some very useful data. It was entering an unknown area of flight which had to be charted if progress was to be made, as it indeed it was. The loss of life of three such experienced test pilots from three prototypes was, however, a very high price to pay for this valuable information.

Chapter 16
LAMINAR FLOW WING RESEARCH

Increasing performance with the arrival on the scene of fast monoplanes led to studies of the flow of air over wing surfaces, and this was heightened with the advent of war. Wings were designed so as to reduce the amount of turbulence over their surfaces, and consequent drag. The condition in which a large proportion of the chord was free from this condition became known as laminar flow. Research into aerofoil section design was a partial solution to the problem, but surface finish was equally important.

One of the firms taking a keen interest was Armstrong-Whitworth Aircraft, whose chief designer, John Lloyd, had started studies early in the war, and in 1942 his firm was awarded a contract by the Ministry of Supply's Directorate of Scientific Research to design and build a smooth contour laminar flow wing which could be tested in the wind tunnel at the National Physical Laboratory. The wing was to have a span of 8 ft and a chord of 6 ft, and would have to be completely smooth. To achieve this, normal methods of construction were reversed, the thick outer skin being built first and held in an accurate jig until the ribs and stringers had all been attached. The design, which had a structural weight within practical limits, proved quite successful, profile drag having been reduced to half the normal value and laminar flow being maintained up to 60 per cent of the chord.

Having successfully proved the concept, AWA were keen to put it into practical use. The first opportunity came with the issue of an Air Staff Requirement in August 1942 for a low-level attack aircraft. The A.W.49 proposal would have been a twin-boom single-engined pusher aircraft, in which the position of the engine would have kept the wing free of turbulence. This was rejected, however, and instead the firm concentrated on the A.W.50 120 ft span flying wing

bomber design, powered by four turbo-jets. To provide aerodynamic data on this type of wing, it was proposed to built a one-third scale flying model glider, to be designated A.W.51.

By early 1944 the A.W.50 had been redesigned, with a reduced span of 112 ft, the wing being appreciably thinner, necessitating the addition of a central fuselage to house the crew, which previously was to have been housed in the centre section of the wing. As a consequence, the glider version also needed redesign, now becoming the A.W.52/G, and work on this was to continue when, soon afterwards, the A.W.50 proposal was dropped.

Whilst the wind tunnel experiments had proved satisfactory, there was no certainty that all would go equally well in practice. AWA were therefore allocated a Hawker Hurricane IIB (Z3687) for flying trials with a laminar flow wing section. It first flew with the new wing in the hands of the Chief Test Pilot, Charles Turner-Hughes, on 23 March 1945, but initial tests were disappointing. Investigation showed the cause to be excessive surface undulations, and this was cured by the use of filler and some careful rubbing down. Further trials at Farnborough showed that the required low drag coefficients had now been achieved, though significantly it was commented that some means should be found of preventing insects adhering to the surface and affecting drag.

Meanwhile a new aerofoil section had been designed by Professor A.A. Griffiths which promised to provide laminar flow from nose to tail if boundary layer suction was used on both upper and lower surfaces. To test the theory, AWA was allotted Meteor III EE445, which flew at Bitteswell in January 1947 piloted by Sqn Ldr Eric Franklin, with outer wings employing both the Griffiths aerofoil and boundary layer suction. The aircraft later went to Farnborough, but

The Armstrong Whitworth A.W.52/G under tow. (RAF Museum 6107-2 & 6107-5)

the programme ended in October 1947 after proving that the Griffiths aerofoil did not come up to expectations. Some useful data had, however, been gained on boundary layer suction.

Progress on the A.W.52/G glider had meanwhile continued. Design work commenced in May 1943 under contract Acft/3125/C.20(a), and construction began ten months later, serial number RG324 having been allotted in September 1943. For speed and economy it was made of wood, the 53 ft 10 in span wing being assembled in three parts. Length was to be 19 ft 4 in and height 8 ft 4 in, the wing area being 443 sq ft. The machine would enable many of the characteristics, such as stability and the effectiveness of the control system of this type of design, to be tested under actual flight conditions. The pilot and observer would be accommodated in a large streamlined canopy housed in the deep centre section, and they would have a full range of instruments for studying flight and control behaviour. The aircraft was to be fitted with a non-retracting tricycle undercarriage.

Despite the relatively simple construction, wartime priorities had to be maintained, and it was not until February 1945 that RG324 was completed, being given the wartime designation Experimental Aeroplane No.233. On 2 March 1945 at Bitteswell, Turner-Hughes, was able to take up the machine for the first time, towed behind Whitley LA951. The first drop was from around 12,000 ft, and later flights went as high as 20,000 ft, giving the pilots about half an hour for tests. Wind tunnel theories proved to be vindicated, and control and stability were perfectly adequate. The only minor modification required was a lowering of the elevon control ratio gear. Much invaluable data was obtained in the many flights subsequently undertaken.

RG324 was damaged slightly while landing at Bitteswell on 25 June 1946, but was repaired in good time to appear that September at the SBAC Show at Farnborough. The tug was later replaced by Lancaster PA366, and on 1 June 1950 RG324 joined 'B' Flight of the Airborne Forces Experimental Establishment at Beaulieu for handling trials. On the closure of that unit, its 'B' Flight became 'D' Flight of the Aeroplane and Armament Experimental Establishment, and on 6 September 1950 this aircraft was ferried to Boscombe Down to continue the trials. It was eventually disposed of on 27 June 1953, when it was sold back to Armstrong Whitworths who regrettably later burnt it.

In the meantime, AWA continued their studies into flying wings, and were particularly keen on the idea of a large flying-wing airliner. Having made some progress in establishing the basic principles, they were encouraged by the Directorate of Scientific Research to build a full-sized machine. In March 1944 they put forward a design study for an experimental tailless twin-jet aircraft of a layout bas-

A fine air-to-air view of the second Armstrong Whitworth A.W.52 showing the futuristic planview. (via M.J. Hooks)

ically identical to the glider and with similar properties and controls, which would then represent a three-fifths scale model of the new design, to be designated A.W.52. At the suggestion of the Directorate of Technical Development it would have two Metropolitan-Vickers F.2 Mk4 engines. Fitted with a tricycle undercarriage, its empty weight would be 15,324 lb and loaded weight 29,800 lb. Span would be 90 ft, length 36 ft 8 in, height 13 ft 9 in and wing area 1,320 sq ft. Estimated maximum speed was 495 mph at 36,000 lb, and cruising speed 325 mph over a wide range of heights. Initial climb was 3,000 ft/min, and the normal range 1,800 miles, which could extend to 2,500 miles with increase tankage.

Draft Specification E.9/44 was then set in hand, but after further discussion with DSR it was proposed in June 1944 to reduce the body size and increase the wing loading in order to improve performance, especially the cruising speed. Span would now be 78 ft, length 32 ft, height 13 ft 6 in and wing area 1,000 sq ft. Empty weight would now become 14,084 lb and all-up weight 31,460 lb. The maximum speed would increase to 520 mph at 30,000 ft, and cruising speed would be improved substantially to 400 mph at 36,000 ft, with initial climb remaining at 3,000 ft/min but range now 2,730 miles. A month later they were told to revert to the original wing size, but to use the new reduced body size, and that DSR would cost two aircraft on that basis.

On 25 August 1944 the company was awarded contract SB.27759/C.4(b) to build two experimental aircraft, TS363 and TS368, with a span of 90 ft and weighing around 30,000 lb. Drawing up of the draft Specification was completed by the end of October, and it was eventually finalised on 18 January 1945. The service ceiling was now to be 45,000 ft, and the engines remained the same, except that provision had to be made for installing Rolls-Royce RB.41s as an alternative. The latter provision was due to doubts as to the F.2 being available in time, and was followed on 23 February by an instruction to fit RB.41s in the first machine. This turned out to be wise, as in fact Metro-vick engines were never fitted.

Armstrong Whitworth later put forward proposals for a tailless swept-wing turbo-jet-powered medium range bomber to meet specification B.35/46, but the contracts for this went to Avro and Handley Page who went on to produce the Vulcan and Victor respectively.

Although tailless, the A.W.52 was not a true flying wing, since it would have a fuselage, and despite being an experimental machine, it was to have provision for up to 4,000 lb of mail. The first aircraft (TS363) was fitted with two 5,000 lb thrust RB.41 Nene 2 engines, and the final measurements were span 90 ft, length 37 ft 4 in, height 14 ft 5 in and wing area 1,314 sq ft. The weight empty was 19,662 lb, and loaded it was 34,154 lb. Piloted by Eric Franklin it had its maiden flight at Boscombe Down on 13 November 1947. Franklin was pleased with the performance, and after satisfying Ministry of Supply requirements that the machine should make five flights and complete three hours flying, the aircraft was flown to Bitteswell by Franklin on 1 December, and modifications were then carried out to cure some vibration problems. The maximum speed was stated to be 500 mph at sea level (M 0·66), and to 480 mph at 36,000 ft (M 0.75). Initial climb was 4,800 ft/min and range 1,500 miles, which could be extended to 1,500 miles with a full fuel load.

RG324 was flown at the SBAC Show at Farnborough in September 1948, the crowd witnessing an impressive display, after which it continued flying from Bitteswell until being taken to Baginton in November for various further modifications.

Meanwhile, the second aircraft (TS368) was completed, fitted with two 3,500 lb thrust Derwent 5s, the reduced power of which were to add to the problems already encountered by its predecessor. It made its first flight on 1 September 1948, just in time for it to be exhibited in the static display at that year's SBAC Show whilst TS363 was showing its paces overhead. In this configuration the empty weight was a little less at 19,185 lb, loaded weight being 33,305 lb. The range was about the same, but performance was considerably less, a top speed being claimed of only 450 mph at 36,000 ft, initial climb only 2,500 ft/min and service ceiling 45,000 ft.

Tests continued on both aircraft, but on 24 March 1949 severe buffeting was encountered by TS368 after entering turbulent air. Fortunately this ceased when the throttles were closed, but worse was to follow. On 30 May 1949, TS363 became uncontrollable while investigating flutter characteristics. During high speed tests, one wing developed flutter and this spread across the entire wing span,

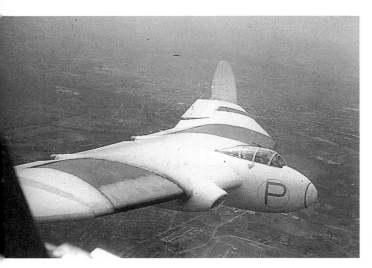

The second Armstrong Whitworth A.W.52 was fitted with Derwents rather than the Nenes of the prototype giving a 3,000 lb thrust power disadvantage. (via M.J. Hooks)

and Experimental Establishment at Shoeburyness to act as a target for weapon firing trials.

The experiment had turned out to be another dead end in aviation research. The problems with stability and control were never completely overcome, and it would have been very difficult to manufacture large wings of the cleanliness and accuracy necessary. Laminar flow was not a practical proposition on a day to day basis, and had proved unsatisfactory on the full scale aircraft. Experiments with the glider had shown that its full effects could not long be maintained once the swept wings had acquired a normal accumulation of dirt and dead flies, and the full-scale machines also proved to have similar limitations. Supermarine came up against the same problem when they were asked to fit a laminar flow wing to their Spiteful fighter.

inducing a pitching oscillation which the pilot, John Lancaster, was unable to bring under control. He consequently achieved the unique but unwanted distinction of making the first successful emergency exit from a British aircraft using an ejector seat, in this case made by Martin-Baker. The machine surprisingly regained its equilibrium, and went on to make a heavy landing in open country, the main damage being caused by the engines having been ripped from their mountings.

TS368 continued the flight test programme, though speed was now restricted to 250 knots. On 1 May 1950 it was allocated for investigation of vibration, pressure plotting of wing and determination of transition on the wing. It was transferred to Farnborough on 3 October 1950, for further research into laminar flow and on airflow behaviour over swept wings. It was damaged while being towed by a tractor on 10 January 1951, but continued trials until being scrapped in May 1954, being then taken to the Proof

Hawker Hurricane Z3687 fitted with laminar flow wings. (via Ray Williams)

Chapter 17
DELTA RESEARCH

Among the many options being considered after the Second World War to take advantage of the great increases in speed which would be available from the development of jet engines was that of delta-winged aircraft. During the first two decades of practical jet flight, numerous British design studies were made in this configuration, and several of these were built for trial purposes, among them products from Avro, Fairey and Handley Page.

AVRO 707

The Avro delta story started with the issue on 25 January 1947 of Specification B.35/46. This was based on Air Staff Requirement OR.229, which was ultimately to lead to a whole host of experimental and operational Specifications. B.35/46, the first of these, called for a post-war jet-powered medium range bomber, but the wording was left deliberately vague so as to allow designers as much scope as possible. It was suggested, however, that the successful designs 'would employ an unusual shape of wing'.

Quite a number of firms found this an attractive proposition, and hopefully submitted initial designs, among them Armstrong-Whitworth, Avro, Bristol, Handley Page, Shorts and Vickers Armstrong. Of these, the delta-winged Avro Type 698 submission and the Handley Page H.P.80 crescent-winged proposal found favour.

Avro had some difficulty in producing a design which could meet the Specification. They tried both conventional shapes and all-wing layouts, without success. The solution was eventually found in a delta-shape layout, requiring no horizontal tail surfaces, a layout which in fact had already been reached in similar research in both Germany and the U.S.A. In the progression of the Avro design, aspect ratio had been lowered by reducing span and increasing

chord. The wing itself was to be quite thick, especially inboard, and thus able to accommodate the engines internally.

In view of the radical departure from previous design practice, it was decided in official circles that flying scale models would help development. The initial proposal was to divide research into three. The Avro Type 707 would be a small aircraft undertaking relatively simple research into handling and stability at low speeds, and the Type 710 would have two Avons for similar tests flying within the limits of the 698s flight envelope of 60,000 ft and Mach 0.95. In addition, a full-scale flying shell 698 would act as an aerodynamic test vehicle, without the normal military equipment. The 710 proposal was soon dropped, however.

Issue 2 of Specification B.35/46, dated 15 June 1948, authorised the construction of two prototype 698s, and seven days later these were ordered under contract 6/Acft/1942, being given serials VX770 and VX777. On the same day two one-third scale 707s (VX784 and VX790) were ordered under Contract number 6/Acft/2205/CB.6(b), and also two half-scale 710s (VX799 and VX808). Specification E.15/48 was drawn up around the 707 design, though this was not finalised, rather belatedly, until 3 November 1948.

There was evidently some vacillation at the Ministry of Supply, as on 24 February 1949 the fresh decision was reached to proceed on the basis of a high-speed scale model and a flying shell, these being covered by Specifications E.10/49 and E.11/49 respectively. There was yet another change of heart on 6 April 1949, when the programme was amended to two full prototypes under B.35/46, one one-third scale high speed flying model under E.10/49 and two one-third low-speed scale models under E.15/48. The high-speed model was ordered on 6 May 1949

Unpainted prototype Avro 707 VX784 at Farnborough. (via M. Stroud)

under Contract number 6/Acft/3395 and was designated Type 707A by the makers, the serial WD280 being allocated. There were potential snags with this arrangement, of course, not least of which was that by proceeding in parallel, the products of any lessons learnt from the 707 could well arrive too late to be of much benefit to the 698.

The design and construction of the 707s went ahead quite rapidly. The first prototype, VX784, was unpainted, being powered by a Rolls-Royce Derwent engine. It had its maiden flight at Boscombe Down on 4 September 1949 at the hands of Avro's deputy chief test pilot, Eric Esler, a small unscheduled hop having been made the previous day. This was just in time for it to be exhibited at the 1949 SBAC Show at Farnborough, but unfortunately on the last day of that month Esler lost his life when the aircraft crashed near Blackbushe. The cause was never really established, control appearing to have been lost while the aircraft was flying at low speed.

Following the loss of VX784, construction of the second machine was suspended for a time. Then, to speed up the programme, a number of short cuts were taken and some inessential frills omitted.

Further official consideration was in the meantime being given to the project, and an internal minute of 6 March 1950 suggested cancelling E.10/49 to save money and allow Avros to put greater effort into the 698 on which

design work was already seriously behind. It was suggested that with redesign work taking place on the 698, the low speed model E.15/48 was out of date and cancellation desirable. An earlier minute of 24 February 1950 had already suggested it was essential that the 707A's wings be redesigned to be an exact copy of those of the 698, thus highlighting another problem with this approach.

The second prototype 707, VX790, painted bright blue, emerged as Type 707B to make its maiden flight at Boscombe Down on 6 September 1950, flown by the new Chief Test Pilot, R.J. 'Roly' Falk, who expressed himself well pleased with its handling. The redesigned aircraft was 12 feet longer with monocoque structure instead of the welded steel tube construction of the prototype, and had a Derwent 8 engine. Its numerous modifications included a completely new nose section with a Gloster Meteor canopy, Avro Athena main undercarriage and a Hawker P.1052 nose gear. The latter proved too short to give a suitable incidence for take-off and was later extended by about nine inches, giving the aircraft a nose-up attitude on the ground, this idea being incorporated in the 698 while it was still at the drawing board stage. Another worthwhile advantage gained from the 707B was that of tilting the jet nozzles downwards and outwards, as trim experimentation had shown that this would minimise the need for changes of trim. Its usefulness in the 698 programme was limited, however, being unpressurised, with manual controls and having engine intakes bearing no resemblance to that of its big brother.

Avro 707B VX790 was painted bright blue. This photograph shows it with air intakes similar to those fitted to the prototype. (RAF Museum 6416-15)

Nevertheless, some useful flying was performed in the 707B. It proved very stable, without any tendency to tumble nose-over-tail which had been feared. It would also hold off the stall at angles of attack which a conventional design could not have attained. Subsequent modifications included fitting of an ejector seat, a redesigned air intake above the wing, a revised hood, all of which had been incorporated by the time Falk demonstrated the aircraft to the press at Dunsfold early in August 1951.

Next to be completed was WD280, which was built at Woodford then transported to Boscombe Down where it flew on 14 June 1951. Initially painted pink, this was later changed to bright red. Similar in outline to the 707A, for the first time scaled-down 698-type wing intakes were fitted instead of the previous dorsal air intakes, the engine reverting to a Derwent 5. This arrangement enabled it to be fitted with a long dorsal fin, and consequently a much more pleasing outline. It still did not have a properly pressurised cockpit, and in practice it contributed very little to the development of the 698, much of the testing being spent in eliminating its own design faults. The main problem was pitch oscillation due partly to out-of-phase movement of the elevators, and difficulties with damping.

A further setback occurred on 21 September when VX790 was involved in an accident at Boscombe Down. Falk had given the local test pilot a full briefing. The test was carried out satisfactorily and the aircraft then made a normal approach, but after touchdown it became airborne again and the nose-up attitude of the aircraft gradually increased until a very high incidence was attained. A wing then dropped and touched the ground, slewing the aircraft round

and damaging the nose. The official investigation afterwards suggested that longitudinally instability when stick free near the ground was very likely a contributing cause. On 13 November 1951 it was authorised to be returned to Woodford for repair, after which it returned to Boscombe Down six months later.

Coincidentally, 13 November 1951 was also the date on which three more machines were ordered under Contract number 6/Acft/7470/CB/6(a), to meet Issue 2 of Specification E.10/49. One of these was to be a second 707A, numbered WZ736 and the other two would be side-by-side conversion trainers designated 707C and given serial numbers WZ739 and WZ744, though WZ739 was later cancelled. WZ736 and WZ744 would both have Derwent 8s, and be assembled at Bracebridge Heath, Avro's repair and overhaul works just south of Lincoln. From there they were easily towed along the road to nearby RAF Waddington. WZ736 followed the theme of having non-standard bright colours, being painted orange, and it was first flown at Waddington on 20 February 1953, flying north to land at the company's main airfield at Woodford. It was followed by WZ744, which was painted the more normal silver, which had its maiden flight on 1 July 1953 at the hands of Sqn Ldr T.B. Wales, this aircraft being then also flown to Woodford. In practice, neither WZ736 nor WZ744 were involved directly in Vulcan development, spending most of their active lives at RAE.

The surviving 707s later became general research aircraft with the Royal Aircraft Establishment at Farnborough and Bedford. VX790 was damaged when landing at Farnborough on 25 September 1956, the port wing, port undercarriage and leg, and the undersurfaces of the fuselage all needing repair, and in November 1957 it was struck off charge at Bedford to be used as spares for the other surviving machines.

WD280 was fitted with a 'cranked' wing at the firm's Bracebridge Heath works, near Lincoln, and on 6 March

The Avro 707B VX790 above the clouds, here seen with dorsal air intake. (BAe)

Avro 707A WD280 banks to demonstrate its delta planform and 698-type wing intakes. (via M. Hooks)

1956 was flown to Renfrew for shipment to Australia in 1956. On 8 May 1956 it was allotted to the Australian Aeronautical Research Council, Fishermans Bend, Melbourne for low speed delta research, most of the flying being undertaken from Laverton, the home of the RAAF's trials flying unit. This task ended, it was struck off charge on 10 February 1967, being disposed of locally for £400 to Geoffrey Mallett

Avro 707C WZ744 side-by-side two-seat trainer was finished in silver. (BAe)

of Williamtown, Melbourne, who then kept it in his back garden.

WZ736 went to the RAF Museum's Reserve Collection at RAF Finningley in 1966, the ground instructional airframe number 7868M being allocated, and is now in the Greater Manchester Museum of Science and Industry. WZ744 also went to RAF Finningley in 1966, being later moved to the Topcliffe satellite, and is now in the Aerospace Museum at Cosford, number 7932M being allocated in this case.

FAIREY FD.1

The delta concept also appealed to Fairey, who were working on a proposed rocket-boosted vertical take-off aircraft for possible shipboard use and saw this as a means of preliminary testing of stability and control characteristics of this layout at slow and medium speeds. They were very interested, therefore, when on 19 September 1947 Specification E.10/47 was issued. Based on Air Staff Requirement OR.252, this sought a delta-winged aircraft capable of undertaking research into 'revolutionary possibilities in the design and operation of fighter aircraft'.

Boulton Paul undertook some work on the specifica-

tion, but the contract went to Faireys who had submitted their 'Delta 1' or Type R design, and on 13 April 1948 they were rewarded with contract 6/Acft/1534/CB.7(b) for three aircraft. These were to have been serial numbers VX350, VX357 and VX364, with the constructor's numbers F.8466 to F.8468, but in the event the order was reduced to one machine and only the first of these was completed.

Forty pilotless radio-controlled models were first built to provide basic data on the delta planform. These were tested first at Aberporth and then from a tank-landing craft in Cardigan Bay and finally from the Woomera-based Long-range Weapons Establishment in Australia.

VX350 was then built at the firm's Heaton Chapel works, fitted with a 3,600 lb thrust Rolls-Royce Derwent 8 engine. It was originally intended for vertical launching with large booster rockets from a short ramp, but the Ministry of Supply later decided against this. Plans for a jettisonable undercarriage were also dropped, the intention having been to fit a skid for landing. Instead the stubby fuselage had a retractable nose wheel fitted under the air intake and two main wheels retracting into the fuselage sides. A large powered rudder was fitted, topped by a small delta-shaped tailplane. The mainplane had inboard airbrakes, elevons and fixed wingtip slots, though the latter were later removed. For landings, a drogue parachute was provided beneath the rear fuselage, in addition to spin-recovery parachute containers at the wing tips.

The fuselage had a length of 26 ft 3 in and span was 19 ft 6½ in, the loaded weight being 6,900 lb. Taxiing trials were commenced at Ringway Airport on 12 May 1950 by Gordon Slade and Peter Twiss, but it was not until 12 March 1951 that the aircraft had its maiden flight at Boscombe Down with Slade at the controls. Much further flying was then undertaken, providing valuable data on longitudinal and lateral stability as well as the rolling capabilities of this planform, and also on the use of braking parachutes.

The maximum possible speed of the aircraft was limited to 345 mph due to structural limitations on the tailplane, but plans to remove this never materialised. It was estimated that if it were removed a maximum speed of 628 mph was possible at 10,000 ft, and 587 mph at 40,000 ft. The initial rate of climb was estimated at 9,300 ft/min, with the ability to climb to 30,000 ft in 4.5 minutes.

The F.D.1 had its limitations, being particularly difficult to fly in anything but calm conditions, and at one time was grounded as being a dangerous aircraft. On 1 May 1953, having completed contractor's trials, it was allotted to Boscombe Down, its life ending when on 6 February 1956 the undercarriage was torn away in an emergency landing by an RAF pilot. Although not a success in itself, it had provided useful experience for the construction and testing of the later F.D.2. Like so many prototypes, it ended its life as a destructive testing machine, being transported on 9 October 1956 to the Proof and Experimental Establishment at Shoeburyness.

HANDLEY PAGE H.P.115

Handley Page involvement originated quite differently. On 5 November 1956 the first meeting was held at Farnborough of a newly-formed Supersonic Transport Advisory Committee, and among the designs considered were submissions from Avro, Bristol and Handley Page, of which the Bristol design was eventually to become the Anglo-French Concorde. At that stage, however, there was some concern at the low-speed characteristics of the slender delta-wings considered likely to be necessary, following the receipt of a report on some wind-tunnel tests in the USA.

Model tests at Farnborough suggested that these results might be misleading, and it was proposed that a piloted glider be built to test the slow speed properties of such a wing. Slingsby Sailplanes drew up an appropriate outline design, and Specification X.197T was then issued for this. There was some disquiet at this approach, however, as such a machine would be of limited use for studying landing and take-off characteristics, or 'dutch rolling'. On 21 December 1959, therefore, a completely revised Specification ER.197D was issued for a powered machine of metal construction, and the work was entrusted under contract KD/2N/02 to Handley Page, who gave it their type number H.P.115.

Design work was carried out in co-operation with the

The stubby lines of the Fairey FD.1 are shown well in this photograph taken en route to 1954 Farnborough Show from the aircraft's base at White Waltham. (via M. Hooks)

The Fairey FD.1 streams its brake-parachute as it comes in to land.

Aero Flight Department of the Royal Aircraft Establishment at Thurleigh, and the machine emerged with serial number XP841 to have its first flight there on 17 August 1961 at the hands of Sqn Ldr Jack Henderson, who spoke into a tape-recorder during the flight. Powered by a 1,900 lb thrust Bristol Siddeley Viper BSV.9 (later 102), it had a wing span of 20 ft and a length of 45 ft, to which could be added another 4 ft 11 in for its nose probe. The wings, which were fitted with elevons, had an area of 432 sq ft, and were of symmetrical section delta shape, having 74.7 degrees sweep and 1.0 aspect ratio. The pilot's cockpit was mounted in a bulbous nacelle extending beyond and mainly below the leading edge of the wings, being fitted with a Martin-Baker ground-level ejection-seat. The engine was fitted centrally above the rear of the wings, and on it was mounted a 60-degree swept fin and rudder.

Before the first flight, Henderson practised extensively on a simulator, then undertook taxiing trials. Coming in to land afterwards, he was full of praise for the machine, which the following month appeared at the annual SBAC Show at Farnborough. It was handed over to the Ministry of Aviation Air Fleet on 23 October 1961, and further tests showed it to be very simple and delightful to fly, well suited to the purpose for which it had been designed, and during the course of the next four years it contributed much to low-speed aspects of the Concorde design. By 1974, however, it was at the end of its useful life, and on 1 February 1974 it joined the collection of historic aircraft then housed at RAF Colerne. On 9 October 1975 it was transferred to Cosford Aerospace Museum, and is now to be seen exhibited alongside the second Concorde (G-BSST) at the Fleet Air Arm Museum at Yeovilton.

Right: **Head-on view of the Handley Page H.P.115. (via M. Stroud)**

Below: **The Handley Page H.P.115 in flight. Close inspection reveals a smoke generator being used on the port wing to visualise airflow. (via M.J. Hooks)**

Rear view of the Handley Page H.P.115 showing its moth-like wing planform. (via M. Hooks)

Chapter 18
The MILES M.52

The Miles M.52 stemmed from Specification E.24/43, first formulated in the autumn of 1943, and officially issued on 26 August 1944, for a high speed research aircraft. This was a very advanced concept for its time.

The Ministry of Aircraft Production awarded contract SB27157/C.23(c) on 13 December 1943 to Miles Aircraft, a firm which, although very talented and imaginative, with an enthusiastic design team, was completely inexperienced in the high speed field. No other firm was asked to compete, giving the double advantages of minimal wastage of scarce design talent and better secrecy. It has also been suggested that the award of the contract was something of a sop for Miles having had their proposals for a transatlantic commercial aircraft turned down, despite being more promising on paper than the officially approved design – which eventually became the Brabazon white elephant.

The order was for a prototype aircraft and an additional bare airframe, to carry serial numbers RT133 and RT136, and a small design team was set up in great secrecy at Woodley. In an earlier joint meeting held at Farnborough on 12 November 1943 had been estimated that the aircraft could achieve a speed of 700 mph at 40,000 ft. Gross weight would be a little under 6,500 lb, including 2,000 lb of fuel. Horse power equivalent from the Power Jets W.2/700 engine was thought likely to be around 6,000 at 40,000 ft, a thrust of 2,375 lb being produced at 1,000 mph.

Despite the many problems such an advanced concept posed, a preliminary design was ready towards the end of 1943. The fuselage would be cylindrical, tapering at the tail and nose. The pressurised cabin was to be in the conical nose of aircraft and would be detachable with cordite charges to project it forward from the aircraft in an emergency, a parachute being attached to slow it down sufficiently for the pilot to bale out with his own parachute. The undercarriage would retract into the fuselage, with the nose wheel being housed between the pilot's feet.

The 25 ft span wings would be very thin and unswept with a symmetrical bi-convex aerofoil section. They would be essentially elliptical in plan form, the tips being cut off at a diagonal, along the line of the outer shock wave. The theory of this shape of wing was given a practical test on the so-called 'Gillette' Falcon, dealt with elsewhere. As such thin wings would be unable to accommodate fuel tanks, it was proposed that these be fitted centrally around the engine, the air intakes being also annular immediately behind the cockpit. Soon afterwards it was proposed to fit an all-moving tailplane which would be tried out on an orthodox aircraft such as a Spitfire.

A meeting was held at Reading on 27 April 1944 during which discussion revealed that there had been a considerable growth in weight. The original proposal envisaged 5,140 lb normal loaded weight, increasing to 6,500 lb overload. This had by now shot up to an estimated 7,754 lb normal increasing to 8,654 lb overload. Part of this increase was due to 70 gallons of extra fuel and part to an increase in the engine installation weight. By July 1944 the position had worsened further.

Meanwhile studies on wing design had shown that, with a take-off weight of 7,493 lb, a higher Mach number could be reached with a conventional type of wing than with the proposed symmetrical bi-convex wing. Either wing would allow supersonic speed to be reached in a dive, but the conventional wing gave more lift and would therefore allow the aircraft to climb to 56,000 feet, which was 6,000 feet more than with the bi-convex wing. Thinner air at the additional height would allow speed to build up faster in the dive, which could last longer, so that Mach 1.07 could be reached by pulling out at 36,000 feet, compared with Mach 1.03 when pulling out with the conventional wing at 32,000 feet.

By the end of 1944 it had become apparent that the Specification could not be met with the design as it stood. At a height of 36,000 feet, drag would be greater than thrust for speeds exceeding 600 mph or Mach 0.90. If it could attain 1,100 mph, however, the reverse would be true, and if it could break through the sound barrier it might well prove possible to reach and maintain a speed of Mach 2.0.

Such a velocity might be reached with a dive from 60,000 feet, but only at the expense of expending all its fuel. Use of a rocket booster was impracticable, as this would have too high a fuel consumption in the climb. Launch from a Lancaster or other large aircraft was also ruled out. Ways therefore had to be sought to increase thrust and decrease drag. The snag with the former was that increased thrust could only be achieved at the expense of increased fuel consumption, which defeated the object of the exercise.

The fuselage design was by now in the mock-up stage, but the cockpit revealed problems for the pilot. The conical shaped capsule had a maximum diameter of 4 ft, tapering down to a point. It was unsuitable for anyone tall, and the pilot would have to sit with his legs astride the nosewheel retraction well, with his feet at the same level as his shoulders. Visibility was very poor, the windscreen slanting only slightly upwards in relation to his line of vision. Landing speed was estimated at 160 mph.

Work continued at Woodley throughout 1945, but events were moving against them. During the closing stages of the war in Europe, and especially after VE-Day, Technical Intelligence teams were able to evaluate German progress on sub-supersonic aircraft such as the Me 262, and particularly the effectiveness of swept-back wings. This threw increasing doubts on the straight-winged M.52 concept, though these misgivings were never communicated to the hard-working Miles team.

By early 1946 the writing was on the wall. In an internal minute of 22 January to the Director General of Technical Development, it was noted that despite a contract having been placed in December 1943 as a matter of urgency, the progress made so far did not seem to have been very rapid. The firm had spent £73,000 up to 30 November 1945 and estimated that it would cost at least £250,000 to complete. In these circumstances, it was suggested that DGTD might wish to reconsider the project. If it was decided that it should continue, approval would be required for additional finance on the basis of the current estimate of the final cost.

The partially complete mock-up of the Miles M.52. (via A.D. Raby/P.H.T. Green)

On 12 February a meeting of the Director General of Scientific Research's Supersonic Committee reached no firm decision, but were unanimous that by this time there was no case for continuing on grounds of obtaining information on transonic or supersonic speed – the original reasons for placing the contract. A case could be made, however, for completion as an engine testbed, with the possibility of gaining useful information on ducted fans and after-burning. But on 25 February 1946 it was finally decided that there was now no objection to cancellation, there being no particular interest in the W.2/700 engine, which had been developed specially for the M.52. The decision was communicated to F.G. Miles in a brief note from the Director, Sir Ben Lockspeiser, and came out of the blue. The official explanation was the need for economy, and the Director expressed his personal belief that an aircraft would not fly supersonically for many years to come.

With the benefit of hindsight, the decision was probably misguided, and lost this country the opportunity of building up a strong lead in this field. Pioneering work in such an area was inevitably costly and liable to unexpected delays. By way of contrast the Americans, who had the benefit of all the calculations and test data relating to the M.52, this having been passed to them by the Ministry of Supply, built the successful Bell X-1 in a fairly similar configuration to the M.52, this becoming the first piloted aircraft to exceed the speed of sound on 14 October 1947. In addition, this and later aircraft disproved the official assumption that swept wings were the answer to supersonic flight, subsequent events proving that they were only at their best in transonic flight, other wing layouts being necessary at higher speeds.

Chapter 19
TRANSONIC DELTA RESEARCH

Further research into delta-wing configurations led to the prospect of speeds around that of sound. This was still a very uncertain area, and official interest led at first to three separate projects being supported. Financial considerations, however, led to the programme being thinned out and therefore, one of these was later dropped.

BOULTON PAUL P.111/P.120

During 1946, Air Staff Requirement OR.241 was drawn up for investigation of the characteristics of delta-wings at transonic speeds. This led later that year to the issue of Specification E.27/46, resulting in contract number 6/Acft/969/CB.7(b) being awarded on 29 November 1946

The Boulton Paul P.111A in flight. (Dowty Boulton Paul Ltd)

The Boulton Paul P.111A. The oval nose intake fed air to a Rolls-Royce Nene. (Dowty Boulton Paul Ltd)

The Boulton Paul P.120, the development of the P.111. Noticeable are the all-moving tailplane, resited braking parachute container and the revised main gear position. (Dowty Boulton Paul Ltd)

to Boulton Paul for the construction of two prototypes, to be given serial numbers VT769 and VT784. A revision of this Specification led to it being reissued on 31 January 1947, and for some reason fresh serials VT935 and VT951 were issued, the originals being cancelled.

The resulting design had a short body powered by a 5,100 lb thrust Rolls-Royce Nene R.N.2 turbojet engine, the nose being fitted with an oval-shaped horizontal air intake. It had built-in pressure-plotting equipment, an automatic observer, a fin-mounted camera to photograph wing tufts and various recording machinery. Non-reversible controls were fitted incorporating spring feel, and a gear change mechanism allowed the sensitivity of the aircraft to be varied by the pilot. The undercarriage retracted into the fuselage sides. The wings, which had a 45 degrees delta shape, had an unusually low thickness/chord ratio for that time, and the tips were detachable to allow comparison between the effects of squared and pointed configurations. The tips of the fin could be similarly detached. For control, the aircraft was fitted with elevons on both the wings and the rudder.

The prototype first flew on 6 October 1950 as the P.111. It had a length of 26 ft 1 in, span of 33 ft 5½ in and wing area of 200 sq ft, empty weight being around 6,500 lb and all-up weight 9,600 lb. The second prototype did not fly until 6 August 1952, and differed in a significant number of respects from its predecessor, being consequently given the new type number P.120. The main external difference lay in the new all-moving tailplane near the top of a completely redesigned vertical tail surface, these increasing the overall length to 29 ft 7½ in. Four airbrakes were fitted around the centre fuselage. Other modification included a braking parachute now housed under the rudder instead of on the port side of the rear fuselage and a new wide undercarriage retracting into the wings. Empty weight was now 10,656 lb and all-up weight 12,580 lb.

It was anticipated that the P.120 would achieve high subsonic speeds during level flight, but this was never put to the test because it developed tail flutter on 29 August 1952 while flying from Boscombe Down and crashed at Grately, near Andover when 'Ben' Gunn, Boulton Paul's Chief Test Pilot, was unable to recover control and had to bale out, landing in a corn field.

VT935 in the meantime had also had its problems. It suffered damage at Boscombe on 20 October 1951, and again on 5 January 1952 when the undercarriage retracted on landing. It was then given a number of minor modifications, including P.120-type fuselage airbrakes. In this guise it became the P.111A, having its first flight on 2 July 1953. Empty weight was now 9,380 lb and loaded weight 11,400 lb, a maximum speed of 650 mph being achieved at sea level and 622 mph at 35,000 ft, the initial climb being 9,400 ft/min. On one occasion it attained Mach 0.93 in level

flight. It went to Farnborough in February 1954, transferring to RAE Bedford in November 1955. On 25 April 1959, its useful flying life ended, it went to the College of Aeronautics at Cranfield for use as a ground instructional airframe and a design sample, until moving to Baginton in July 1975 for the new Midland Air Museum.

FAIREY F.D.2

In September 1947, Fairey, who were already pursuing the F.D.1 and relevant scale models, were also invited to look into the possibilities of transonic flight by a ground-launched VTO machine. After some investigation they

Right: **The first prototype Fairey FD.2 high in the clouds.**

Below: **Worms-eye view of the Fairey FD.2 first prototype.**

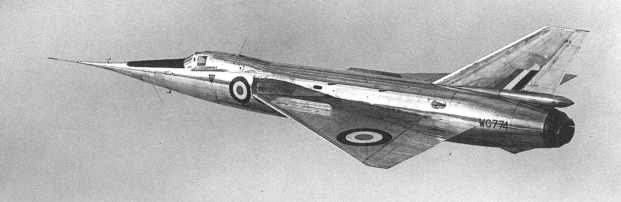

formed the view that the exercise would only be of real value if it was directed towards obtaining specific information on a layout representative of a typical possible piloted supersonic aircraft. Design studies led to a design similar in layout to the parallel work at EEC which led to the P.1 Lightning.

Early in 1949 the Principal Director of Scientific Research (Air) approached the firm about the possibility of a rather different design, based if possible on a single engine. By the end of that year the new design had settled to delta-wing planform of aspect ratio 2, not very dissimilar to the aircraft which was eventually built. Being the second delta-wing design from Fairey, it was generally referred to as the Delta Two or F.D.2.

For a time the design was regarded as being in competition with Armstrong Whitworth's reworked A.W.58 design, but this fell by the wayside. On 26 September 1950 the situation was formalised with the issue of Specification ER.103 specifically for the F.D.2. The requirement was described as being a delta-wing transonic research aircraft which would enable investigations of problems associated with flight at transonic and supersonic speeds up to Mach 1.5 and at altitudes of between 36,000 ft and 45,000 ft. It was to be fitted with a single Rolls-Royce Avon R.A.5 engine, with provision for reheat, though an alternative of an Armstrong Siddeley Sapphire engine could be considered. The aircraft should be capable of exceeding Mach 1.3 in level flight with reheat to 1500°K at 36,000 ft.

A blueprint of the layout was filed early in July, and on 27 July 1950 two aircraft were ordered under Contract number 6/Acft/5597/CB.7(a), to carry serial numbers WG774 and WG777, with constructor's numbers F.9421 and F.9422 respectively, a static test machine being also ordered. The firm was by that time heavily engaged in design work for the Gannet, however, so work on the new delta design took a low priority and did not really start in earnest for about two years.

On 26 September 1950 a revised Specification was issued, specifically mentioning 60 degrees sweep and amending the height requirement to 'up to at least 45,000 ft'. The engine was now specified as an Avon R.A.3 of 8,300 lb thrust, still with reheat to 1500°K. By February 1951, however, Fairey were referring to the power plant as being an R.A.8 with reheat, and the design was now known as Project No.34 Type 'V'.

Construction began at the end of 1952, and the machine which began to emerge was the smallest which could be designed to house the pilot, engine and fuel. Overall weight and frontal area had been kept to the minimum possible, with only relatively small air intakes in the wing roots. Yet it had to be capable of normal handling both on the ground and in the air, with sufficient fuel capacity to be able to carry out flights of sufficient length to produce worthwhile results.

The aircraft had a length of 51 ft 7½in and a wingspan of 26 ft 10 in, the wing area being 360 sq ft. An innovation was the design of the nose portion of the aircraft. The length of the pointed nose was likely to obstruct the for-

ward view of the pilot during landings, and to overcome this the whole of the nose, including the pressurised cockpit, was made to be hydraulically drooped by 10 degrees.

In August 1954, tests were carried out on WG774 in the blower tunnel at Boscombe Down to assess the jetti-

son characteristics of the cockpit hood. It was also necessary to assess the possibility of injury to the pilot or damage to the aircraft in the event of an emergency jettison being made in flight. It was found that the hood jettisoned safely in flight at speeds between 100 and 280 knots,

The first prototype Fairey FD.2 repainted to mark its achievement in breaking the absolute world speed record on 10 March 1956. (RAF Museum 6769-2)

and the application of small amounts of yaw would not seriously affect the jettison characteristics. It was also concluded that the pilot was unlikely to experience any difficulty in reaching the ejection seat blind after the hood had been jettisoned. There were some minor criticisms, but these could easily be corrected, and regular ground jettison tests should ensure that the hood was capable of correct release and had not developed excessive friction in the operating mechanism.

The completed machine, now powered by an Avon R.A.14, was taken to Boscombe Down, and on 6 October 1954 Peter Twiss took her up for the first time in a flight which lasted 25 minutes. Further trials were going well when on 17 November the engine lost all power due to a system fault and the resulting fuel starvation. Twiss was by that time at 30,000 ft and 30 miles from Boscombe Down, but elected to try to get the machine back there despite worries over the hydraulic-accumulator pressure being insufficient to maintain control. Heading home, he glided down and when the machine emerged from cloud six miles from the runway it was pointing straight towards it, and still with 2,500 ft height in hand. When he selected undercarriage-down on final approach, however, there was only sufficient pressure to lower and lock the nosewheel, and he did not have the benefit of airbrakes or the 'droopsnoot'. Nevertheless he brought the machine to a halt with only relatively minor damage after it swung off the runway and dug in the starboard wing. For this brave feat he was subsequently awarded the Queen's Commendation for Valuable Service in the Air.

The machine was taken back by road to the manufacturers at Hayes for examination and repair, a wing from the static test machine being exchanged for the damaged one. Flight trials were resumed in August 1955 and no troubles were experienced with the substitute wing. The first supersonic flight was made on 28 October, and it was soon found that Mach 1.1 could be reached without the aid of after-burning. By the following month WG774 had attained Mach 1.56, being 1,028 mph at over 36,000 ft, which was well above the absolute world speed record, which at that time was held by a North American Super Sabre at 822 mph. On 10 March 1956, operating from Boscombe Down, Twiss flew the machine on a measured course between Chichester and RNAS Ford on two timed runs. Flying at its best height for speed of 38,000 ft, the aircraft established a new record of 1,132 mph, considerably exceeding the previous record and becoming the first holder of a record of more than 1,000 mph.

Meanwhile WG777 had been completed, also fitted with an Avon R.A.14, being first flown by Twiss from Boscombe Down on 15 February 1956. It had minor differences in equipment and instrumentation, and from 13 April 1956 was based at RAE Bedford for measuring and handling trials in a follow-up aerodynamic research programme, now fitted with a 9,300 lb thrust Avon R.A.28 engine, capable of 13,100 lb with reheat. The poor English weather and environmental considerations limited supersonic tests with WG777, and on 11 October 1956 it was

flown out from Bedford to the French air base at Cazaux, near Bordeaux, where the population was sufficiently sparse for supersonic bangs to cause little complaint, and the aircraft could take advantage of the Mediterranean sun. Between 15 October and 15 November the aircraft flew 52 sorties, including six hours logged at Mach numbers in excess of 0.96. Soon afterwards the aircraft were able to take advantage of a new supersonic track running from Bedford to the Wash.

Research work continued, though the Bedford pilots did not find the aircraft very easy to fly, requiring constant attention up to sonic speeds, after which difficulties with lateral trim gave pilots the impression of continuous dutch roll. It remained at Bedford, eventually completing a total of 429 flights, until officially released in June 1966. On 8 September 1967 it was transported to Finningley for exhibition purposes, being given ground instructional number 7986M, and is now exhibited in the Cosford Aerospace Museum.

Meanwhile WG774 was taken over for Concorde development. Specification ER.193D had been issued on 31 December 1959, for a high speed research aircraft to evaluate the ogee wing of the Concorde, and on 5 September WG774 moved from Bedford to the Filton Division of BAC to help facilitate research study. The work was covered by contract KD/2E/06/CB.7(c), which was extended on 30 May 1961 to include conversion, the machine being redesignated BAC-221 in December 1963.

WG774 was now fitted with a completely new sharpedged ogival wing, a lengthened fuselage and many other modifications, including new systems and telemetry as well as a long-stroke undercarriage. Its overall length was now 57 ft 7½ins and wingspan 25 ft. The Specification was later replaced by ER.221D, issued on 18 July 1961, and the muchmodified aircraft first flew at Filton on 1 May 1964, fitted with an Avon R.A.28. There was a minor mishap on 13 Sep-

Above: **The slender BAC.221 with 'Dunlops dangling'.(BAC)**

Left: **The BAC.221 incorporated the first 'droop-snoot', later to be adopted on Concorde, although in the earlier aircraft the entire cockpit moved together with the nose. (BAC)**

tember 1964, but on 20 May 1966 it joined the Aerodynamics Flight at RAE Bedford, providing a lot of useful data on the high-speed handling behaviour of this wing planform. At the end of its useful life, it was transported by road on 6 November 1974 to the Royal Scottish Museum at East Fortune. From there it was reallocated in January 1980 to the Science Museum-administered Concorde Exhibition at RNAS Yeovilton, where it is currently displayed alongside Concorde 002 (G-BSST).

ARMSTRONG WHITWORTH A.W.58

The third aircraft in this proposed trio stemmed from Air Staff Requirement OR.282, which was drawn up in 1948 for a research aircraft to capable of investigating problems associated with flight at both transonic and supersonic speeds. In August of that year Armstrong Whitworth received contract 6/Acft/2751/CB.7(b) requiring them to produce a design study for such an aircraft with the capability of reaching a speed of Mach 1.2 and the potentiality to be adapted at a later stage to become a fighter fitted with full armament as well as radar.

The firm looked into the possibilities of both single- and twin-engined designs, and within three months was able to submit an outline study for a single-engined machine powered by either an Armstrong Siddeley Sapphire or a Rolls-Royce Avon. The streamlined single-seat fuselage sported a swept fin with a high-mounted all-moving tailplane, and the swept wings had drooped leading edges and wing fences.

After some consideration, Specification E.16/49 was drawn up, and a draft issued by MOS on 14 May 1949. This required a single-seat machine, fitted with a Rolls-Royce Avon engine with reheat and capable of both transonic and supersonic speeds. The fuselage was to have a pressure cabin, there should be provision for two 30 mm guns and the outer wings should feature elevons. It was anticipated that extensive alterations might be necessary to the lifting and control surfaces during development, therefore the design should be capable of adaptation. A maximum level speed of not less that Mach 1.12 was called for without the use of reheat.

On 25 May 1949 serial numbers WD466 and WD472 were allocated for two prototypes under contract number

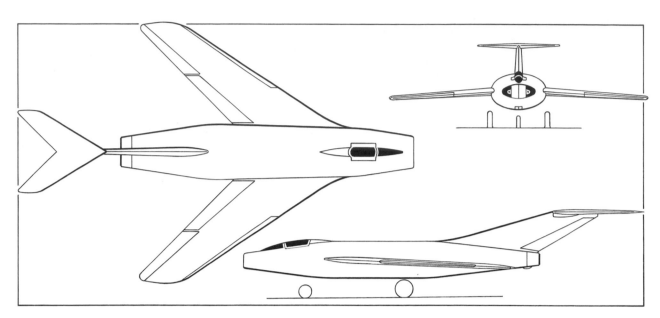

Above: **Three-view of the original Armstrong Whitworth A.W.58, the first design to meet Specification E.16/49.**

Below: **Three-view of the later Armstrong Whitworth A.W.58, proposed to meet the requirement for a delta design.**

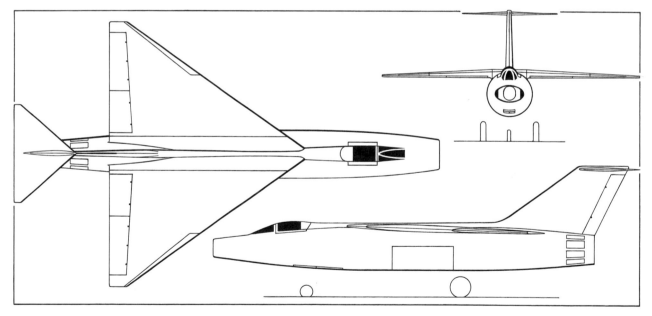

6/Acft/3913/CB.7(b), the maker's designation A.W.58 having been given by then. The initial design study produced a machine with a 59 degrees swept wing of 3.03 aspect ratio, having a length of 45 ft 2 in, span 24 ft and wing area of 190 sq ft. Powered by the specified Avon engine, it was realised by mid-July that it would only have been capable of speeds up to Mach 1.07 without reheat, and it was therefore decided to utilise an Armstrong Siddeley Sapphire instead.

As the design developed, consideration was given to replacing the original straight edges of the wings with cranked ones, and in this version the span was to have

been 27 ft 6 in and the length 48 ft 1 in, all-up weight being around 16,000 lb. On 22 September a revised version of Specification E.16/49 was issued, and on 1 October work commenced on a mock-up. Later that month the firm asked to revert to the Avon, as in their view this had more development potential than the Sapphire and was likely to be capable of producing sufficient thrust by the time the airframe was ready, but at the end of the month this was rejected by the Ministry.

Meanwhile, unbeknown to the firm, events had been moving against the project. On 12 November they received a letter from the Director of Military Aircraft

Research and Development telling them that due to financial stringencies it was necessary to cancel one of the three projects then being undertaken in this field, and the A.W.58 had been selected as the victim of this cutback. In the same letter, however, they were asked to submit a new study for a high-angle delta design to meet the performance requirements of Specification E.16/49, the proposals to include one design based on a Sapphire. This would be considered in competition with Fairey, who were then working on their F.D.1 design.

By the end of that month a provisional reworked design was under consideration, still identified as the A.W.58, with a 55 degree leading edge sweep. Construction was also about to start on a three-eighths flying scale model fitted with an Armstrong Siddeley Adder. Some dis-

cussion then took place with the Ministry before it was decided to fit a tail, and the design emerged with a span of 27 ft and length of 44 ft 8 in. It had an all-up weight of 13,200 lb, which compared with an estimated 11,800 lb for the F.D.2, and featured a 10,000 lb thrust Armstrong Siddeley Sapphire engine, giving a likely capability of speeds up to Mach 1.5.

Again their efforts came to nought, however, a letter being sent to the firm on 16 May 1950 telling them that their design had been unsuccessful, Faireys having been awarded the contract. The flying scale mock-up appears to have been temporarily overlooked, though, as some paperwork was required three months later before it could be officially authorised for disposal, putting a final end to the scheme.

Chapter 20
PRONE PILOT RESEARCH

One of the options being looked into for fast flying in the early post-war years was that of prone flying. To this end, in September 1948 the Air Council purchased from Reid & Sigrist, the Desford-based firm of instrument manufacturers, one of the only two aircraft of their own design ever built by their aircraft department. This was a two-seat fixed-undercarriage low-wing monoplane tandem trainer, registered G-AGOS and first flown in July 1945 with the company designation R.S.3, being named the Desford after its base. Powered by two 130 hp de Havilland Gipsy Major Is, it had a wingspan of 34 ft, a length of 25 ft 6 in and wing area of 186 sq ft.

Bought under contract 6/Acft/2695/CB.9(a), the service number VZ728 was allotted, and work commenced on modifications, the machine now becoming the R.S.4 Bobsleigh, an obvious analogy for the toboggan-like position of the horizontal pilot. Refitted with Gipsy Major 8s, the aircraft's nose was extended to house the prone pilot position, and as a safety precaution a normally-seated pilot position was retained, the forward cockpit being removed, and the aft cockpit fitted with a windscreen and sliding blown canopy, the overall length now being 26 ft 6 in.

The first flight in this new configuration was made on 13 June 1951, and a number of tests were carried out at Farnborough, where it went on 23 August 1951 for investigation. There was insufficient space for rudder pedals in the nose cockpit, and therefore it was fitted with a spectacle-wheel type of control column for all three axes, which in practice made the machine somewhat difficult to fly. It was sold in January 1956, reverting to its original civil registration and being subsequently used for photographic work by Film Aviation Services.

This line of research was later resumed when Armstrong Whitworth undertook conversion of a Gloster Meteor F.8 (WK935) with a greatly extended pointed nose housing the unpressurised prone-position. To compensate for the extra nose length a larger Meteor NF.12 type of rudder was installed so as to maintain stability. This aircraft made its first flight at Baginton on 10 February 1954, the prone pilot lying on a couch and having a full set of controls. As with the Bobsleigh, a second pilot always sat in the normal cockpit position as a precaution. In the Meteor the pilot was not entirely prone, his legs being bent lower than his trunk, and in this instance he had the benefit of rudder pedals – though he could be in some difficulty if a foot slipped from one of these as he would be unable to see them. Freedom of movement was limited, and hydraulic boost was therefore applied to all controls.

Trials were undertaken for the Institute of Aviation Medicine at Farnborough and for the Bristol Aeroplane Company, the latter for a proposed rocket-powered interceptor, the Type 185. It was found to be no more difficult to fly than from the normal Meteor cockpit, though the pilot was likely to become numb from the cold and end up with sore ribs. The Bristol 185 project was dropped, however, and on 3 March 1955 the prone-Meteor went to 15 MU Wroughton for spares recovery action, being later transferred to 33 MU Wroughton. It was given the ground instructional airframe number 7869M in January 1965, when it was allocated for display purposes and sent to RAF Colerne, moving in February 1977 to the Cosford Aerospace Museum, where it is still exhibited.

The Reid and Sigrist Bobsleigh prone pilot research aircraft seen in April 1951. (via M. Stroud)

The Gloster Meteor 8 prone pilot research aircraft. (via J.D. Oughton)

Chapter 21
COMMERCIAL VENTURES

During the Second World War the Allies had of necessity to rely on the United States to meet their need for many hundreds of transport aircraft. This gave America the opportunity to build up an unassailable lead in the commercial transport field. Nearly four decades were to pass before European manufacturers began to make any significant inroads into this, but if two large advanced aircraft from the Filton design team had been more successful the story might have been very different.

BRISTOL BRABAZON

Towards the end of 1942 the Ministry of Aircraft Production set up a meeting of chief designers to discuss the possibility of designing a long-range commercial aircraft. Bristol were not represented at this initial meeting but were allowed to attend the next meeting on 14 January 1943, and were able to produce outline proposals for a transport having 5,000 miles range, adapted from an earlier design study for a proposed multi-engined heavy bomber.

Meanwhile an interdepartmental-committee had been set up under the chairmanship of Lord Brabazon of Tara to decide the types of British civil aircraft likely to be needed in the immediate post-war period. The Brabazon Committee, as it became known, recommended five basic types, of which priority was to be given to the first, the Brabazon Type I, this being an express airliner able to fly direct between London and New York without refuelling, the needs being formulated in Air Staff Requirement OR.171.

Ideally, the Type I would have been built by a firm which already had considerable experience in building large bombers, but none of these had spare capacity, and therefore in March 1944 it was decided that Bristol should

have the contract, provided they undertook that their other work was not affected. The British Overseas Airways Corporation advised that 18 hours was the limit for passenger toleration, and each should have at least 200 cu ft of space, rising to 270 cu ft for luxury travellers.

Initial thoughts for the Type 167, as it had become, centred around a 25 ft diameter body with two levels of accommodation. Day seats could be provided for 150 passengers, but this dropped to 80 if sleeping berths were required, there being a dining room, promenade area and bar. This size of fuselage, however, would produce too much drag for the engines then available, and the concept was changed to a 20 ft diameter single-deck layout. In this version the dining room would disappear, and accommodation would be reduced to 96 by day and 52 by night.

On 22 November 1944 the requirement was formally issued to Bristol as Specification number 2/44, based on OR.171 Issue 1. Fitted with four pairs of coupled Bristol Centaurus engines, empty weight was estimated as 143,597 lb and all-up weight as 250,000 lb, with a resulting range of 5,000 miles at 20,000 ft at a cruising speed of 250 mph. A later version, however, fitted with eight Bristol 'Pilot' turbine engines, would have an empty weight of only 129,247 lb, and with the same all-up weight it could fly a similar trip at a speed of 295 mph, giving a substantial reduction in journey times.

In February 1945 the military serial numbers TX376 and TX381 were issued for two machines under contract number 6/Acft/4124/C.20(a), but these serials were later cancelled.

Nine months later the Director General of Technical Development in correspondence with the Controller of Research and Development was concerned to see the first

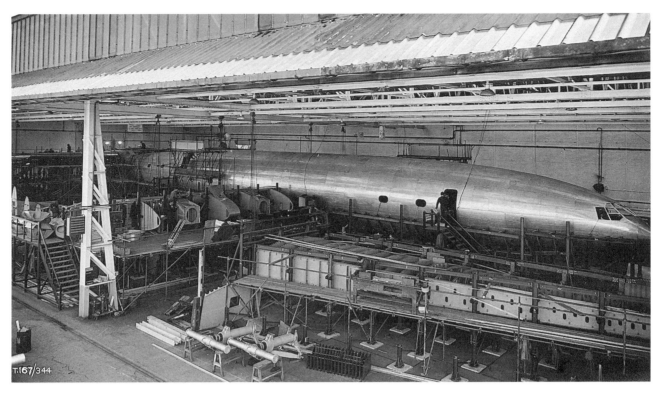

The Bristol Brabazon under construction.

prototype get into flight with the least possible delay. He did not expect the turbine-engined version to get into the air for about a year after the first machine was due to fly and was anxious to gain as much flying time as possible in the meantime. He thought it abundantly clear that the second prototype must have the high compression turbine installation, and this requirement must therefore be stated to Bristol in unequivocal terms. He went on to suggest that the present order be extended from two prototypes to five, comprising one Centaurus-engined machine plus four with gas turbine engines, though this never materialised.

By 1946, O.R.171 Issue 2 had resulted in the drawing up of Specification 2/46 for the turbine-powered version. The nomenclature of the two versions was settled at Brabazon I MkI for the Centaurus version, and Brabazon I MkII for the gas turbine-engined machine, both the Bristol Theseus and Bristol Proteus being under consideration for the latter, though by April 1946 this had narrowed down to the Proteus.

The two-deck concept had not been entirely discarded by Bristol, and in May 1946 their Chief Designer, Dr A.E. Russell wrote to the Ministry of Supply about the result of investigations into a double-bubble MkII. They had found that the aircraft was equally economic with either one or two decks when operating on the route for which the aircraft was specially designed. He suggested, however, that the sole advantage of the double-deck body seemed to be that it carried rather more passengers, which might be useful for bank holidays and rush hours, but it would take longer to construct. The double-decker

would take three hours longer to get to New York than the single-decker, without counting stopping times at intermediate landings.

In August 1946 it was reported that on a half-scale structural model the wings failed at 54 per cent of the design load (gust case). The failure took the form of shearing the rivets attaching the skin to the bottom boom of the port front spar, extending from inboard of the undercarriage bay to the fuselage. Surprisingly, this does not seem to have been considered serious, except insofar as it was delaying a decision on whether the wings as a whole were strong enough.

The design was fairly orthodox, but every effort was made to save weight during both design and construction. It had been hoped to build the prototypes at the firm's Weston-super-Mare factory, but tests on the subsoil showed it to be unsuitable for the lengthy runway which would be required. Construction therefore had to be undertaken at Filton, which led to much local recrimination as the necessary construction of a strong and lengthy runway involved closing a new dual-carriageway by-pass and demolishing part of a village, the resulting furore helping to delay the first flight. It was also necessary to construct a special three-bay eight-acre assembly hall, this too being a cause of delay when its completion was held up by the bitter winter weather of early 1947.

Various component tests were made on different aircraft during construction. The hydraulic actuators for the flying controls, for instance, were tested on Lancaster RE131, and the combustion heaters for de-icing the wings and tail were flight-tested on Buckmaster RP164. The first prototype was rolled out in December 1948. Having the constructor's number 12759, it had been allocated military serial number VX206 earlier that year, but in the event it was to carry civil registration G-AGPW which had been reserved as early as June 1945. It was fitted out as an unfurnished test-bed equipped with assorted data-recording equipment, though the possibility was not ruled out that it might be converted later for commercial use.

Powered by eight 2,360 hp Centaurus XX engines, G-AGPW finally took to the air on 4 September 1949 at the hand of the Chief Test Pilot, Bill Pegg, and performed like a lady. The only incident of note occurred on 16 January 1950 when hydraulic failure led to a landing with flaps up, but the use of reverse pitch on the airscrews and the lengthened Filton runway prevented any actual damage. The aircraft was demonstrated at Farnborough in September that year, and for demonstration purposes it was fitted out with 30 reclining-type BOAC seats with which it was possible to show how such a large airliner could increase comfort and quietness for its passengers.

The aircraft had a span of 230 ft, length of 177 ft, height of 50 ft and wing area of 5,317 sq ft. Empty weight was 145,100 lb and all-up weight 290,000 lb. Maximum speed was 300 mph at 25,000 ft and the range was 5,500 miles at a cruising speed of 250 mph. Initial climb was 750 ft/min and service ceiling 25,000 ft. For commercial purposes it would have had a crew of 14 and could carry 94 passengers.

The promise was never fulfilled, however. By November 1952 the Brabazon project was getting nowhere, with the Americans getting most of the post-war commercial orders. Bristol were well into Britannia production by then, and badly needed extra space. They therefore pressed for permission to take the two Brabazons out of the hangar by the following March. They intimated that they would offer no objection to an instruction to abandon the whole Brabazon project and dispose of the two aircraft, considering that the type had been overtaken by progress and its prospects for the future were a diminishing quantity.

They were taken at their word, probably with much relief all round. G-AGPW had accumulated less than 400 hours of flying time, and was eventually scrapped at Filton in October 1953, authority for this having been given on 17 August. The second machine, c/n 12870, had the civil registration G-AIML issued in December 1946 and the military serial VX343 in April 1948, but was never assembled before it too was scrapped. It was slightly longer at 178 ft 10 in, and wing area had increased to 5,422 sq ft although the span remained the same. It would have had eight 3,500 hp Bristol Proteus 705 turboprop engines giving a range of 5,460 miles at 350 mph.

This spelt the end of a sad story which had started with such promise. The work was not entirely wasted, however, as the Bristol design team gained valuable expertise which was put to use in the Britannia and later in Concorde.

BAC CONCORDE

In 1956 the newly-formed Supersonic Transport Advisory

The Bristol Brabazon MkI photographed in February 1950. By this time modifications had been made including the fitting of small additional stabilisers to the tail plane. (via M. Stroud)

The Bristol Brabazon in flight. (RAF Museum 6369-3)

Committee commenced what turned out to be a three-year study, 'to initiate and monitor a co-operative programme of aimed research designed to pave the way for a possible first generation of supersonic transport aircraft'. The 28 members of the committee included representatives of all the major British aircraft and engine companies as well as the two main airlines, BOAC and BEA.

By March 1959 it was able to report that with the developing technology then becoming available, it would be feasible to start serious work on a long-range supersonic commercial transport. A 100-seat machine with a range of 1,500 miles could be designed with a speed of Mach 1.2, whilst a trans-Atlantic 150-seater version with a range of 3,000 miles was estimated to be capable of Mach 1.8. Various wing outlines were considered, including compound-swept ('W' and 'M') and slender delta, the latter being the only one suitable, with surprisingly good performance up to just over Mach 2, this ultimately resulting in the now familiar slender ogival delta-wing planform.

Comparative feasibility studies were undertaken by Hawker and Bristol, the former being given the task of producing a design with a thick wing merging into the fuselage, whilst Bristol worked on a thin wing attached to a highly streamlined fuselage. The latter was found to be the better of the two, and Bristol were awarded a design study contract leading to their Type 198 design, a 132-seat machine with six Bristol Olympus under-wing engines and a take-off weight of 380,000 lb. Two versions of this were proposed, the 198A being of aluminium alloy structure and the 198S of steel, it being estimated as being able to reach Mach 2.3, with a range of 3,500 nautical miles. The Type 223 was to be a smaller version of this with only 100 seats and a reduced all-up weight of 250,000 lb, but still capable of crossing the Atlantic.

In 1960 Bristol became part of the British Aircraft Corporation, and a contract was awarded for a design study, but in view of the cost and likely risk it was made conditional that an international partner be found. Germany showed no interest, while the Americans were working on the lines of a Mach 3 machine constructed of steel and titanium, and therefore the slower Bristol design was of little interest to them. Bristol had in fact submitted for comparison purposes their Olympus-powered Type 213 along these lines, but this would have involved too big a venture into the unknown. The French firm Sud Aviation, however, already busy with orders for their subsonic Caravelle, were thinking in terms of a Mach 2 Super Caravelle with a 1500-mile range and were therefore more receptive.

Negotiations took place, with the British side arguing that the best proposition was an aircraft with the capability of flying the Atlantic on, say, the Paris-New York route. Sonic boom problems would be minimal and the time-saving aspect of the journey would be much more attractive to customers. The French still stuck to their original concept, however, and neither side would back down, but eventually, on 29 November 1962, ministers of the two countries signed a treaty in London giving the French team the lead on the aircraft design and the British team, in the shape of Bristol-Siddeley (later merged into Rolls-Royce), the lead on the engine. There was some compromising on this, with the French engine SNECMA firm taking responsibility for the engine nozzle, and the BAC being largely responsible for the nose, tail and nacelles. Construction was to be of aluminium alloy.

There was much in common between the two approaches, it being particularly notable that the two design teams had come to very similar conclusions about the optimum wing form. The only important differences were in the wing position and the nose structure. Sud were thinking in terms of a low wing and a normal windscreen with adequate visibility. BAC favoured a mid wing and a nose hinged downwards to improve the pilot's view during landing, an idea originally developed and patented for the Fairey F.D.2, and inherited by Westland in 1960 when they took over Fairey. Ultimately the low wing was chosen, and in 1967 BAC bought the 'droop snoot' invention from Westland for incorporation in the Concorde.

Development costs were optimistically estimated at between £150 and £170 million, and assembly lines were to be set up at Filton and Toulouse, but the French effort was somewhat dissipated in the early stages by their insistence on continuing in parallel with their Super Caravelle project, which was not finally dropped until 1965. The main problem, however, was lack of cohesion between the two nationalities, with the post of chairman of the airframe committee alternating on an annual cycle, and nobody at a lower level wishing to be subordinate to his counterpart, so that decisions dragged on whilst they were fought out on jingoistic lines, often irrespective of their merits.

Whilst in retrospect it would be easy to decry all this, it must be borne in mind that there was no precedent for such a major undertaking in Anglo-French collaboration, or indeed internationally. Many lessons had to be learned the hard way, but the long drawn out nature of the discussions and arguments did have the advantage of allowing time to iron out many of the potential difficulties, with the result that when it came to the flight development stage this went extremely smoothly. Perhaps even more important, the ground rules were laid for future international collaboration on expensive projects, with particularly great benefit to the Sepecat Jaguar and the Panavia Tornado.

The name Concorde was adopted soon after the signing of the treaty. It had been suggested by the son of the Bristol Publicity Manager, and the spelling found easy acceptance by the French – but not by the British Government who swam against the tide on this issue, not being willing to drop the anglicised spelling Concord until the end of 1967.

Costs, meanwhile were shooting up, and the British team were being proved right on the non-viability of the smaller design proposed by the French. Re-designing eventually increased the capacity to up to 140 economy-class seats, necessitating adding more than 20 ft to the originally planned length. Greater power was demanded of the Olympus engines to cope with this, the all-up weight being now in the region of 400,000 lb, and the initial cost estimates paled in comparison with the final research and development bill of £970 million, shared equally between the two countries.

The Americans in the meantime were still pursuing their dream of a Mach 3 counterpart, and a contract was awarded to Boeing. In the end it proved too advanced even for their resources, and they eventually dropped out of the picture with the withdrawal of funding by the Senate. By the time their involvement ended in 1971, Boeing were well established as the world's leading builder of mass air transport and they shed very few tears.

The Anglo-French project soldiered on, with cost escalation and design difficulties bringing calls for its cancellation – but it was the subject of a binding international treaty, and had to continue. Much of the rising cost was due to its being developed at a time of steadily rising inflation, but this apart, the original estimates had been hopelessly low for such an advanced design.

The first of the two short-length prototypes, 001 (F-WTSS), eventually flew at Toulouse on 2 March 1969, piloted by André Turcat, Director of Flight Test for Aérospatiale, followed on 9 April 1969 by 002 (G-BSST) at Filton in the hands of Brian Trubshaw, and these undertook most of the test programme. They were followed by two pre-production machines, 01 (G-AXDN) being flown by Trubshaw at Filton on 17 December 1971, and 02 (F-WTSA) at Toulouse on 10 January 1973. Full-production aircraft then began to roll off the line, alternate aircraft being assembled in France and Britain.

The eventual design which had emerged proved to be a triumph of advanced technology. Initial production machines were powered by four Rolls-Royce/SNECMA Olympus 593 Mk602 engines providing 38,050 lb thrust with reheat at take-off, and 6,800 lb thrust at a cruising altitude of 60,000 ft. The wing span was 83 ft 10 in, length 203 ft 9 in, height 37 ft 1 in and wing area 3,856 sq ft. Basic operating weight was 172,500 lb and maximum weight at take-off was 389,000 lb. Range at a cruise of Mach 2.05 was 3,853 miles, and up to 144 passengers could be accommodated depending on the seating arrangements.

Perhaps if something like the original optimistic timescale had been maintained the technical success might have been translated into a commercial triumph, but by the time the aircraft was ready to go into service the world was in the throes of an oil crisis. Added to this environmental problems led many countries to refuse it airspace, mainly due to the frequent sonic booms to which they would be subjected. Potential customers dropped out one by one, and eventually only the two national lines, British Overseas Airways Corporation (later British Airways) and Air France ordered it.

BAC Concorde G-BSST under assembly. (via M. Stroud)

Even the Americans would not allow it in at first, adopting the dog-in-the-manger attitude that as they could not have their own SST they would do their best to stop the Anglo-French one. British Airways could therefore only operate it initially on the Heathrow-Bahrein route, but hearings by the US Government eventually allowed a trial service to Washington in 1976, and the following year a regular service was permitted into New York's Kennedy Airport. This gradually proved that the environmental problems were not as great as the many protesters had claimed, but it was too late to remedy the situation, and only 14 production machines were ever built. All are still in service and proving a boon, especially to business travellers wishing to get to their transatlantic destinations with a minimum of unproductive time spent in the air. G-BSST is currently exhibited in an annexe to the Fleet Air Arm Museum at Yeovilton.

Concorde 'SST bearing the names of the joint manufacturers. (via P. Jarrett)

Chapter 22
VERTICAL TAKE-OFF & LANDING

With increasing power becoming available from the development of jet engines, the prospect opened up of harnessing this for some form of vertical take-off in which rotors would be unnecessary. Helicopters and other forms of rotorcraft were developing rapidly, but they could not be expected to combine their advantage of taking off from small areas with that of high speeds.

ROLLS-ROYCE FLYING BEDSTEAD

In the early fifties Rolls-Royce, in conjunction with the Royal Aircraft Establishment, investigated the possibility of a controlled form of vertical take-off and landing, now familiar as VTOL. A test-bed was built, officially described as the Thrust Measuring Rig, but more colloquially known as the 'Flying Bedstead', the design of which was carried out under the direction of Stan Hart, the chief installation designer. The project was a joint one, with RAE taking responsibility of the control and autostabilisations system and Rolls-Royce for the design of valves and linkages for these systems.

The requirement called for the rig to have a thrust-to-weight ratio of 1.25 to 1 when carrying a full fuel load, the latter being sufficient for only 15 minutes testing, and it had to be capable of remaining off the ground for at least five minutes without overheating. It also had to be capable of attaining a height of 50 feet and of moving anywhere within an area of not less then 100 feet square.

The resulting machine consisted of a tubular framework powered by two Rolls-Royce Nene 101-IVs horizontally opposed to nullify gyroscopic torque. They were exhausted downward to provide lift, the jet pipes being sited near each other to keep rolling and pitching to a minimum. Control of pitch, roll and yaw was by means of air tapped from compressors and fed to puffer pipes at the corners of the machine, 9 per cent of the compressor delivery air being bled off from one of the engines for this purpose.

The rig was subject to contract number 6/Eng/5910/CB.13(c), and was first rolled out at Hucknall on 3 July 1953, making its first tethered flight six days later. The rig did not fully measure up to requirements, the thrust margin of 25 per cent not being reached, with a maximum ratio of the order of only 1.16 to 1 being achieved, and even less than this on take-off, gradually rising as fuel was expended. Problems were encountered initially with the undercarriage structure, the oleo legs not extending evenly at first, and all-metal wheels were substituted for the original rubber-tyred ones.

The problems were gradually ironed out, but it was not for more than a year that the first free flight was made, on 3 August 1954 at the hands of Captain Ronnie Shepherd. No serial number had been allotted initially, possibly due to the fact that the rig was built under an engineering contract, and not one for an aircraft, but on 23 November 1954 it became XJ314. By the time it had its last test at Hucknall, on 15 December 1954, it had made 224 tethered flights totalling nine hours, and 16 free flights lasting 105 minutes in all. The free flights had gone as high as 50 feet and in winds of up to 20 knots, forward speeds of up to 10 knots having been achieved. By the time the Hucknall tests had been completed the rig had been developed to become very stable with no difficulty being experienced in maintaining the hover – although the gradual loss of fuel could transform an intended gentle descent into an equally gentle climb unless thrust was reduced slightly to compensate for this.

After overhaul, the rig was despatched to RAE Farn-

The Rolls-Royce Flying Bedstead aloft at Hucknall.
(Rolls-Royce Ltd)

borough on 13 January 1955 to continue trials, transferring to RAE Bedford on 21 June 1956. It made many further successful flights until 16 September 1957, when a mechanical failure in the auto stabilisation system resulted in the full application of pitch control, and it crashed. It never flew again, but was rebuilt for exhibition purposes, and on 9 January 1961 was allotted permanently to the Science Museum, being currently on loan to the Fleet Air Arm Museum at RNAS Yeovilton as part of the VSTOL Exhibition.

In the meantime a second machine had been completed, under contracts 6/Eng/8409 and 6/Eng/7814/CB.13(c), and this too received a serial number, XK426 being allocated on 22 April 1955. It was rolled out on 19 August 1955, and began tethered flight on 17 October 1955, the first free flight being made on 12 November 1956. On 22 November 1957 it was allotted under contract number KD/X/05/CB.10(a) to RAE Bedford for assessment of the effects of atmospheric turbulence and to obtain further information on ground effects. This never happened, however, as five days later, during its last tethered flight at Hucknall, the rig crashed after loss of control due to the rig's striking the gantry, killing the pilot Wg Cdr H.G.F. Larson. It had by that time made 156 tethered flights, totalling 13 hours, and four free flights amounting to 21 minutes. It was never rebuilt, and on 8 December 1964 the remains were sold to a scrap merchant. Despite the setback of losing both machines in such a short space of time, the principle had long since been proved successful and it paved the way to more practical developments.

SHORT SC.1

Although the Rolls-Royce Thrust Measuring Rig did not appear until July 1953, thinking was already going ahead to a proper aircraft with VTOL capability, and on 25 September 1952 Specification ER.143T was issued for a more normal research aircraft capable of full transition from level to vertical flight and vice versa. Two years later sufficient knowledge had been gained from the TMR for the Ministry of Supply to feel sufficiently confident to award Contract number 6/Acft/11094/CB.7(a) on 10 July 1954 to Short Brothers & Harland of Belfast for the construction of two prototype aircraft. Work had initially proceeded under the designation PD.11, PD indicating Preliminary Design, but this was later superseded by the type number SC.1, the aircraft being allocated serial numbers XG900 and XG905, with the respective manufacturer's numbers SH.1814 and SH.1815. An unsuccessful contender for this contract was the Percival P.94 design.

Power for the SC.1 was to be provided by no less than five of the newly-developed Rolls-Royce RB.108 engines each giving 2,010lb of thrust, which would provide the superb thrust/weight ratio of 8:1. Four of the engines were mounted around the centre of gravity with their effluxes directed vertically downwards, air for these being drawn in through a curved rectangular grill built in above the centre fuselage, a close-meshed wire grill reducing the danger of ingesting debris. The other engine was for horizontal propulsion, with a normal jet efflux in the tail of the aircraft, air being drawn in through an intake immediately forward of the vertical tail surfaces. Because the RB.108 was designed to work in the vertical position, this fifth engine was fitted at an angle to avoid the necessity for major modification to the engine systems.

The pilot would have an excellent view downwards, being positioned in a large helicopter-type transparent canopy right at the front of the aircraft. He was to be provided with all the usual conventional controls, plus a throttle lift lever to control in unison the four vertically mounted lift engines. The machine was also to be fitted with automatic-stability control gear, power controls and specialised landing gear, all of which entailed much design and development work. Sharply tapered horizontal wing surfaces were minimal in size, but sufficient to maintain the aircraft in forward flight without the use of the vertical motors. They had a span of only 23 ft 6 in, against a basic length of 24 ft 5 in, the wing area being 211.5 sq ft. There were no horizontal tail surfaces.

The first metal was cut in 1955, and by late 1956 XG900 was basically complete, ground engine tests being possible on 7 December with only the propulsion motor installed. No problems were encountered, and ten days later Tom Brooke-Smith, the firm's Chief Test Pilot, began extended taxiing trials. On completion of these the aircraft was despatched by sea to Boscombe Down, being embarked in SS *Copeland* on 6 March 1957 for what turned out to be a rather rough two-day passage around Land's End to Southampton. Continuing by road, the aircraft reached its destination on 11 March, and by 2 April

Short SC.1 XG905 under tether at Belfast. (Short Bros & Harland Ltd)

was ready for a series of flight tests involving normal take-offs and landings.

In the meantime the second machine (XG905) had been completed, being given a raised dorsal fin above the horizontal engine as a result of the trials on XG900. All five motors were installed, and on 3 September 1957 the lift motors were run for the first time. These had been swivel-mounted so that they could tilt within a range of 35 degrees fore-and-aft. When tilted aft they helped in transition from vertical to forward flight, and when tilted forward provided rapid deceleration for vertical descent.

As a precaution, early hovering flights with XG905 were made with the aircraft tethered, the first of these being made on 23 May 1958, again by Tom Brooke-Smith, and this was followed by similar flights, involving also Jock Eassie and Sqn Ldr S.J. Hubbard of RAE Bedford. By 25 October sufficient confidence had been gained for the first free hovering flight to be made, and the following month it landed safely on the soft turf of a football pitch.

By September 1959 sufficient confidence was felt to have an aircraft carry out a hovering demonstration at the SBAC Show at Farnborough. No allowance, however, had been made for the efficiency of the local grass-cutting services, and Tom Brooke-Smith in XG900 found it necessary to descend with unintended rapidity when the horizontal intakes became clogged by newly-mown grass

Short SC.1 XG900 in front of the Boscombe Down wind tunnel during cockpit canopy jettison trials. (via M. Stroud)

stirred up in a cloud by his take-off.

In early 1960 XG905 was shipped to RAE Bedford, and here it made the first transition from vertical to horizontal on 6 April. Soon afterwards, XG900 received its four lift engines and auto controls, and both machines had various modifications including fitting fairings to the oleo legs.

The second Short SC.1 in free hover clear of its special platform. (Shorts)

Brooke-Smith was able to demonstrate publicly full transition when XG905 appeared at the next Farnborough Show in September 1960. On 23 March 1961 XG900 went to RAE Bedford, and appeared at that year's Farnborough Show, this time piloted by Short's new Chief Test Pilot, Denis Tayler. A minor incident was a fire in the area of the starboard wheels on 22 May 1963.

Shorts continued to fly XG905, and over 80 flights were made at Belfast, ending on 2 October 1963 when it went out of control, pitched into the ground and overturned, killing J.R. Green, an RAE test pilot. The aircraft was not written off, however, being returned to the factory and eventually flown again in 1966. On 4 June 1967 it was shipped to Boscombe Down, from where it went 12 days later to RAE Bedford for V/STOL control and instrument systems tests with the Blind Landing Experimental Unit.

This concept of vertical flight had by now been superseded, however, by that of the Hawker P.1127, which had proved that vertical flight did not require multiple engines. XG900 was relegated to ground running only in March 1969, and two years later the two machines were withdrawn from Bedford, XG900 going to the Science Museum on 22 June 1971, and XG905 being returned to Shorts until it went for exhibition to its current home, the Ulster Folk and Transport Museum at Cultra Manor, Holywood, on 4 June 1974. XG900 is currently displayed in the VSTOL exhibiton at Yeovilton. A proposal by Shorts for a PD.43/SC.8 two-seater trainer variant with six RB.108s attracted no official interest.

HAWKER P.1127

Early in 1957 leading French designer Michel Wibault put to the American Mutual Weapons Development Programme office in Paris a suggestion for an aircraft engine which would provide both vertical and horizontal thrust through controllable discharge outlets. His proposal centred around a Bristol BE.25 Orion engine, and was therefore passed by MWDP to Bristols with an assurance of substantial financial backing for its development.

Soon after starting work, Sir Sydney Camm, chief engineer of Hawkers, approached Bristols about the possibility of installing such an engine in a V/STOL combat aircraft able to carry a 2,000 lb warload. His firm had recently been heavily involved in a proposed P.1121 design for which Ministry of Supply development funding was no longer forthcoming, and were therefore looking for some other project more likely to attract NATO interest. A V/STOL machine seemed a likely prospect with its ability to dispense if necessary with a runway, or alternatively to use its vertical thrust to take off from a normal runway with a big overload.

First thoughts centred around twin rotating nozzles at the side of an aircraft being fed by-pass air, with a conventional tail pipe discharging the hot exhaust. Discussion between the two firms resulted in the jetpipe being bifurcated, leading to another set of rotating nozzles, the resulting engine design being given the title BS.53 Pegasus.

MWDP fulfilled their promise of financial help with the engine, agreeing in June 1958 to pay 75 per cent of the cost of its development. Hawkers were not so lucky, falling foul of a recent ruling that research projects could only be financed if they had a civil application, but they went ahead on a private venture basis.

Official interest was nevertheless maintained, and in April 1959 draft General Operational Requirement GOR.345

was issued, work starting soon afterwards on formulating the consequent Specification ER.204D. The metal for the first prototype was cut in May 1959, and five months later Hawkers was awarded £75,000 to finance design work. The Specification was formally issued on 29 February 1960, and on 27 June 1960 an order was placed under Contract number KD/2Q/02/CB.9(c) for three machines, two of which were to carry serial numbers XP831 and XP836, the third being used for static tests. This order was quickly followed by another under the same contract for four development machines, to be serialled XP972, XP976, XP980 and XP984.

An opportunity arose for developing the concept when, in August 1961, NATO formulated a basic military

Hawker P.1127 prototype XP831 in the hover.

requirement (NBMR.3) for a possible supersonic V/STOL light strike fighter, to replace the Fiat G.91 around 1966. Hawkers came up with the P.1154 design for an improved P.1127 fitted with a derated Bristol Siddeley BS.100 engine, its main competitor being the French Mirage III-V Balzac, powered by a set of Rolls-Royce lift engines. Both the RAF and Fleet Air Arm took a keen interest in the P.1154, and for some time the outlook seemed reasonably hopeful, but the two services were unable to agree on a compromise version to meet both their interests, and the NATO requirement gradually died, so that eventually in February 1965 this promising project was finally cancelled.

With the possibility of a supersonic P.1154, RAF interest in the subsonic P.1127 had waned, but the programme continued and prototype XP831 made its first tethered hop on 21 October 1960 in the hands of Bill Bedford at Dunsfold, powered by a 10,400 lb thrust Pegasus 1. The aircraft was of basically conventional design, but was comparatively small, its length of 41 ft 2 in and wingspan of 24 ft 4 in both being appreciably less than that of its Hunter stablemate. Two large side intakes immediately behind the pilot led directly to the engine, which occupied much of the centre fuselage. The bicycle-type undercarriage consisted of a nose-wheel and twin main-wheels under the fuselage, the machine being steadied on the ground by two small wheels on outrigger struts at each wingtip. Puffer pipes

at the aircraft's extremities controlled pitch, yaw and roll in the hover and during slow-speed flight, and anhedral on the wings counteracted any tendency to dutch roll.

The first free hover with XP831 took place on 19 November 1960, it then being re-engined with a 12,000 lb thrust Pegasus 2 for its first conventional flight, which took place at RAE Bedford on 13 March 1961, both piloted by Bill Bedford. Minor damage was caused when it slewed round after failing to take off on 22 September 1961, but otherwise initial trials went fairly smoothly.

XP831 was used for hovering and engine development by the respective manufacturers, a 13,500 lb thrust Pegasus 3 being fitted during 1962. Successful trials were carried out aboard HMS *Ark Royal* on 8 February 1963 in front of representatives of the RAF, Fleet Air Arm, US Navy and Royal Australian Navy. It became the cause of considerable embarrassment, however, when on 16 June 1963 it crashed with Bill Bedford at the controls at the Paris Air Salon, right in front of the Balzac. Damage was extensive, but it was worth repairing, and on 2 February 1965 it went to RAF Bedford for experimental and research work, being eventually transported on 13 November 1972 for display at the RAF Museum.

Meanwhile the second prototype made its appearance, fitted with a Pegasus 1, XP836 having its first tethered flight on 7 July 1961, followed by the first free flight on 12 September. This machine was retained by Hawkers for conventional flight trials, but its life turned out to be a short one, as on 14 December 1961 the port front cold nozzle broke off, and the pilot had to make a low-level ejection while attempting to make a precautionary landing at RNAS Yeovilton. This aircraft was eventually struck off charge on 13 November 1962.

XP831 continued the trials with both Hawkers and Bristol Siddeley, being again re-engined in 1962, this time with a 13,500 lb thrust Pegasus 3. Fortunately work was well advanced with the next four aircraft, XP972 being flown on 5 April 1962 with a Pegasus 2 engine. This machine was also retained by Hawkers, and was evaluated for possible use by the Luftwaffe, but like its immediate predecessor it had a short life, a wheels-up landing at Tangmere after engine failure on 30 October 1962, with Hugh Mereweather at the controls, resulting in heavy damage. The remains were returned to Hawker's Kingston factory for repair, but a year later work had still not commenced, and eventually it was struck off charge on 15 September 1964. The firm had in the meantime become part of Hawker Siddeley Aviation in 1963.

Hawker and Bristol Siddeley were able to continue development flying with the next aircraft, XP976, which successively had a Pegasus 2, 3 and then 4. It was used at various times for performance and handling trials, engine development and pilot conversion as well as familiarisation flights. On 26 July 1965 it went to the Blind Landing Experimental Unit at RAE Bedford for research work, including work on head-up displays, returning to Dunsfold on 5 November 1965. It was finally struck off charge there on 1 February 1968, following which it went to 71

MU at Bicester to be shown at various functions as a static display aircraft. After a spell in store at Aston Down it was cannibalised for spares for XP980, then used for a time at RAE Farnborough as a test rig before being dumped there in 1974.

Next came XP980, which had its first flight on 24 February 1963, introducing a taller fin design. This had a very active development life, being used intensively for development and engine trials before going to Boscombe Down on 27 January 1966 for systems trials, stores carriage and airfield performance trials. Its flying life ended when in April 1970 it was allotted to Flight Refuelling Ltd for modification to ground drone standard, using the wings of Harrier XV751 which had suffered damage at West Raynham on 5 August 1969. On 7 October 1971 it was delivered to RAE Bedford to be used for crash barrier trials, before going to Dunsfold on 7 June 1972 for rough ground trials, these being continued the following year at Gaydon. Later in 1973 it went to 71 MU Bicester for possible conversion as a 'Harrier' display aircraft. This failed to materialise, and in October 1980 it went to the RN School of Aircraft Handling at Culdrose, repainted to represent a Sea Harrier with the ground instructional serial A2800. It is now on display at the FAA Museum at Yeovilton as part of the VSTOL Exhibition.

The final P.1127 development aircraft, XP984, was completed to a new standard, having a 15,000 lb thrust Pegasus 5 engine with improved intakes, a larger fuselage, a taller fin, an anhedral tailplane and two wing hard-points. It had its first flight on 13 February 1964, and was then used at RAE Farnborough for airframe and engine development

work. It suffered some damage in a forced landing at Thorney Island on 9 March 1965, but repairs were completed by October, and in November brief stalling and spinning trials were carried out at Boscombe Down to confirm the advice given in Pilots' Notes on recovery from spins. The spinning trials were somewhat restricted, however, as it was not fitted with external tanks, unlike later aircraft.

The conclusion reached at the end of the trials was that the aircraft would spin readily upon application of pro-spin control, but fully developed spin was not established within two complete turns of the spin. Recovery from the incipient spin was immediate upon application of recovery control. Engine surge was encountered in a high proportion of spins, sometimes taking the form of rapid 'popping'. More frequently, however, was what became known as a 'locked-in' surge, which precluded stalling with the aircraft in the landing configuration.

XP984 was then fitted with Harrier-type swept wings, with which it flew on 23 March 1966. It then went back to Farnborough for aerodynamic trials, including spins and stalls, carrying out demonstrations aboard HMS *Bulwark* between 18 and 20 June 1966. On 13 September 1966 it went to RAE Bedford for VTOL research flying, returning to Dunsfold late that month. On 11 September 1968 it went back to Farnborough, transferring to RAE Bedford on 21 April 1972 for flight trials of a nozzle inching system, as well as HUD and yaw auto-stabiliser. After suffering an accident there on 31 October 1975, it was relegated to ground

The first development Hawker P.1127, XP972, banking for the camera.

Hawker P.1127s of the Tripartite Evaluation Squadron. (BAe)

instructional duties, being sent on 10 February 1976 to HMS *Thunderer*, the RN Engineering College at Manadon, Plymouth, to become A2658.

In the meantime, the P.1127, unlike many of the aircraft described in this book, had become a continuing success story. Nine further aircraft had been ordered, of a similar standard to the XP984, and these were given the name Kestrel FGA.1. They were flown by a Tripartite Evaluation Squadron set up as part of the Central Fighter Estab-

lishment at West Raynham, where they were flown by RAF, US Navy, US Army and Luftwaffe crews. At the conclusion of the trial, six of these aircraft went to the United States, where they received the designation XV-6A. The Luftwaffe lost interest in the type, but in due course developments of the machine went into production in both Britain and America, being used by the RAF as the Harrier, the Fleet Air Arm as the Sea Harrier, and the US Marine Corps as the AV-8. The British versions served with distinction in the 1982 Falklands Campaign, which could probably not have been carried to a successful conclusion without them. Later versions are still in production in both countries.

Chapter 23
WING EXPERIMENTS

The speeds likely to be achieved by jet power led to much varied research into wing theory. In addition to new shapes such as swept wings and deltas, various other configurations were looked into, as well as the possibility of generating more lift. Various firms were involved, and the following are among the aircraft which participated in this form of research.

MILES GILLETTE FALCON

In April 1938 the Air Ministry had bought a Miles M.3B Falcon Six for use in comparative wing tests. Serial number L9705, it was fitted with six different sets of wings, three with the standard Falcon taper ratio of 1.6 to 1, but with different aerofoil section, and three with the higher taper ratio of 4.45 to 1.

When the M.52 project got under way, this machine was returned in 1944 to Miles, and fitted with a full-scale wooden mock-up of the bi-convex wing designed for the M.52. Its razor-thin shape led to the aircraft becoming known as the Gillette Falcon, powered by a de Havilland Gipsy Six II engine and given the official appellation Experimental Aeroplane No.237. It made its first flight in this form at Woodley on 11 July 1944 in the hands of Hugh Kennedy.

To retain the planform intact a special undercarriage was constructed, mainly using Miles M.38 Messenger components and attached to the lower fuselage. In its initial form the standard Falcon tailplane was retained, but this was later replaced by the type which would be used on the M.52 though fitted with conventional elevators, until replaced by an all-moving tailplane.

The Falcon spent some time at Farnborough from April 1945, with the occasional return to Woodley for vari-

The Miles Gillette Falcon.

ous modifications to be executed. It was soon found to have the greatest reluctance to take off in a normal distance for such a light aircraft, and would readily return to earth when attempts were made to ease it into the air. Left to itself it would eventually take off but, to overcome a pronounced ground effect, it then became necessary to move the stick forward a few inches to be able to climb at a reasonable angle. It had a poor rate of climb, however, and was difficult to handle.

Nevertheless, the tests produced nothing to show that a full-scale bi-convex wing would produce any great difficulties for the pilot of the M.52 when in low speed flight. The RAE report suggested, however, that the step from flying the Gillette Falcon to coping with the M.52 on its first test flight was likely to be a difficult one, and the test pilot concerned could therefore have found himself in considerable trouble.

HANDLEY PAGE H.P.88

At the end of 1947 the Handley Page B.35/46, destined to become the H.P.80 Victor, was in the early design stages. The shape of the control surfaces had not yet been fina-lised, and to help development of these it was proposed to build a 0.4 scale model of the proposed wings and tail on to an existing jet aircraft. The type initially selected was the Supermarine Attacker, but this was changed to a Swift from the same stable, due to its having fuel tanks com-patible with 45 degrees of sweep at the wing-roots. This proposal was approved, and on 5 April 1948 contract number 6/Acft/2243/CB.6(b) was issued for two aircraft to be built to Specification E.6/48 and to carry serial num-bers VX330 and VX337, though the second machine was later cancelled. The Handley Page type number H.P.88 was allotted.

Due to lack of drawing office capacity, the responsi-bility for the design of the wing and tail was passed to General Aircraft Ltd of Feltham under sub-contract. This firm, however, was merged into Blackburn Aircraft Ltd on 1 January 1949, the resulting combination being named Blackburn & General Aircraft Ltd, with headquarters at Brough, Yorks. Under the SBAC system of type nomencla-ture, the machine was given the Blackburn designation YB.2.

The specification produced a design for a single-seat low-wing monoplane powered by a 5,100 lb thrust Rolls-Royce Nene 3 engine. It had swept stressed skin wings with a single spar, and the tail surfaces were also swept back. There was no centre section, the crescent-shaped wings being attached direct to the fuselage, each being fitted with a Fowler flap and two Kruger nose-flaps. The tail was of all-moving design mounted near the top of the fin, the junction being faired by a 'bullet', the rear portion of which housed an anti-spin parachute. The cockpit was pressurised and situated forward of the leading edge of the wings, the aircraft being comprehensively equipped with flight instrumentation, and a Martin Baker Type 1A ejection seat was fitted, adjustable for height to suit the pilot.

The Supermarine-built fuselage had been given yet another designation, in this case Type 521 in the series

The Handley Page H.P.88 in flight showing the unusual reverse crescent wing shape. (via A. McMillin)

of their parent company, Vickers. Despite earlier intentions, it had ended up as essentially an Attacker fuselage, with the wing roots, instrument layout and fuel system of a Swift. Both wing span and overall length were 40 ft, and the all-up weight was 14,460 lb.

The fuselage was completed at Hursley Park, then transported by road to Brough on 25 February 1950, sus-taining slight damage while being unloaded. By June 1951 the completed machine, painted glossy royal blue over-all, was ready for taxiing trials at Brough, following which it was taken to the long runway at Carnaby, where it had its first flight on 21 June at the hands of the Chief Test Pilot, G.R.I. Parker.

Early trials established that the machine suffered from longitudinal instability, the tailplane being excessively sen-sitive to small stick movements. 'Sailor' Parker found that bumpy weather induced pitching, the problem being exacerbated by pilot over-correction which resulted in

The Handley Page H.P.88 with flaps and airbrakes deployed.

porpoising. This sensation became quite serious at 230 kt, but the progressive addition of angle strips to the tailplane had put back the onset speed to 450 kt by the time of the seventeenth flight on 5 August. The aircraft was then flown to Stansted, but on 26 August 1951, whilst making a low level speed calibration prior to an appearance at the annual SBAC Show, the aircraft broke up, tragically killing the pilot, Duggie Broomfield of Handley Page. Broomfield had earlier discovered that the porpoising effect could be overcome by going 'hands off' and allowing the aircraft to damp it out.

The subsequent investigation established that there was no inherent fault in the H.P.88 design, and the loss of the test aircraft had only a minimal effect on the programme, assembly of the two full-size prototypes being by then well advanced. The accident had in fact resulted from the fitting of a bob-weight at the end of the elevator control run to meet an RAE requirement, being intended to limit accelerations due to stick movement. This and the powered flying controls had produced a coupling which induced fatal pitching oscillations.

SHORT SHERPA

Geoffrey Hill, who before the war had been searching for perfect inherent stability and control with his Pterodactyl designs, retired in 1948 to Ulster, and here he was able to continue his aerodynamic work in conjunction with Shorts. No financial support was forthcoming from the Ministry of Supply, but the firm decided to go ahead anyway. The cheapest way of testing Hill's 'aero-isoclinic' wing idea, as he called it, was to build a glider of fairly simple spruce construction.

Shorts were interested in the proposals mainly to solve some of the problems connected with high speed subsonic flight, particularly in tailless aircraft such as the Vulcan. One of the main problems involved was distortion of the wing and control surfaces, this aeroelastic difficulty being greatest with swept wings, which would bend upwards when the aircraft executed a tight turn or was pulled out rapidly from a fast dive, with resultant loss of lift at the tips. This could create a vicious circle in which the remainder of the wing had to take up even more load, and with a high aspect ratio wing there was a danger the wingtips could try to meet above the aircraft!

The glider, which had rotating wingtip controls, was built in secret for reasons of commercial security, being completed with the Class B registration G-14-5 and designated SB.1. It emerged in July 1951, and the firm's Chief Test Pilot, Tom Brooke-Smith, made winch launches at Aldergrove on the 14th and 17th to get the feel of the controls. No problems were encountered, and on 30 July he strapped himself in again, this time to be towed by Short Sturgeon VR363, piloted by colleague Jock Eassie. The aircraft climbed to 10,000 feet, and after a descent in which the pilot was able to gain some experience in familiarisation and handling, was able to make a safe landing. His only reservation was the amount of turbulence from the

This view shows well the planform of the Short Sherpa (via M.J. Hooks)

The Short SB.1 taking off under tow from a Short Sturgeon. (MAP)

Sturgeon, and for the second flight, on 14 October, a longer tow rope was used. This had an adverse effect, however, and difficulty was soon encountered. Pulling up through the wake to gain clearance from its effects proved difficult. Brooke-Smith cast off and attempted to sideslip laterally, but the glider hit the ground at about 180 mph in a nose-down attitude. It then bounced nose-up, causing the pilot to lose control, and crashed.

The machine was not a total loss, however, it being possible to re-use the wing and tail. The company therefore decided to continue its researches, despite continuing lack of official interest. This time a powered machine was contemplated, with the usable surfaces being built on to a new light alloy fuselage. Blackburns provided two small Turboméca Palas turbojet engines which were mounted immediately to the rear of the wings and pointing slightly outwards. Brooke-Smith made the initial flight of this new configuration from Aldergrove on 4 October 1953. As type SB.4 it now bore the registration G-14-1 and the name Sherpa, the latter being partially derived from the recent conquest of Everest, which happily fitted the concocted title 'Short and Harland Experimental Research Prototype Aircraft'.

The Sherpa flew quite well, but the promised aerodynamic advances were considered insufficient. One will never know what might have happened if Shorts had been successful in bidding for a contract where the concept could have been put to full use and tried out properly. In any event, designers were now beginning to learn to produce conventional wings capable of operating successfully at high subsonic speeds.

After completing the flight test programme G-14-1 went to the College of Aeronautics at Cranfield where it was reregistered G36-1, commencing post-graduate research flying in 1957. The aircraft was transferred to the Bristol College of Advanced Technology in 1964, for use as a laboratory test specimen. In May 1966 it was presented to the Skyfame Museum at Staverton, from where in December 1977 it was transferred to Duxford on loan to the Imperial War Museum, being placed in store.

MARSHALLS M.A.4

In the mid-fifties, the Ministry of Aviation decided to sponsor a small research programme which was to be undertaken by Cambridge University into boundary-layer control by suction. It was decided to allocate an Auster T.7 for the project, and on 6 September 1955 machine VF665 arrived at Cambridge aerodrome from Rearsby, for conversion by the locally based Marshalls Flying School.

The aircraft retained its normal 145 hp de Havilland Gipsy Major VII engine, but was fitted with a new square cut high-aspect ratio wing having a porous surface, an enlarged tail unit and a stronger undercarriage. Suction for the wing perforations was provided by a small gas

The Marshalls M.A.4, a much modified Auster T.7 used for boundary layer control experiments. (MAP)

turbine engine fitted within the rear fuselage, resulting in greatly increased lift.

The work was covered by Specification ER.184D, which was not finalised until 22 January 1957. VF665 was first flown in its new form early in 1959 but the work was undertaken in some secrecy, and its existence was kept secret until about 18 months later. The aircraft had a wing span of 40 ft, length of 24 ft, wing area of 160 sq ft, and an all-up weight of 2,850 lb. Much was learnt from the experiment, but VF665 was finally written off in a crash on 8 March 1966. The remains were transported to Farnborough for investigation on 22 March, and the aircraft was finally struck off charge on 21 November 1966.

HUNTING H.126

Between 1952 and 1954 the National Gas Turbine Establishment at Pyestock, Hants, carried out research into a possible new method of utilising the power of a jet engine. This involved channelling the exhaust jet to emerge downwards as a thin sheet of gas through the trailing edge of the wings. Originally it was proposed to duct all the exhaust jet in this manner, not only to provide all the propulsion, but also to produce a 'jet-flap' of high-velocity gas which in theory would permit increases in lift coefficients when flaps and ailerons were lowered. The advantages seen were substantially lower take-off and landing speeds.

Later experiments suggested, however, that much improved lift coefficients could be obtained by bleeding off only a relatively small proportion of the exhaust jet, relatively cold air being then ejected through 16 fishtail nozzles around a radiused trailing edge. The rear stagnation point could be moved forward by blowing air forwards through the lowermost slit. The remainder of the exhaust gas was ejected through two nozzles on the lower fuselage to provide propulsion and lower the thrust line.

Hunting Aircraft had been involved in this concept, producing Jet Flap Research designs studies, numbered from JFR.1 to at least JFR.12. One design, produced in 1956, to meet Specification ER.175D, was to have been a de Havilland (Canada) Otter fitted with a new tapered wing, and having a Wasp engine at the front in the normal position, plus two Rolls-Royce RB.108 engines in the fuselage to provide exhaust jets for the jet flaps. It was decided, however, that this approach was unsatisfactory, and that it would be better to design a completely new aircraft.

On 20 May 1959, therefore, Specification ER.189D was issued for such a machine, and this was followed on 16 June 1959 by an order for two aircraft under Contract KD/23/01/CB/10(c), to be numbered XN714 and XN719, though the second of these was later cancelled during construction. Several design variants were considered, the one chosen for construction being designated H.126/50, though generally referred to simply as the H.126. XN714 was fitted with a Bristol Siddeley Orpheus 805 engine, mounted in a rather inelegant stub-nosed fuselage measuring 50 ft 2 in in length. It had a tall angular fin and rudder, with a high-mounted tailplane, overall height being 15 ft 6 in. Long thin wings were mounted towards the top of the fuselage aft of the single-seat cockpit, and it had a span of 45 ft 4 in. The ducting system for the hot gases was the subject of much study, it being necessary to insulate and heat-shield the normal light alloys. A fixed undercarriage consisted of a nosewheel and two main wheels on legs beneath the wings.

XN714 was rolled out in August 1962, by which time its manufacturer had become part of the British Aircraft Corporation. Limited taxiing trials were carried out by the firm's chief test pilot, Stanley Oliver, after which the aircraft was dismantled and transported on 12 December to nearby RAE Bedford for reassembly. No attempt was made to fly the aircraft during a particularly bad winter, but on

26 March 1963 the weather improved and Oliver was able to take her up for the first time, accompanied by a Meteor chase aircraft. XN714 flew in a characteristic nose down attitude and no difficulties were encountered.

On 13 October 1964 the aircraft went to Boscombe Down for tests in the blower tunnel, then went back to Luton on 3 November, making an appearance at the Paris Air Salon at Le Bourget in June 1965. It returned to Bedford on 18 March 1966 for further high-lift flight research with the Aerodynamics Flight, then in July 1967 it was earmarked to go to the USA for full-scale wind tunnel tests by the National Aeronautical and Space Administration. In the event this happened at a rather leisurely pace, the aircraft going on 22 July 1968 to Holme-on-Spalding-Moor for preparatory 90-hour servicing by Hawker-Siddeley, and did not actually leave for America until 3 April 1969, being flown out aboard Short Belfast XR366 to the Ames Flight Research Centre at Moffett Naval Air Station, California. It returned to Holme for temporary storage on 14 May 1970, and from there went back to RAE Bedford on 4 December 1970, but was never uncrated. In June 1972 it was offered for disposal, being eventually allocated on 30 April 1974 to the Cosford Aerospace Museum for display purposes.

The concept was dropped after Hunting Aircraft became absorbed into the British Aircraft Corporation,

The Hunting H.126 shows off its side view. (via Eric Morgan)

The Hunting H.126 during its maiden flight on 26 March 1963. (via M. Stroud)

though a jet flap variant of the Jet Provost was mooted, the BAC.165 being a proposal for a COIN (counter-insurgency) attack aircraft.

YOUNGMAN-BAYNES
HIGH LIFT RESEARCH AIRCRAFT

On 22 January 1947 the Ministry of Supply placed an order under contract Acft/5414/CB.6(b) with Alan Muntz & Co. Ltd of Heston for a special high-lift wing. This was to be fitted to a redesigned Proctor 4 fuselage fitted with a 250 hp

Youngman-Baynes High Lift VT789 which was based on a Proctor 4 fuselage. (MAP)

de Havilland Gipsy Queen 32 engine, the combination being given the Percival designation P.46.

The concept was the brainchild of R.T. Youngman, who saw his new full-span slotted-flap system as solving some of the problems hitherto associated with lateral and longitudinal control in full-span flaps. The design of the wing was entrusted to Muntz's aircraft section, led by Mr L.E. Baynes, and the completed combination was the responsibility of the Heston Aircraft Co. whose chief test pilot, Ralph Munday, first flew the aircraft, by then numbered VT789, on 5 February 1948.

Overall dimensions were somewhat different from the Proctor 4, being a span of 33 ft, length of 29 ft and wing area of 179 sq ft, compared with the Proctor's respective figures of 39 ft 6 in, 26 ft 4 in and 202 sq ft.

The front half of the chord of the special wing was fixed, including the leading edge, but the remainder was movable. The next quarter comprised a full-span flap, and then a half-length trailing flap was built into the inner section of the rear quarter chord. The latter moved to a greater angle than the main flap, to which were attached ailerons. The main flap was operated by shaft driven by a Croydon Engineering $1\frac{1}{2}$hp electric motor, and the ailerons maintained their angle relative to the main flap irrespective of its position.

The system operated reasonably well in tests, a tendency to wallow on approach being of only minor importance since it could be cured by a certain amount of redesigning. The main advantage was that high lift was provided at low speed, with consequent reduction in landing distances, a factor which could have particular applications for carrier-borne aircraft.

Chapter 24
NAVAL AVIATION RESEARCH

The Fleet Air Arm has, on the whole, tended to get either spin-offs from aircraft initially developed for the RAF, or fairly orthodox aircraft developed to meet its own requirements. On occasion, however, it has had the opportunity for original research. Here are detailed two projects, both purely naval in origin, but both abortive.

FOLLAND E.28/40

By late 1940, the advent of newer types of naval aircraft was leading to problems associated with their increasing weight during deck landing. The Directorate of Technical Development decided that a research aircraft was required, specifically to undertake a full scale investigation of the problems involved. Air Staff Requirement OR.101 was accordingly drawn up, and on 17 February 1941 Specification E.28/40 was issued calling for a mock-up to be completed within two months.

The aircraft had to be suitable for operation in any part of the world and had to be designed so that it could be equipped to operate from an aircraft carrier on reconnaissance, torpedo attack or both level and dive bombing duties. It was at first intended for either accelerator or catapult launching, and also crash-barrier landing if necessary, but the first of these requirements was amended on 16 August 1941 to call only for assisted take-off capability. Folding wings were to be fitted, capable of being handled on deck in a wind of 35 knots.

The engine was at first laid down as a Napier Sabre, but the August 1941 amendment altered this to a Bristol Centaurus, which had to be capable of satisfactory operation in temperate, tropical and arctic conditions.

For the purposes of initial flight trials, the prototype was to be fitted with flying and engine instruments, wireless telegraphy, navigation facilities and recognition equipment. Other equipment, likely to be included in an operational aircraft, was to be simulated by representations of similar weight and taking up a similar amount of space. Included in these would be a mock-up turret which would, however, have to be aerodynamically representative and capable of being rotated in flight.

The contract was awarded to Follands, who gave it their designation FO.116, and work started on a single prototype, the serial number DX160 being issued. The design evolved as a mid-wing monoplane, the wings being fitted with leading-edge slots and Fowler trailing-edge flaps to provide the maximum possible lift. To avoid the consequent necessity for a steep landing, and therefore a long-stroke undercarriage, the wings were of variable incidence, enabling the pilot to set them at the appropriate angle in relation to the fuselage, which would remain in the horizontal plane throughout.

The aircraft, which had a span of 52 ft 6 in and a length of 44 ft, was to be fitted with a 2,400 hp Bristol Centaurus III engine, giving an estimated top speed of 263 mph. The all-up weight was calculated as 18,250 lb, which would have given a minimum speed too high for carrier work had it not been for the special wing. The maximum range was likely to be 800 miles at 230 mph.

By 1943 the first machine was well advanced, but by that time events had moved on, and many of the problems had already been solved in practice. Had events moved differently it might have eventually carried out attacks against the Japanese homeland, but in the event the contract was cancelled, and all work stopped, the firm turning its attention to the FO.117A, an abortive project for a proposed fighter with a contra-rotating propeller to Specification F.19/43. A second E.28/40, to be serialled DX165, was never built.

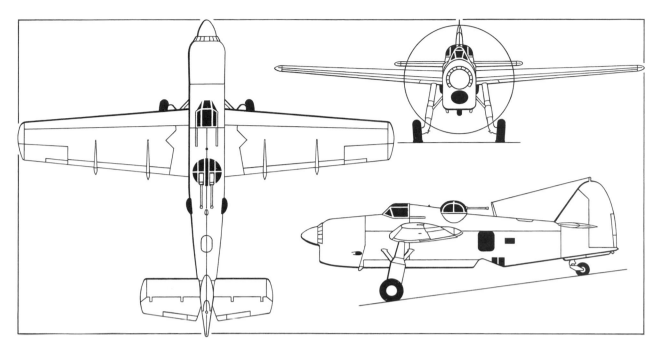

Three-view of the Folland E.28/40.

D.H. VAMPIRE (FLEXIBLE RUBBER DECK)

On 3 October 1944 the Director of Technical Development at the Ministry of Aircraft Production, N.E. Rowe, wrote to W.S. Farren, the Director of the Royal Aircraft Establishment to the effect that he had seen a report of the Messerschmitt Me 163B rocket-propelled fighter, which apparently jettisoned its undercarriage on take-off. He suggested that RAE should look into possibilities of using this method for aircraft up to 40,000 lb weight. Three weeks later the scope of the investigation was widened by a letter asking for an appreciation of the advantages to be gained by operating high-speed jet aircraft from aircraft carriers without undercarriages, and by December this was being directed specifically at jet aircraft of about 10,000 lb weight.

An undercarriage represented a substantial proportion of the weight of an aircraft, being as much as seven per cent in the case of naval aircraft, so the carrier aspects took priority from the start, and by early 1945 opinions and advice were being sought from the industry. One of those approached was Westlands, who on 27 March 1945 submitted a detailed document entitled 'Proposal for improvements in aircraft carriers and carrier-borne aircraft'. They appear to have had little or no subsequent involvement, however.

The preamble to the report referred to investigation having been made into the possibilities of improving the performance of carrier borne aircraft by getting rid of the landing gear. It was suggested that the principal modification would be to transfer from the aircraft itself to the deck of the carrier the shock-absorbing gear necessary to deal with the high rates of descent, which might be of the order of 12-14 ft sec. As a secondary change the arrester gear might also be removed or consist entirely

of some mechanism on the deck. It was commented, though, that any methods of assisted landing that made modifications to the deck should be such as not to impede handling of the aircraft on the deck by mechanical means. Three possible main schemes were proposed, all with jet aircraft in mind. In each of these the fore part of the deck would be left clear, so that aircraft could take-off either normally or with some means of assistance, such as rockets or accelerators.

The first scheme envisaged fore and aft wires, spring-loaded at the ends to absorb the kinetic energy of the aircraft when making a normal landing, the forward speed of the aircraft being dealt with by the usual system of transverse arrester wires. The undersurfaces of the wings and fuselage would be suitably reinforced with $\frac{1}{8}$ in sheet steel, and the arrester 'wires' would actually be 150 ton cables of approximately $1\frac{7}{8}$ in diameter. It was anticipated that there would be problems with the weight of the cables and also with manhandling of aircraft on deck, particularly in the event of an emergency.

The second scheme was quite different, consisting of a deck with sponge rubber absorption. The deck would be clear and level, the surface being either of rubber or plastic-impregnated fabric, supported on a thick layer of sponge rubber of the connected-cell variety. This, in addition to providing elastic energy absorption, would have a considerable damping effect by reason of air flow through the inter-connected cells. Because of the soft nature of the surface, aircraft would need only a small amount of reinforcement to land without appreciable damage. Final arresting would be by means of a crash-barrier consisting of several arrester cables, superimposed vertically and faced with a thick cushion of sponge rubber similar to that used on the deck. The nose and wing leading edges of the aircraft would be suitably reinforced to

De Havilland Vampire VG701 picks up a wire as it comes in to land on the rubber deck aboard HMS *Warrior* in February 1949.

act as buffers.

The third scheme was a variation of the second, in which the decking would be supported by a series of inflated rubber bags, the damping and energy absorption being assisted by dash-pots attached to the deck in the spaces between the adjacent bags. The deck would be either a continuous rubber or reinforced fabric surface as in the previous scheme, or else formed of a series of thin laminated planks. In this scheme the main vertical travel would be only of the order of 1 ft and normal arrester wires could be used. The aircraft would be provided with retractable skids so that with the more rigid deck the required landing attitude could be more easily obtained.

Comparison showed that the second and third schemes possessed inherent advantages, in that no new piloting techniques were required, the deck could be easily used for landing conventional wheeled aircraft if required, while the absence of any obstructions above the surface would allow unrestricted movement of personnel and equipment, such as towing or lifting trailers. Some variation or combination of the two schemes might also be possible.

Around the same time a letter was received by MAP from Hugh Conway, Chief Engineer of Messier Aircraft Equipment Ltd of Warrington, who enclosed some notes, but commented that his only original contribution was the suggestion (which he thought was probably not novel) that vertical thrust devices might be used, these being switched on when the aircraft was a few feet from the ground, providing the force necessary to change direction of motion to horizontal. This suggestion was not pursued, but on 19 June Conway, now Chief Engineer of Dunlop's Aviation Division at Coventry, wrote regarding proposals for skid undercarriage development. As a result of his continuing interest, MAP subsequently decided that he was the most suitable person to undertake investigation of the scheme, since he could pull in Dunlop experts on rubber, and was himself familiar with the mechanical aspects.

At a meeting on 18 April 1945 it was stressed that the problem of operating aircraft without undercarriages from carriers was not the only objective, reminding those

present that it was also the aim to have land-based aircraft operating without undercarriages. Nevertheless, the main emphasis remained on carrier-borne landings.

On 9 August 1945 DTD agreed in principle that both de Havilland and Supermarine be asked to co-operate in development, and both expressed an interest, though in fact the latter company subsequently dropped out, five Vampires and Sea Vampires being subsequently modified for the trials. By this time the favoured scheme involved a pneumatically supported deck. By January 1946 it had been decided to build two decks in grassed areas at Farnborough, each comprising a one-piece 200 ft x 60 ft flexible landing area consisting of a rubberised cord fabric of sixplies, approximately five-sixteenths of an inch thick. Each deck would be supported along its 200 ft length on two parallel rows of steel drums, these being in 6 ft lengths, pitched 59 ft apart. The drums for the pneumatic deck would be of 1 ft 6 in diameter and those for the suspended carpet would be 2 ft in diameter.

Of the two schemes to be built, the first was constructed in the space between the three main runways (07, 18 and 30) and an existing dummy deck, being surrounded by paving and steel decking, with arrester gear alongside. The second scheme was to be on the north side of the aerodrome near Meadows Gate. In the first scheme the 200 ft x 60 ft carpet was supported by three layers of air bags laid athwartships, whilst in the other it would be suspended between two rows of drums without any other support, there being athwartships tension. The Home Office agreed to provide 24 miles of $7\frac{1}{4}$ in diameter deluge hoses from surplus wartime stores – though it was commented that only 25 miles had ever been constructed! 12 miles of this would be required to construct the deck. In later stages of the trial this hosing was replaced by tubes made from rubber dinghy fabric.

Dropping trials were carried out at Farnborough using a heavily ballasted surplus Hotspur glider (BT752) suspended from a crane and with Lt Cdr 'Winkle' Brown in the cockpit. In addition, a Bell Airacobra (AH574), the only aircraft available with a nose-wheel, was fitted with catapult gear and an arrester hook so that it could be used for flyover trials, both at Farnborough and over a carrier in preparation for the full-scale Vampire tests. It did in fact make one touch-down on the carrier concerned, HMS *Pretoria Castle* on 4 April 1945.

Conversion work on the Vampires involved was undertaken by de Havilland at Leavesden, these being the last aircraft to leave No.2 Factory before it went over to engine production. Vampire F.1 TG285 was sent to Farnborough in June 1947 for crash barrier trials and then earmarked for flexible deck work. The first attempt at a flexible deck landing at Farnborough took place on 29 December 1947 with Sea Vampire F.21 TG426 with Brown at the controls, but this resulted in a major accident, the aircraft being damaged beyond repair. It was followed in February 1948 by Sea Vampire F.21 VT802, which was damaged in another accident on 2 June. In June and July 1948 four more F21s arrived in the shape of VG701, VT795,

De Havilland Vampire VG701 being hoisted by crane during rubber deck trials aboard HMS *Warrior* in February 1949.

VT803 and VT805.

By March 1948, HMS *Warrior* was being converted to take a flexible deck, and it was hoped to transfer one of the Farnborough decks about June of that year. It was not until 2 November, however, that it put to sea from Portsmouth for its first trials, which lasted until 8 December. VT802 was still under repair at Hatfield, awaiting spares, but the other four machines were available. The first five landings were made by TG286, followed by landings by VT795, VT803 and VT805. The tests were not without incident: on the fourth landing, for instance, the aircraft bounced after just failing to pick up the arrester wire, though with no embarrassment to the pilot, who landed successfully on the second attempt. As a result of these

trials a number of alterations were made, including modifications to the aircraft arrester hooks and replacement by airbags of the hard forward edge of the flexible deck. Trials were suspended over the Christmas period, but resumed on 25 January 1949. VG701 was involved from 15 February, minor damage being caused to its flaps the following day when they fouled a wire, but it was able to complete the programme. The sea trials ended on 31 May 1949.

In January 1950 it was proposed to continue with development of the flexible deck using four Sea Hawks, it being envisaged that a prototype, N.7/46, would be available by March 1951, and that by the end of 1952 it would be possible to earmark at least three fully operational machines. As far as is known, however, only one Sea Hawk test was carried out at Farnborough, the machine being catapulted off and landing on the flexible deck without the undercarriage being lowered.

In the end nothing came of the experiment, which would have involved costly modifications and new installations with insufficient gain.

Bell Airacobra AH574 was used at Farnborough during rubber deck trials. (via J.D. Oughton)

Chapter 25

THIRD GENERATION JETS

By the end of the second World War, the design of jet aircraft was sufficiently established for requirements to be formulated in respect of machines which it was hoped would see both the RAF and the Fleet Air Arm through to the early fifties and possibly beyond. As well-established suppliers of fighter aircraft for both services, Hawker and Supermarine each had their sights set on continuing this tradition, with a consequent steady flow of design studies. Both firms ultimately succeeded in their objectives, Hawkers producing the Hunter and Sea Hawk, and Supermarines the Attacker, Scimitar and Swift.

HAWKER P.1052

In October 1945 Hawkers submitted a design study for a swept-wing aircraft. Based on the P.1040 design, which was eventually developed into the Sea Hawk, it was designated the P.1047 and featured a rocket motor. This met with some interest, both at Farnborough and in naval circles, and resulted in a research requirement, number OR.243, for a swept-wing version of the P.1040 for naval use, but powered by a normal jet engine.

After substantial discussion, draft Specification E.38/46 was drawn up and received by the company on 16 January 1947, the final version being issued on 18 March 1947. A provisional order was placed in May for the construction of two prototypes, and in March 1948 serials VX272 and VX279 were allocated for these machines, to be built under contract 6/Acft/1156/CB.7(b), the new design being termed P.1052.

The fuselage was to be essentially that of the P.1040, accommodating amidships the same power plant, a 5,000 lb thrust Rolls-Royce Nene 2, there being wing root intakes and bifurcated jet pipes. The attraction of the aircraft for

Farnborough was that it would be their first pressure-plotting high-speed swept-wing machine, the 35 degree swept-wing providing a higher usable Mach number than the P.1040. Pressure plotting essentially meant that the sweep and aerofoil thickness were carefully designed to maintain the pressure constant along a line parallel to the leading edge, the wing and fuselage intersection being also carefully shaped to reduce induced velocities. This reduced the boundary layer thickness and thus the drag.

The design had a broader root chord than its predecessor, and to counteract the bending and torsional loads inherent in swept wings deeper spars were fitted. The attachment points for the wing spars were also strengthened, the front points being moved further forward. The P.1040 tailplane was retained, except that the tips were made more blunt.

In February 1948 it was proposed that an arrester hook be fitted to the P.1052 for deck-landing trials, and in October came a prospect of it going into quantity production, but it was decided instead to wait for other designs then in the pipeline.

VX272 was ready at Kingston by November 1948. It was then transported by road to Boscombe Down, where after taxiing trials it was flown on 19 November by Sqn Ldr T.S. Wade. It had a span of 31 ft 6 in, a length of 37 ft 9½ in, a height of 10 ft 1 in and wing area of 258 sq ft. VX279 had its maiden flight, also in Wade's hands, on 13 April 1949, and the following month set up a record by flying from London to Paris in 18 minutes.

On 28 June 1949, VX279 went to Boscombe Down for assessment, returning to the maker's aerodrome at Langley on 30 August. Although originally intended only for flight research, considerable interest had been evinced in the aircraft's possibilities for development into an intercep-

The first prototype Hawker P.1052 picks up a wire as it lands aboard HMS Eagle during deck trials in May 1952. (BAe)

tor fighter, and brief handling trials were therefore undertaken to assess its fighter potentialities. The aircraft was liked by all the test pilots who flew it, and was generally considered to be a pleasant aircraft to fly, being free from any vices likely to endanger the safety of the aircraft. It had a high performance, including a good rate of climb. The swept back wings produced the high usable Mach number of 0.9, with no features likely to affect adversely the aircraft's operational characteristics. Stalling characteristics were also good for a high speed aircraft. During trials, speeds of the order of 650 mph were achieved in level flight.

Directional disturbance, however, resulted in both lateral and directional oscillation (dutch roll), and although this could be damped by the pilot, further tests were considered necessary to determine the effect on the aircraft's qualities as a gun platform. The only major criticism was of the elevator, which was much too heavy for a fighter aircraft, and would rapidly tire the pilot in combat.

The cockpit layout was thought to be good, with controls and instruments neatly and tidily grouped. The cockpit was roomy, but ventilation was inadequate for high speed

flight at low altitude and there was not enough cockpit heating in the region of the rudder bar and throttle when at high altitude. The Malcolm ejector seat was found to be uncomfortable by all the pilots who flew the aircraft, and its associated equipment came in for considerable criticism.

The opportunity was taken to give the aircraft a preliminary deck-landing assessment. It was found to be very easy and pleasant to fly in simulated deck landings at the loading condition tested, and was considered at least as good as the N.7/46 at the same weight. The dutch rolling which could occur in disturbed air conditions might, however, be found disconcerting if encountered at a late stage on the approach to an actual landing. If the aircraft was to be developed for naval use, some form of stall warning would be required. It was also considered that with current arrester gear, the high speed approach would necessitate windspeeds across the deck which would be impractically high, especially for service operation.

The programme suffered a setback on 29 September 1949 when a sheared fuel pump drive resulted in a forced landing at Farnborough with considerable damage. The machine went back to Kingston, and during a Ministry visit there on 21 October it was proposed that whilst under repair a new rear end be fitted with provision for an Armstrong Siddeley Snarler rocket motor. It was also

The second prototype Hawker P.1052, VX279, in flight. (BAe)

decided to fit air brakes and an electrically operated adjustable tailplane. In the event, structural tests which had been carried out on a non-flying third P.1052 led to further reinforcement of the wings spars and main spar fuselage frames, further delaying repairs and curtailing the possibility of other modifications.

The Snarler idea, which would have resulted in redesignation as P.1078, was dropped, and VX279 was fitted instead with a new rear fuselage incorporating a straight jet pipe in place of the bifurcated one, a new fin and

Head-on view of the Hawker P.1081, the rebuilt VX279. (BAe)

rudder, and a swept-back variable-incidence tailplane. The flying controls had been modified to suit the new units, and the wings strengthened by fitting additional stringers. In this form, which was a private venture by Hawkers, it was termed the P.1081, flying again on 19 June 1950, being later given further modifications, including an electric tailplane actuator, boundary layer wing fences and further tail alterations.

By this time the Navy were taking an active interest in the machine. It had been their practice to adopt a belt and braces approach to replacement of an aircraft already in service, more than one project being considered for its successor. Both the Attacker and Sea Hawk would eventually need to be replaced, but only one new fighter design was at present in prospect. Supermarines were busy developing their N.9/47 design for the next generation, but new Staff Requirements had recently been introduced for this Specification which the firm might not find it easy to meet, with the possibility that an unsuccessful design might emerge at the prototype stage. It was stressed that there had not yet been an opportunity for assessing the P.1081 for deck landing, and in any case it would be necessary to introduce new features, such as saddle tanks to regain the endurance sacrificed in abandoning the bifurcated jet pipe. Nevertheless, if the firm had early knowledge of the possible requirement, it should be relatively easy for them to pass from the Sea Hawk to the fully navalised P.1081, since many parts would be interchangeable.

This idea was quickly discouraged, however, so as not to divert Hawker's attention from existing project work. Instead, it was suggested that the Navy be offered navalised versions of the Swift or Hawker Hunter, or alternatively a navalised version of a proposed Australian P.1081. In the event they eventually received the Supermarine Scimitar.

The Australians had originally attempted to buy the P.1052, but Hawker's would not agree to this and offered the P.1081 instead. The Australian team sent to Kingston reported, however, that the latter required some extra work

The Hawker P.1081 showing the modified tail. (via F.K. Mason)

on the tail unit, due to vibration problems, and in any case there was concern about Hawker's ability to provide proper support for one of its designs being built abroad under licence. In the event, North American Sabres were built instead.

On 31 October 1950, VX279 was given a 40 minute test by Neville Duke. He reported severe rudder pedal vibration at 26,000 ft between 350 and 400 knots IAS. He also encountered considerable vibration on retraction of the undercarriage after take-off, which he put down to the nose-wheel spinning and rubbing the tyre in the undercarriage bay, but this problem was not encountered if the wheels were lowered and raised in flight.

Meanwhile the work on VX272 was completed by March 1950, and two months later it was authorised to be released to Farnborough for tests on longitudinal stability and wing dropping at high speed. On 17 July, however, it suffered an engine failure on approach and crashed into a bicycle shed, necessitating further repairs at Kingston. Seven days later VX279 suffered undercarriage failure during a forced landing at RAF Odiham.

As if there had not been enough setbacks, VX279 was lost on 3 April 1951, the machine being totally destroyed when it dived into the ground at considerable speed on Plashett Park Farm, Ringmer, near Lewes, catching fire on impact. The pilot, Trevor 'Wimpy' Wade, managed to eject, but was still strapped into his ejector seat when it struck the ground. It appeared that Wade's seat was rotating at a speed which was probably high enough to incapacitate him as he left the aircraft, and he was killed on impact. The cause of the accident remained obscure.

The damage to VX272 had greatly delayed the intended fitting of an arrester hook and long-stroke undercarriage, and yet another postponement occurred on 5 September 1951 when, in its first flight after repair, more damage was occasioned during a crash landing after the undercarriage had become stuck in the up position.

By January 1952 Farnborough were getting extremely

concerned at all the delays, the P.1052/P.1081 being one of the very few swept-wing research aircraft on which important problems of speed could be investigated. It had also been earmarked for deck trials very early in its life, which had recently been planned for 4 December 1951 at Spithead, yet they had still not taken place. It was suggested that the machine be returned to standard and allotted to the RAE Aero Flight for continuation of the high-speed investigation which was in progress when it crashed. This was agreed to on the basis that it would be reconverted later for trials in HMS *Eagle,* subject to six weeks warning.

Conversion to deck-landing standard finally took place at Hawkers in April of that year, and on 27 and 28 May successful trials took place aboard HMS *Eagle.* The pilots involved reported that in the deck conditions prevailing the aircraft was comparatively easy to deck-land. It was comfortable to fly at chosen airspeeds and the view of the deck was excellent. They suggested, however, that the aircraft's dutch roll characteristics might have proved embarrassing had the trials not been done in exceptionally stable air conditions.

Immediately after the trials VX272 returned to Hawkers to be finally fitted with the variable-incidence swept tailplane, with which it returned to Farnborough on 27 May 1953. The chapter of accidents continued, however, when on 1 September 1953 the aircraft had to land with one wheel retracted, causing damage to the port wing and dive brakes. This was not too serious, however, and on 1 December it was back for further trials, these finally coming to an end when in February 1955 it was relegated to ground instructional duties at RAF Halton, being renumbered 7174M. It is now on exhibition at the Cosford Aerospace Museum.

SUPERMARINE 510

In late 1946 work began on formulating several Specifications for advanced jet fighters and bombers. One of these was E.41/46, which was issued on 26 April 1947 for a swept-wing version of the Supermarine E.10/44, to be used for high-speed flight research, but which could also be adapted as a single-seat fighter. The firm was accordingly awarded a contract, numbered 6/Acft/1031/CB/7(b), for two aircraft to carry serial numbers VV106 and VV119, a maximum design speed of 700 mph being specified.

Both were built at Hursley Park, and each was based on an Attacker fuselage installed with a Nene 2 engine, and fitted with research instrumentation. When VV106 had its first flight by Mike Lithgow from Boscombe Down on 29 December 1948, it became the first British jet aircraft to take to the air with swept surfaces on both wings and tail. The span was 31 ft 8½ in, length 38 ft 1 in and wing area 273 sq ft. Engine failure necessitated a wheel-up landing there on 16 March 1949, but damage was not serious, and the machine was soon flying without difficulty at up to Mach 0.93. With the engine at 12,300 rpm a maximum level speed was achieved of 630 mph at 10,000 ft (M 0.86) and 635 mph at 15,000 ft (M 0.88).

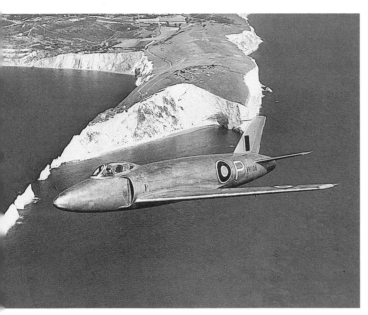

The first prototype Supermarine 510 flying over The Needles. (RAF Museum 6349-2)

The second prototype Supermarine 510 with noticeably longer nose, and modified air intakes and wingtips. (via M. Stroud)

The cockpit hood jettison mechanism was modified after one was lost in flight, and a more pointed nose was fitted later, further improving the speed. After an appearance at the 1949 SBAC Show at Farnborough it undertook assessment trials at Boscombe Down, where the effect of the sweep-back received favourable comment, the drag characteristics having improved considerably at high Mach numbers, though this was offset by longitudinal instability just prior to the stall. There was no tendency to 'snaking', the ailerons were light and crisp, and overall it was relatively easy and simple to fly, with no sign of the dangerous problems many people had expected of swept-wings. A tricycle undercarriage was recommended, however, and Attacker-type front engine mountings were later installed, as well as improvements to the intakes to improve airflow.

Carrier trials were carried out aboard *HMS Illustrious* from 8 November 1950, ending six days later when the port wing struck the ship's port gun turret when a rocket failed during a RATOG take-off. Fortunately Lt Cdr D.G. Parker, RN of Boscombe Down managed to maintain control and the machine returned to Chilbolton for repair.

Fitment of a special tail unit to VV106 in 1951 turned it into the Type 517. In this configuration the rear fuselage was hinged so as to be adjustable through four degrees up or down, which proved be a very effective trimmer.

On 26 September 1952 the aircraft went to Farnborough for high speed research, but was soon back at Chilbolton after making a wheels-up landing at Farnborough on 14 November when piloted by T. Gordon Innes, an RAE test pilot. On 3 September 1953 it returned to Farnborough for research into high Mach numbers, until being relegated to ground instructional duties, being despatched to No.1 School of Technical Training at Halton on 17 February 1955, renumbered to become 7175M.

Meanwhile VV119 had taken to the air on 27 March 1950, being flown by Lithgow from Boscombe Down, initially as Type 528, which was very similar to the 'needle nose' version of the Type 510. Two months later it was taken in hand for extensive modification, including being fitted with reheat and the recommended nosewheel, the length now having increased to 42 ft 11 in. In this guise it emerged as the Type 535, flying again on 23 August 1950 and soon afterwards appearing at the annual SBAC Show. On 28 December it flew with wing fences, and in July 1951 a speed of 622 mph was recorded in level flight at 15,000 ft. It joined VV106 at Halton in September 1955.

This swept-wing development of the Attacker had by now attracted the interest of the RAF. Two production prototypes were ordered on 9 November 1950 under contract 6/Acft/5986/CB.7(b), to be given serial numbers WJ960 and WJ965. These were quickly followed by an order for 100 machines under contract 6/Acft/5969/CB.7(b). Named the Swift, a total of 176 production machines eventually appeared. VV106 is now exhibited by the Cosford Aerospace Museum.

Chapter 26
SMALL ROTORCRAFT

Rotary-wing development in Britain largely ceased by the summer of 1940, when priority perforce had to be given to the rapid manufacture of fighters, bombers and training aircraft (see Chapter 5).

By 1940 the Cierva Autogiro Company had virtually ceased to exist and in fact had never been a manufacturing concern in its own right. Promising developments by Hafner had come to a sudden end when Hafner was interned as an alien.

The most advanced rotary-wing development was being undertaken by G. & J. Weir Ltd on the experimental helicopters W.5 and W.6, but in 1940 the decision was taken by the company to conclude these activities as more important work on the war effort could be performed within the company's other engineering operations. This decision seems to have been unilateral, though possibly even against the wishes of the Air Ministry, and it effectively stopped progress on the development of helicopters in this country for at least three years.

Raoul Hafner was, in due course, released from internment and managed to continue his rotary-wing experiments with the Airborne Forces Experimental Establishment at Sherburn-in-Elmet. This work was primarily concerned with 'autogyro' applications to vehicles for the delivery of troops and equipment from the air.

Cierva C.30 and C.40 autogiros were taken into RAF use for radar calibration duties, but as no new autogiros were being produced it would only be a matter of time before replacement machines would be required.

The only source then available was America, and so moves were made to obtain some Pitcairn PA.39s through the British Air Commission in America, and Wing Cdr 'Reggie' Brie was sent to across for this purpose. It was not long before Brie came to hear of the experimental helicopter work being undertaken by Sikorsky on the VS-300 and later the R-4. Brie was instrumental in arousing British interest (particularly on the part of the Fleet Air Arm), and large orders were soon placed for Sikorsky helicopters.

This development soon became known in British aviation circles, and was heatedly opposed by James Weir of G. & J. Weir Ltd and his designer C. G. Pullin. It was their contention that the Sikorsky helicopters were unstable and therefore dangerous. It was also argued that it would be most unwise to continue the situation where no British helicopter development work was being undertaken, so that America would have an enormous lead in this field by the end of the war.

Matters came to a head in 1943 when the opposition of Weir to the Sikorsky designs was such that it began to affect the previously good relationship with Sikorskys that the British Air Commission had enjoyed.

At this time there is little doubt that the Air Ministry would have preferred that Raoul Hafner should become the leading figure in British rotary-wing development. They were probably annoyed that Weir had managed to raise the issue at such a high level, and seemed to have felt that his contentions that the Weir design would be an advance on Sikorsky would not prove to be true.

Hafner could not be released from his work at AFEE in 1942, and in any case the Air Ministry considered that he would have to undertake future helicopter development in conjunction with one of the major British aircraft manufacturers, as his own A.R.III Construction company did not have the financial or physical resources to undertake this work alone.

The Cierva W.9 being demonstrated during the SBAC Show at Radlett in September 1946. (RAF Museum 6137-16)

CIERVA W.9

Thus, the Air Ministry felt itself compelled to award Weirs a contract to construct a helicopter to its own design, and the first 'Experimental' specification for a British helicopter — E.16/43 — was issued to the Cierva Autogiro Company in 1943. Two aircraft were originally planned, to be numbered paradoxically as W.9 in the Weir sequence, serials PX203 and PX207 being allocated on 3 August 1943 under contract SB.51216, though the second of these was later cancelled.

G. & J. Weir had long been associated with the Cierva company through shareholdings from the Weir family, and in 1939 G. & J. Weir Ltd had obtained a controlling interest in Ciervas - although too late to resurrect the affairs of that company in the prevailing circumstances. Pullin, who had been the designer of the Weir W.5 and W.6 experimental helicopters, became Chief Designer of the revived Cierva company and also Managing Director.

It is interesting to note that despite the Weir Company's deciding to cease rotary-wing activities in July 1940, James Weir's enthusiasm for the helicopter had manifested itself again by November 1941 when investigation began of the W.8 project (see Chapter 5). A 'new' Aircraft Department was formed by Weirs in December 1941 at Cathcart, near Glasgow. In 1943 this Department was moved to the premises of Mollart Engineering (who had manufactured components for Cierva in the past) and later to its own premises at Thames Ditton. Finally in 1946 a move was made to Eastleigh aerodrome, Southampton.

This was after the first flight of the W.9 (PX203), the exact date of which has not been recorded. It may have been as early as October 1944, but Ken Watson, who supervised the early ground-running, puts it as early 1945. The aircraft controls at this stage were manual, and when full power was applied on one occasion the rotor went virtually out of control, and in the subsequent massive vibration Watson went partly through the roof of the cabin and almost into the rotor blades. The resultant damage caused a significant delay before first flight. The company did not have the resources at this time to employ a test pilot, so that the W.9 was taken to Henley-on-Thames where the Cierva Rotas of 529 Squadron were based. The squadron commanding officer, Sqn Ldr Alan Marsh, then conducted the first flight.

The appearance of the W.9 changed quite dramatically around this time. It would seem that it first emerged with a highly streamlined totally enveloping fuselage with a 'futuristic' appearance. It is still not clear whether the first flight was made in this guise, or whether the degree of damage suffered in the ground-running accident was such that a major rebuild was then necessary.

The engine fitted to the W.9 was the original 205 hp Gipsy Six Series II taken from the Weir W.6 helicopter. Dimensions were rotor diameter 36 ft, length 36 ft 9 in and height 10 ft. The gross weight was 2,647 lb, and a maximum speed of 115 mph was predicted.

It was not until 22 June 1946 that the existence of Cierva W.9 was publicly announced, and this came about in a fairly public way at an air pageant at Southampton Airport. By this this time only 30 hours flying had been achieved, Alan Marsh being now employed by Ciervas as a test pilot. Test flying continued in a fairly low-key way, as by this time the company was heavily involved in the design and development of the Skeeter and Air Horse helicopters.

The final appearance of the W.9 was much different from the original streamlined totally enclosed fuselage. Early in the flight programme, the front fuselage structure had been cut back and a much smaller but longer rear fuselage added. At this time, however, there was still a fairly enveloping front-fuselage back to the beginning of the tail boom. Further modification of the front fuselage led to most of the fuselage structure and rotor pylon covering being discarded.

In its original format the rear fuselage ended in an upward curve at the top of which the most unusual feature was a jet-efflux duct, canted to port. In the later configurations the duct was set at right-angles to the line of the fuselage, but still at the extreme end of the tail boom.

This, at the time, was a unique feature and represented the Cierva Company's attempt to dispense with a tail rotor. Directional control was however not fully satisfactory. Engine cooling air from a fan driven by the engine was ducted along the inside of the tail boom, joined and heated by the engine exhaust gases and ejected through the tail 'pipe'. Two horizontal shutters at the fan intake controlled the efflux of air to control the reactive thrust. The initial fixed pitch fan and shutters were inadequate and were replaced by a multi-bladed variable pitch fan coupled to the rudder pedals to vary the jet velocity. There was in fact no 'rudder' as such, only a small tail fin, and this was not always fitted, especially in the early stages. It was discovered that about 25 per cent of the engine power was absorbed by this early attempt at 'Notar' (no tail rotor).

The main rotor system of the W.9 stemmed from theoretical and experimental work undertaken earlier in the war by Weirs. It was styled the Aerodynamically Stabilised Rotor (ASR) and the whole rotor was carried on one rotating universal joint or gimbal. A swash-plate connected to the pilot's control was linked to the blades to effect change of pitch in the cyclic sense. The blades were bridled together so that differential flapping was suppressed — thus variations in coning only produced a change of col-

lective pitch. This latter gave an automatic change-over from helicopter setting to that needed for autorotation. A torque meter was installed – the first time ever in a helicopter. Ken Watson's incident led to hydraulic servo controls being fitted. There was, as indicated above, no collective pitch and lift was varied by use of the engine throttle – speeding up or slowing down the rotor rpm. This led to a lag in response which did not assist the hovering process.

At some stage in 1948, the decision was taken to install dual controls so that other pilots could fly the W.9. On 20 January 1948 Alan Marsh decided to 'have a go' from the starboard seat, having done all the previous flights from port. This meant changing hands on the controls, with the result that he rolled the machine over on the first take-off. As the initial flight programme was virtually completed the machine was not repaired. In fact a part of the fuselage was turned into drip-trays and they were somewhat ignominiously employed thereafter under the Skeeter and Air Horse.

There is no doubt that the Cierva W.9 was an important element in the development of post-war British helicopters, despite its purely experimental nature. At that time (the mid-war period) all helicopters were largely experimental, in any event, and it was to be several years before helicopter specifications were to be issued with anything other than an 'E' prefix. The remains of PX203 were sold to the Cierva company on 26 May 1948.

BRISTOL SYCAMORE

If Britain was to have a serious post-war helicopter capability it could be seen that there would be the need for more than one firm to be involved in rotary-wing development.

The only other 'helicopter-capable' design team from late 1930s had been Hafner's A.R.III Construction Company, and efforts had, in fact, been made by Flt Lt Welsh of that company to obtain a contract so that parity with the Cierva/Weir team could be maintained. The major problem, however, was the fact that Raoul Hafner's work at the Airborne Forces Experimental Establishment on the Rotachute/Rotabuggy designs was considered to be of vital national importance and for some time the Air Ministry refused to consider releasing him from these projects.

It was not until 1944 that this release was accomplished. A contributing factor to the delay was the memory of the late 1930s, when the promise shown by Hafner's rotary-wing experiments was negated by the absence of capital in the A.R.III Construction Company. This had been overcome by the 'shot-gun' marriage between Hafner's company and the Pobjoy Aircraft and Engine Company, the latter having become a subsidiary of Short Brothers.

Before any significant contract could be given to Hafner, though, it was imperative that he should obtain the backing of a major industrial concern – preferably within the aircraft industry. In fact, Hafner approached a number of companies, including the Nuffield Organisation (Morris Motors). The latter were looking to develop their aviation

The first prototype Bristol 171. (via Eric Myall)

activities (mainly then concerned with Tiger Moth production and the repair of damaged service aircraft) in the post-war years, and were already considering production of a range of light aircraft engines for post-war civil aviation opportunities.

In the event, the Bristol Aeroplane Company decided to form a helicopter division, bought up the assets of the AR.III Construction Company, and installed Raoul Hafner as Chief Designer of the new division.

Work immediately commenced on the design of a four-seater helicopter. This had probably been given the original Hafner designation 'P.D.9', but became known as the Bristol Type 171 and was later named the Sycamore.

The helicopter which eventually emerged from the Hafner drawing board was a 'conventional' design along the classic Sikorsky layout, i.e. one main rotor with a tail rotor at the end of the fuselage. Nevertheless, all helicopters were considered experimental at that time, and the Specification which was eventually awarded to Bristols came within this category, i.e. E.20/45, for an experimental four-seat machine. It was finalised on 25 July 1946 'To cover the design and manufacture of two prototype helicopters for research and experimental work on helicopter design in general, with specific reference to the development of a helicopter suitable for use by civil operators as a taxi or by the RAF for communications or AOP duties.' The engine specified was a 450 hp Pratt & Whitney Wasp Junior modified as required to provide the necessary drive to the rotor, an earlier attempt to utilise

the 500 hp Bristol Aquila engine having been abandoned. The Armstrong Siddeley Cheetah, Alvis Leonides, and Fedden flat-6 were also given some consideration.

The serials VL958 and VL963 were allocated on 4 September 1945 under contract C/Acft/5490/CB.9(a) to the two helicopters (Bristol c/ns 12835 and 12836), the first of these flying on 27 July 1947, following ground tests commencing on 9 May, and the second on 2 February 1948. In April 1949 the civil registration G-ALOU was allotted to the second prototype, no doubt in connection with the 'civil' aspects of the Bristol 171s development programme, but also to permit demonstration and display flights to potential customers. A Certificate of Airworthiness was issued on 25 April 1949.

Well before this, however, a second Specification had been issued for Type 171 development. This was Specification 34/46 and was based on the earlier E.20/45, but in this case to cover the design and manufacture of a prototype suitable for developing into a helicopter for general civil use. The power plant specified was the Alvis Leonides LE.1M of 550 hp. It is interesting to note that the 'E' prefix was missing from the initial and second drafts of the Specification (the latter dated 27 January 1947), but that by July 1947 both official reports and correspondence incorporated this prefix. In the event, the third Bristol 171 prototype emerged as VW905 (c/n 12869), this serial having been issued on 7 October 1947, though the machine had been allocated the civil registration G-AJGU as early as February 1947. The first two prototypes became known as Series I machines, while the third was classified as a Series II. VW905 first flew on 3 September 1949, some two years after the first prototype, but its rotor disintegrated

Right: **The second prototype Bristol 171. (via Eric Myall).**

on its second take-off that day.

From initiation of project work on the Bristol 171 in August 1944 to the first flight of the first prototype took approximately three years, which must be considered a satisfactory rate of progress, given the circumstances of its birth and gestation. A substantial amount of testing of components took place during this period. Rotor testing was carried out on a tower built for this purpose, and lengthy transmission trials were also undertaken before the flying programme commenced.

All three Type 171s were involved in manufacturer's trial for some time. VL958 was then tested at the Airborne Forces Experimental Establishment at Beaulieu in March 1949 and was later operated at both Boscombe Down and Farnborough. VL963 was also operated by Farnborough, while VW905 was flown not only by Farnborough and Boscombe Down, but also at RAE Bedford, where it was used as a static test-vehicle for early deck rolling platform trials. None of these three prototypes survived, all having accidents while in the service of the RAE.

The design went into limited production for both military and civil use, the Sycamore 3 being the first production version. Three machines were ordered under contract 6/Acft/2505 and serials WA576, WA577 and WA578 allotted on 10 November 1948. Between April and August 1951, WA577 undertook preliminary performance and handling trials at Boscombe Down, fitted with an Alvis Leonides LE.23 HM engine, to assess the suitability of the type for use in temperate climates. The general conclusion was that the cockpit layout was quite satisfactory and the aircraft pleasant and easy to fly, and by helicopter standards its stability was good. The main criticism was that although the main flying controls were duplicated, the pilot flying from the left- hand seat had to change hands on the cyclic pitch control to adjust the trimmers. The existing 80 lb trimmer springs were unacceptable for certain flying manoeuvres because of the heavy lateral stick forces which occurred and which required to be trimmed out for maintenance of full control of the aircraft. Fitting lighter (50 lb) springs, however, reduced these lateral forces within the compass of the pilot, and then flying from the left-hand seat became acceptable for all flight conditions. It was suggested, though, that it would better if trim adjustments could be made from this seat without changing hands.

Both WA576 and WA577 eventually became ground

The third prototype Bristol 171. (via J.D. Oughton).

instructional machines, renumbered 7900M and 7718M respectively. WA578 was completed as an HC.10 and undertook tropical tests in Malaya, crashing after its return to the United Kingdom when on 3 July 1956 it overturned on landing near Tidworth, Wilts.

The third initial production Bristol 171 emerged as the Sycamore HC.10.

Chapter 27
LARGE ROTORCRAFT

Once helicopters had started to become a practical proposition, the thoughts of several designers turned to the possibility of designing large commercial machines. Bristol, Cierva and Fairey all had their own ideas on how the concept should be tackled, and all spent some years in pursuit of this objective, but only the Bristol designs ever led anywhere, and then mainly in the military field.

CIERVA AIR HORSE

Following its work on the W.9, the Cierva design staff set its sights on a much larger design. In July 1945 it issued a brochure for the W.11 heavy lift helicopter, powered by a 1,600 hp Rolls-Royce Merlin 32 engine and weighing 14,000 lb overall. To try to overcome earlier problems with torque reaction, it was to be fitted with an unusual arrangement of rotor layout, comprising three rotor heads with associated rotor blades and control system, each rotor having a diameter of 40 ft. The machine had a crew of two, and with a payload of 5,000 lb was intended for such varied tasks as heavy crane lift, passenger transport, air ambulance and agricultural use such as crop spraying.

By September the design had been revised to become a pure crop-sprayer, intended to meet the requirements of Pest Control Ltd of Cambridge, whose Managing Director, Dr. Ripper, saw this method of dispensing liquid as more efficient than by ground vehicle. The rotor wash would tend to deposit some of the liquid on the undersurfaces of the leaves, and as the helicopter would not land it could not damage the plants. The all-up weight of this version was 15,000 lb, the maximum speed was estimated at 115 mph, and the cruising speed at 100 mph.

Ciervas adapted a Sikorsky Hoverfly I with a rudimentary spray bar system to substantiate these theories, and this resulted in a specification being drawn up by the Agricultural Research Council of the Ministry of Agriculture and Fisheries in conjunction with Pest Control Ltd, for a crop-spraying helicopter with a 100 cubic foot capacity for insecticide. After further discussion, involving the Ministry of Supply and the Ministry of Civil Aviation, the original Pest Control Ltd requirement was adapted and issued on 28 June 1946 as Civil Aviation Operational Requirement CAOR.3/46.

In the meantime development of the W.11 had gone ahead, a mock-up being constructed at Eastleigh Airport, Southampton. Known at that stage as the 'Spraying Mantis', it had two three-bladed rotors at the front and another at the back, each being mounted on skeletal frame outriggers to which were attached spray bars and associated nozzles. Automotive Products Ltd had provided a special long stroke undercarriage capable of absorbing shock loads of 39 ft/sec at 15,000 lb weight in an emergency landing without damaging the airframe.

The Colonial Office also now took an active interest, for possible overseas use, and in July 1946 a development contract was issued for one prototype machine under Contract number 6/Acft/704/CB.10c to the requirements of Specification E.19/46, which had been formulated around CAOR.3/46. Wind tunnel tests that summer at Farnborough on the three-rotor configuration were fairly successful, though it was suggested that the effectiveness of the fore and aft control could be increased by having the single rotor at the forward end instead of aft, a modification that became definitive in September. At the same time it was decided to have the fuselage fully enclosed, so as to widen its scope for use as a cargo carrier or passenger transport, it being now known as the Air Horse.

The first prototype Cierva Air Horse showing off its paces in 1949. (RAF Museum 6359-4)

A second machine was ordered early in 1947, the two aircraft having constructor's numbers W.11/1 and W.11/2. Overall length was to be 88 ft 7 in, and overall width 95 ft. Financial restrictions hampered development, but in the summer of 1948 the civil registrations G-ALCV and G-ALCW were allocated, and the first machine was earmarked for static display at the annual Farnborough Show, where it appeared as G-ALCV, powered by a 1,620 hp Rolls-Royce Merlin 32. On 10 September, it was allocated military serial number VZ724, which was applied back at Eastleigh when it returned there for ground running and tethered hovering trials. These began in October at the hands of Alan Marsh, and by the first week in December the machine had worked up to Experimental Flight Clearance.

On 8 December 1948 the first untethered flight was made, Marsh lifting her off at an all-up weight of 14,600 lb, thus setting up a record for the largest weight to be supported in rotary-wing flight at that time. Some 50 minutes flying was completed that day, and very few problems were encountered during initial flight trials. During the Spring of 1949 it was stripped down for examination, and various alterations were made, including modifying the main rotor booms to change the resonance characteristics and increasing the area of the stabilising fins.

Steady progress was made with the flight characteristics during that summer, and VZ724 made its public debut in September at the 1949 Farnborough Show. On 12 October Marsh lifted her off at 17,500 lb, the heaviest yet, and the Air Horse showed promise of a further increase in payload potential. Empty weight was 12,140 lb, and the maximum speed was estimated as 140 mph at sea level.

Range was judged to be 320 miles at a cruising speed of 116 mph, initial climb 790 ft/min and service ceiling 23,300 ft. In December auto-rotation trials commenced at a height of 1,000 feet with a rate of descent at 15,000 lb weight of 21 ft/sec at 35 knots.

By February 1950 the second machine had been completed under contract number 6/Acft/4024/CB.10(c), also powered by a Merlin 32 engine, and instead of its civil registration it bore serial WA555, which had been allotted on 8 November 1948. It successfully completed tethered tests the following month, by which time VZ724 had flown 38 hours without serious incident. By then, however, Pest Control Ltd were having second thoughts, improvements in spraying techniques making smaller aircraft such as the Hiller UH-12 more suitable. Fortunately for the firm, the Colonial Office were still interested in the Air Horse's overseas possibilities, making a grant of £45,000 to assist in development costs, total development costs being estimated by the Ministry of Supply at £350,000.

Disaster then struck, for on 13 June 1950, while on its way to the Airborne Forces Experimental Establishment at Beaulieu, VZ724 crashed on a farm near Eastleigh owing to failure of the front rotor hub assembly, killing the pilot, Sqn Ldr 'Jeep' Cable, the second pilot, Alan Marsh, and the technical observer, H.J. Unsworth. A small hinged drive link on top of the pylon had failed, and one of the rotor blades hit the starboard rear rotor boom, which broke off causing disintegration of the rear rotor.

By the time of the crash, VZ724 had successfully completed 80 hours flying, and WA555 had managed 20 hours of ground running. The wreckage of VZ724 was taken to Farnborough for examination, whilst WA555 was stripped down to components, being later reassembled for further strain gauge tests, during which it flew a total of 1 hr 1 min, presumably in hovering flight close to the ground. Saunders-Roe took over the Cierva Company early in 1951 as the nucleus of its Helicopter Division, and the Air Horse programme was soon abandoned so as to concentrate on the Cierva Skeeter. WA555 went to the Ministry of Supply sub-depot at Chelford on 15 June 1954, being stored there until sold on 28 February 1958 to Staravia at Ascot as scrap.

FAIREY ROTODYNE

By July 1949 the Ministry of Supply was beginning to take an active interest in jet-driven rotors. These were seen as offering the possibility of eliminating all the clutches, free wheels, gearboxes and other paraphernalia associated with the normal mechanical transmission to a rotor, as well as the necessity for torque compensating devices, all of which introduced additional weight and power losses. The snag was that it had not yet proved possible to produce small jets of the turbine type, and alternatives such as ram jets and centrifugal pressure types with combustion chambers at the blade tips had a high fuel consumption. Nevertheless they offered the promise of being very practical during initial take-off, climb and landing, and also for cruising with the jets shut down and the aircraft operating as a gyrodyne.

The Ministry had already found, however, that neither Rotol nor de Havilland Propellers were very interested, apart from an initial burst of enthusiasm, due to their technical staff already being fully committed on day-to-day requirements and the development of new types of propellers. On the other hand Faireys were keen on this use of jet propulsion and were already carrying out some basic research with the assistance of a German scientist, August Stepan, later Chief Development Engineer of MBB Helicopters at Ottobrunn, and it was proposed that they be given Departmental sponsorship.

It was around this time, as previously mentioned, that the Rotodyne idea was beginning to take shape, though the complexity of its design was such that it took around ten years from these initial thoughts until its first flight. Although there were contemporary proposals for large helicopters, it was almost certainly the first serious project aimed at producing a rotary-wing airliner for scheduled inter-city routes.

The 1947 proposals were for a 15-seat machine powered by two Leonides engines and weighing some 20,000 lb. By 1951 the passenger capacity had increased to 23 and a number of other power plants had been considered, including the Rolls-Royce Dart, the Armstrong Siddeley Mamba and the projected de Havilland H.7, the weight having now increased to 31,000 lb. BEA, however, issued their 'BEAline-Bus' specification that year, requiring a capacity of 35/40 passengers, and to meet the further increase in size and weight the Napier Eland was

The Fairey Rotodyne flying in its original unpainted guise.

chosen as the power plant.

On 12 June 1953 contract 6/Acft/5831/CB.10 was awarded for a single prototype, to carry serial number XE521, and six months later the Ministry of Supply finalised Research Helicopter Specification RH.142D. The issue of a serial indicated that a potential military role for battlefield support was seen, but the main purport seems to have been directed at the civil requirements. XE521, which had constructor's number F.9429, was regarded as a pure prototype and became known as 'Type Y'. A second prototype was envisaged as 'Type Z', with the basic designation FA-1, to meet Air Staff Requirement OR.334 for a vehicle carrier to meet Army needs, the serial XH249 being allocated. This machine would have been powered by two Rolls-Royce Tynes with two R-R RB.176s as separate propulsion engines and gas generators, and could also have been fitted with up to 70 seats, but it never materialised.

When completed, XE521 had a fuselage length of 58 ft 8 in, a wing span of 46 ft 4 in, a height of 22 ft 2 in, and a rotor diameter of 90 ft. Its main features were a box-like fuselage surmounted by a large sail-like rotor pylon, and large twin fins at the rear extremity. Rear clamshell-type doors were fitted to allow easy loading of vehicles or freight. A large four-bladed rotor, with the now well-developed, though noisy, pressure-jets at the tips, gave vertical flight ability, and two underslung 3,150 shp Napier Eland N.El.3 engines on substantial stub wings provided forward propulsion and compressed air for the pressure jets.

The aircraft had been largely built at Hayes, but Fairey's Stockport factory was entrusted with the tail, final assembly being at White Waltham. Substantial ground testing of power plants and rotors was carried out at both White Waltham and Boscombe, then on 6 November 1957 the machine made its first untethered flight. Test flying was undertaken by Sqn Ldr Ron Gellatly and Lt Cdr John Morton.

The first transition flights commenced on 10 April 1958 and were successfully completed by October of that year. Some confidence in the project was demonstrated on 5 January 1959 by an attempt on the 100 km closed-circuit record, an average speed of 190.0 mph being achieved, well in advance of any contemporary pure helicopters. Public demonstrations of the Rotodyne had commenced at the 1958 Farnborough Show and continued at the 1959 Paris Aeronautical Salon.

During these years of flight testing, interest in the Rotodyne project came from a number of quarters. A licence agreement to manufacture the Rotodyne in America was negotiated by the Kaman Aircraft Corporation, and strong interest in operating the type came from Okanagan Helicopters in Canada, New York Airways and Japan Air Lines. There was also keen interest from the US Army, with talk of a possible order for 200 machines.

Meanwhile the enforced merger of all the British helicopter manufacturing interests into Westlands had been effected in 1960. Westlands stopped development of their

The Rotodyne – here with splayed fins – seen starting the tip jets. (via J.D. Oughton)

own Westminster project in favour of the Rotodyne, but one practical effect of the merger was to introduce some degree of delay and uncertainty into all current projects.

To develop the Rotodyne into the enlarged machine now contemplated would have involved additional Government aid, and the first casualty was the potential military version, mainly on cost grounds. British European Airways then felt that they could not continue with the project as the principal, and possible sole, customer and in the absence of any firm order (as distinct from letters of intent), Westlands decided to withdraw. Formal notification of the cancellation of the project followed on 26 February 1962.

XE521 had been allocated to Westlands at White Waltham on 22 February 1961 for use in the flight development programme as part of the design work required for the Type 'Z', against Contract number KD/X/05/CB.10(a). It was no longer required, however, and on 7 May 1962 was released from the contract. On 8 December 1964 it was sold for scrap to R.J. Coley Ltd, though in the event several large components eventually found their way to the British Rotorcraft Museum at Weston-super-Mare, where they are preserved as the few relics of what might have been. It has been suggested that one of the main factors affecting cancellation was that of noise, especially from the rotor tip jets, but the firm were confident that this problem could have been overcome by the time commercial operations started.

Many people thought at the time, however, that the company was excessively optimistic in this view. Some four years of very intensive effort was put into noise reduction, yet produced what can only be described as qualified suc-

The Fairey Rotodyne in full paint, proceeding dramatically!

cess, reducing the noise from above the threshold of pain to the point where it was simply intolerably noisy. One engineer, wearing both ear plugs and ear defenders (muffs), and working about 100 ft from the blade tips, was deaf for about eight hours afterwards!

With the benefit of hindsight, it can be seen that given the difficulties in producing even small reliable helicopters at the time of the initial proposals, larger projects would inevitably run into serious problems. These were not only technical, but economic, and at the end of the day the Rotodyne can be said to have failed on both counts - though it almost succeeded, and there are many who believe that with more finance and perseverance it would have done so.

BRISTOL 173

Civil helicopter activities in this country in the early post-war years were covered by operational requirements promulgated by the Ministry of Civil Aviation. A demand was seen for three particular types, these being a four-seat helicopter for air-taxi work, a ten-seat helicopter for air transport/airline operations and a large cargo helicopter, these three types being covered by Operational Requirements CAOR.1, 2 and 3 respectively.

Bristol's Type 171 was submitted in response to the first of these, and in response to the second requirement Raoul Hafner commenced the design of the Bristol Type

173 early in 1947, against competing designs from Fairey and Cierva. A tandem twin layout was chosen incorporating as many parts of the Type 171 as was feasible. These parts included the engines/mountings, the front fuselage/cabin, the rotor hubs and the heads, the latter being handed for opposite rotation. Hafner's design was successful in gaining a contract and was produced to Specification E.4/47, the first draft of which was issued on 29 April 1947. It called for the design and manufacture of a prototype ten-seat helicopter, with two Alvis Leonides LE.1M engines.

A definitive Specification followed on 30 June, and a mock-up was completed by December 1947. The relative complexity of the design at this time is illustrated by the fact that the mock-up was still subject to detailed modifications in January 1949, although construction of the prototype had already commenced in 1948. Despite the advantages obtained by using Type 171 components, and the flight experience obtained on this type from 1947 onwards, the gestation period of the Type 173 was lengthy and it was not until 5 May 1951 that the prototype commenced ground-running trials, at Filton.

In July 1948 the civil registration G-ALBN had been allocated to the first prototype (c/n 12871) confirming the civil origins of the type, and it was in this guise that the first flight was made on 3 January 1952, tethered flying trials having commenced in November 1951. Some ground resonance problems had been encountered during these tethered flights, but after modifications and some trouble-free ground taxiing, the problems appeared to have been solved and the first free flight was mainly successful. On

The first prototype Bristol 173 in civil guise as G-ALBN. (RAF Museum 6495-2)

the second flight, the following day, however, ground resonance manifested itself with a vengeance between the front rotor and the rear undercarriage, and the prototype was significantly damaged on touch-down. It was not ready for further flying until the end of July 1952.

Meanwhile military interest in the aircraft had become clear, both from the Royal Air Force and the Fleet Air Arm. The first-named service was not only pursuing a transport requirement but also envisaged an air-sea rescue role, while naval interest centred around the anti-submarine capabilities of the Type 173. This latter manifested itself when the serial XF785 was allocated on 23 October 1953 to the prototype under contract CB.1001. Deck-landing trials were carried out on HMS *Eagle* that autumn, confirming naval interest. Military interest at that time was such that the prototype never reverted to its former civil status and retained its service serial XF785 thereafter.

Nevertheless, British European Airways Helicopters maintained a strong involvement in the programme, having for some time had plans to use helicopters on short-haul United Kingdom and European routes. It was probably this factor which led to the order for a second prototype. The position is not entirely clear, but this was probably still within the parameters of Specification E.4/47. Nevertheless a number of improvements over the first prototype were incorporated. The major visible difference was the addition of stub wings at the front and rear ends of the fuselage, the latter pair having vertical fins and a greater span. These wings were designed to off-load the main rotors in forward cruising flight. This brought the design into the compound helicopter category, the first British application of this configuration. The first flight of G-AMJI (c/n 12872) was on 31 August 1953. Thereafter the first prototype was known as a Series I machine, while G-AMJI became the Series 2.

G-AMJI was painted in full British European Airways Helicopters livery for the 1953 SBAC Display, serial XH379 being allocated on 20 August 1954 under contract 6/Acft/1597/CB.10(d) for further service trials, particularly the Fleet Air Arm. The stub wings were found to make deck handling difficult, so they were removed and the upswept tailplane of the first prototype incorporated. Service trials occupied much of 1954/55, but in 1956 the aircraft was loaned to British European Airways for route proving trials. These commenced on 20 July 1956, but on 16 September 1956 the second prototype was badly damaged when the nose dropped during backward flight at speed. By this time a further modification had been made to the tailplane assembly. This was undamaged in the crash and was donated to the first prototype.

The latter thereafter continued development flying until 1959, when it was withdrawn from use at Weston-super-Mare. It became a ground instructional airframe at the RAF Technical College, Henlow with maintenance serial 7648M, and still survives. The second prototype was also offered to the College, but was abandoned.

By this time it had long been apparent that Alvis Leonides engine was not sufficiently powerful to meet the increasing weight demands as the design progressed and both civilian and military customers expanded their requirements. The stage was therefore set for the develop-

The first prototype Bristol 173 after adopting military markings, now fitted with horizontal stabilizer endplates. (via M. Stroud)

The second prototype Bristol 173 silhouetted by the sun on a murky day. (via M. Stroud)

The first Bristol 173 Srs.3 (XE286) in low flight. (via M. Stroud)

ment of the Series 3 Bristol Type 173, and an order was placed for three aircraft of this type, to be powered by 870 hp Alvis Leonides Major engines. Civil registrations G-AMYF/G/H were allocated and the type was to be known as 'Rotorcoach' in B.E.A. service, a 16-seater civil transport version being required.

Initially designed with the stub wings of the Series 2, the first of the Series 3 machines appeared without them and bearing the military serial XE286, which had been allotted on 12 May 1953 under contract 6/Acft/8425/CB.10(d).

Flight testing commenced at Filton with a successful first flight on 9 November 1956. Cooling problems with the Leonides Major manifested themselves, and XE286 was grounded in 1958. The other two Series 3 prototypes did not fly and all three were used in various guises as ground-test rigs for the Bristol Type 191/192 programme which eventually led to the production of the Type 192 as the Bristol Belvedere for the R.A.F., but to a different Specification. Civil interest in the design also ceased in the late 1950s, when the economics of civil helicopter operations at that state-of-the-art were recognised to be problematical.

XF785 is currently held in store at Henlow by the RAF museum.

Chapter 28
ROTARY WING VARIATIONS

Out of the mainstream of post-war British single rotor helicopter development came two designs from Fairey and one from Percival. The Fairey products had a limited amount of success, but that from Percival turned out to be a complete disaster.

FAIREY GYRODYNE

The Gyrodyne, or 'gyratory aerodyne,' had its origins in a proposal by Dr J.A.J. Bennett which he put forward in answer to pre-war Specification S.22/38 as an alternative to fulfilling that Specification with a 'pure' autogyro design (see Chapter 5).

By 1943, Bennett was working for the authorities and was soon to be posted to Sikorskys as Resident Technical Officer, becoming the chief liaison link between Britain and Sikorsky.

As previously mentioned (see Chapter 27), it was the contention of Cyril Pullin, Weir's Chief Designer, that the Sikorsky R-4 was a dangerous, unstable machine, and this had led to a serious deterioration in the Sikorsky/British relationship at one time. In the circumstances it would have been surprising if Bennett had resumed his former association with Weir/Cierva when he returned to the United Kingdom at the end of the war. Instead, he soon established a relationship with the Fairey Aviation Company, and his pre-war 'Gyrodyne' concept was resurrected, the design becoming known as the FB.1 (Fairey-Bennett 1).

The concept of the Gyrodyne was basically the substitution of the tail rotor configuration by a propeller at the end of a stub-wing, partly to counteract any yaw produced by the main rotor and so facilitate directional control and partly to promote forward flight, thus reducing the loading on the main rotor. For forward flight the propeller

absorbed much of the power of the single-engine. On take-off, landing and hovering, however, the power was progressively applied to the main rotor and the propeller absorbed merely enough power to counteract yaw. In forward flight the stub wings contributed to lift and further reduced the main rotor loadings. The configuration of the rotor head was relatively simple in comparison with that of a 'true' helicopter, and was based on Cierva's tilting-head principles.

The first Specification issued for the Fairey Gyrodyne was E.4/46, but an official note dated April 1947 indicates that although this specification had been issued there were no Ministry of Supply orders in prospect at that time. Nevertheless, the company was building two prototypes as a private venture, probably in response to civil requirement CAOR.2/46. The Gyrodyne is described in E.4/46 as a four-seater all metal helicopter, which was something of a misnomer as it was not a helicopter in the real sense of the word. It is believed that the Gyrodyne was first considered by Fairey's as a possible contender for the A.2/45 Specification for an Air Observation Post aircraft. At this time the proposed power plant had been an Armstrong Siddeley Cheetah.

The Army/AOP connection recurred later when Specification A.7/47 was issued to Faireys, again based on the Gyrodyne concept. At the same time A.6/47 was issued to Bristol's for their Type 171 (Sycamore) design. Westlands were also looking for an outlet for their version of Sikorsky's S.51 – the Westland Dragonfly – but for some time it appeared that the Fairey Gyrodyne was the front runner in the field. The military serials VW796 and VW797 were allocated to Fairey against this Specification under contract 6/Acft/1414/CB.9(a) dated 5 September 1947, which interestingly preceded by one month that issued for the

The first prototype Fairey Gyrodyne (G-AIKF) seen flying over the course at White Waltham on which it established a new helicopter speed record on 28 June 1948. (RAF Museum 6261-3)

Type 171, namely VW905.

Official interest in the further development of the Fairey Gyrodyne came with the issue of Specification E.16/47, and it is presumed that from this time onwards the design came within the aegis of the Ministry of Supply. The serial VX591 was allocated to the first of the two Gyrodynes then under construction, being issued on 19 June 1948 under Contract 6/Acft/2102, the constructor's number being F.8465. This serial was soon cancelled, however, and the aircraft bore the civil registration G-AIKF when it was rolled out at Hayes. Powered by a 515 hp Alvis Leonides LE.22HM engine, which was the only suitable power plant at that time, it made its first flight at Heston, on 7 December 1947, in the hands of Basil Arkell, but had already appeared as a static exhibit at the 1947 SBAC display at Radlett three months earlier. It had a fuselage length of 25 ft, a width over the stub wings of 16 ft 8 in and and a rotor diameter of 51 ft 9 in. Its empty weight was 3,600 lb and loaded it weighed 4,800 lb. The estimated maximum speed was 140 mph, with an initial rate of climb of 1,000 ft/min and a service ceiling of 17,000 ft.

G-AIKF had the company designation FB.1, and the second prototype, which was apparently identical to the first, was registered G-AJJP and had the designation FB.2. G-AJJP, also identified by the normal Fairey c/n F.9420, is believed to have flown for the first time in the Spring of 1948. On 28 June 1948 G-AIKF established an FAI (Class G) 3 kilometre speed record of 123.4 mph, in the hands of F.H. Dixon. An attempt on the 100 kilometre closed-circuit record ended in tragedy, however, when on 17 April 1949 this same aircraft crashed at Ufton, near Reading, on a practice run, killing both crew members, F.H. Dixon and Derek Garroway.

The cause of the accident was believed to have been fatigue failure of the flapping link assembly retaining nut of the number 1 rotor blade, allowing the blade to become detached in flight. When the investigation into the crash was completed, the Gyrodyne programme was effectively cancelled, and the second prototype grounded, only to become involved in a new project.

FAIREY JET GYRODYNE

It is important to consider the Jet Gyrodyne primarily as a predecessor to the Rotodyne, and not as a development of the Gyrodyne. The accident to G-AIKF effectively marked the end of the Gyrodyne as a distinct type although not as a concept.

To place the Jet Gyrodyne in proper context, it is

necessary to go back to 1947, when first thoughts on the Rotodyne as a large transport aircraft were being assembled. This early study, followed by a patent in 1949, was the work of Dr Bennett and Captain A.G. Forsyth. It was not until 1951, however, that the name Rotodyne was first mentioned. At the end of that year British European Airways put forward a specification for a short/medium haul 'BEAline Bus' and it was around this that the Rotodyne project first crystallised.

Well before then, however, G-AIKF had crashed, and Fairey's were left with no role for the second prototype Gyrodyne (G-AJJP) if the Gyrodyne concept was not to be developed. In the early 1950s, however, the rotary wing emphasis of the firm turned to the Rotodyne, Dr G.S. Hislop taking over control of this side of the firm in 1953. The concept received official blessing on 7 December 1953 with the issue of Specification RH.142D, which probably also

covered work on the Jet Gyrodyne as a 'proof-of-concept' vehicle, contract 6/Acft/7270/CB.9(a) for the latter being issued on the same date. Due to an administrative error, the Jet Gyrodyne was initially allocated serial number XD759, but when it was discovered that the number had already been issued to one of a batch of Canadian-built North American Sabres, it was replaced by XJ389.

Although XJ389 looked superficially similar to the Gyrodyne, it was a much different beast, though it retained the constructor's number F.9420. In the Gyrodyne the three-bladed rotor had been shaft driven, but in the Jet Gyrodyne a larger two-bladed rotor was driven by a Fairey pressure-jet at the tip of each blade. The starboard tractor propeller of the Gyrodyne was removed, and to provide forward propulsion and directional control a variable pitch pusher propeller was fitted at the end of each stub wing. The engine remained an Alvis Leonides 54 (later 55), but the flight controls were changed to a more conventional helicopter type. The engine also powered two Rolls-Royce centrifugal compressors (from Merlin engines), which supplied air under pressure to the rotor tips where

The Fairey Jet Gyrodyne at White Waltham in September 1959. (RAF Museum 6638-3)

kerosene was fed in and the mixture ignited.

As forward speed increased, the amount of compressed air to the tips was decreased by coarsening the pitch of the propellers, which effectively increased the amount of power taken by them. Eventually the pressure jets were flamed-out, the compressors were declutched, and the rotor free-wheeled in autorotation, so that the aircraft became to all intents and purposes an autogyro. This procedure was reversed as forward speed decreased and with the pressure jets relit the aircraft reverted to helicopter flight for hovering and landing.

First tethered flights began early in January 1954 at White Waltham with John Dennis as test pilot, and a first free flight was made towards the end of that month. It was soon found, however, that the machine was underpowered, all the modifications having brought the gross weight up to 6,000 lb. It took some time to overcome this problem, the first transition from helicopter to autogyro cruising flight not being made until 1 March 1955, but eventually such transitions became routine and by September 1956 a total of 190 had been achieved and 140 autorotative landings made.

The flight test programme had been largely completed by the time the Rotodyne first flew in November 1957, after which further flying was largely superfluous. XJ389 was still at White Waltham when the firm merged with Westlands in 1960, and was authorised to be sold as scrap on 1 December 1960. though it probably remained there until 1965 when flight testing was transferred to Yeovil. It was later passed to No.424 Squadron, Air Training Corps and displayed at their Southampton headquarters before being taken over in 1979 by the Cosford Aerospace Museum, where it is currently exhibited.

PERCIVAL P.74

Shortly after the Second World War the Ministry of Supply were looking into the possibility of large single rotor helicopters, but foresaw difficulties in providing mechanical drive for such machines if the all-up weight exceeded 15,000 lb. It was suggested, therefore, that a rotor-tip drive might provide a solution. One problem was to find power plant firms willing to experiment in this field, due to existing commitments with engines for the many new fixedwing aircraft, but Napier agreed to take on this task, developing the NOr.1 750 hp gas generator which later became the Oryx.

In the meantime Hunting Percival at Luton Airport had established a Helicopter Division, which in 1950 started looking into the best use of gas turbines. After some study it was decided that there were advantages in ejecting the whole exhaust of the engine through the tips of the rotor blades.

This would have the advantage of eliminating the need for anti-torque measures used by normal helicopters, resulting in a more compact configuration. It should also reduce considerably the complexity of gearboxes, drives and other components needed, thus reducing vibration

problems and their consequent fatigue, which in turn ought to simplify and cheapen maintenance.

The Ministry of Supply had let it be known that they were interested in the concept, and were financing a suitable engine, and in November 1951 Hunting Percival joined forces with Napier to embark on a design study for a projected design under the type number P.74. In the meantime the Ministry were working on covering Specification EH.125D, and this was finalised for issue on 8 May 1952, a single testbed machine being ordered under contract 6/Acft/7054/CB.8(a), to carry serial number XK889 and be fitted with two Oryx engines.

The design emerged as a portly looking machine, initially fitted with a large fin having an inclined-hinge rudder with which it was hoped to provide yaw control by using the downwash from the rotor. This theory proved impracticable, however, and a more normal tail rotor was fitted instead, thus increasing the number of mechanical parts. A crew of two could be accommodated, and portholes were provided each side for use by passengers, of which there would have been eight or 12, depending on the internal seating. A large Perspex crew canopy helped to give the machine a frog-like appearance.

The engines were mounted in parallel underneath the cabin floor, with access through detachable side panels, and each drawing in air through four panels immediately behind the front wheels. Gas generated by the engines was to be mixed with cold air, then forced through side ducts to the rotor hub, and then through the hollow stainless steel non-feathering rotor blades to be ejected from the tips. During start-up the exhaust gases were initially to be discharged through a round orifice in the fuselage sides above each engine, a valve then gradually closing to divert them to the blades once operating speed had been attained.

For testing purposes a large pit was constructed by July 1954, so as to reduce external noise levels and provide some protection in the event of a rotor failure. Two possible aerofoil sections were considered for the rotor, and one of these was tested in the pit on an old Sikorsky Hoverfly helicopter. The tests were never completed, however, as the heavy loads imposed on the Hoverfly's clutch caused it to burn out.

Difficulties also arose over the gas flow, which turned out to be insufficient, leading to a complete redesign of the rotor hub mechanism, which took more than a year. The chosen laminar flow aerofoil section also gave cause for concern, as it depended on cleanliness for effectiveness, and this would be difficult to maintain day to day by normal commercial operators due to insects. Another difficulty was argument as to whether to undermine the intended simplicity of the machine by incorporating power assistance, eventually settled by a compromise decision to provide this for only the collective pitch system.

Despite the problems and delays, XK889 was eventually rolled out in May 1956, and initial engine runs were undertaken without the rotor. It was then moved out on to the aerodrome and tethered down for ground running

The Percival P.74 under construction. (via Mike Keep)

The Percival P.74 being inspected. (via Mike Keep)

tests. The firm did not have suitable pilots of its own, but secured the loan from Faireys of Ron Gellatly and John Morton, who had experience with the Gyrodyne and Ultra Light helicopters, both of which had rotor tip power. They soon discovered that the machine showed not the slightest inclination to leave the ground, and in any event had numerous design faults. There was too much drag from

The Percival P.74 on the aerodrome at Luton. (via Mike Keep)

the thick aerofoil section and the machine was unlikely to take off without power assistance in the cyclic pitch.

The firm went back to the drawing board and produced a design study for a redesigned version of the P.74 powered by the much more powerful Rolls-Royce RB.108 power plant and designated P.113, but they were too late. Rationalisation of the British aircraft industry was in the air, the Ministry of Supply was looking towards centralisation of helicopter manufacture, and they withdrew support in this field from Hunting Percival.

Chapter 29
THE FLYING BOAT FIGHTER

Flying boat research was never pursued on a major scale, but during the Second World War, Saro produced a revolutionary concept for a flying boat fighter. As luck would have it, this came on the scene too late to stand any real chance of going into production. One wonders, though, whether it might have proved an asset in later smaller struggles, if it had been properly developed.

SARO SR.A1
During 1943 Saunders-Roe, under the inspiration of Sir Arthur Gouge, conceived the idea of a small jet-propelled flying boat fighter. The war against Japan was by then at a turning point, and it was envisaged that such a machine could be invaluable in an island-hopping campaign, where land bases might be unavailable and in any case would be prone to enemy attacks. All that would be required was a sheltered stretch of coastal water, which would suffer no such vulnerability.

By the end of that year the scheme was sufficiently advanced for the firm to put a proposal to the Ministry of Aircraft Production, and these were woven into Air Staff Requirement OR.170, which then formed the basis of Specification E.6/44. Without waiting for this to be finalised, contract Acft/4122/CB.9(b) was issued on 29 April 1944 for three prototypes, allocated serial numbers TG263, TG267 and TG271. Originally designated the SR.44, under the new SBAC system of nomenclature it had the company designation SR.A1, but was referred to colloquially as the 'Squirt'. The Specification was not in fact finalised until 6 November 1944.

Discussion with the Ministry during May 1944 indicated that the aircraft was to be made as small as was practicable, and to be suitable for operation in any part of the world and at a great height, the latter requirement making a pressure cabin a necessity. As originally envisaged, the hull was to be divided into seven compartments with canvas stretched across the bulkheads, and bilge pump fittings were required for the hull and wing floats, the pumps to be ground equipment. The firm was also asked to investigate the possibility of installing photo-electric cells in the hull compartments, with indicators in the pilot's cockpit to tell him what damage had been sustained to the hull during combat.

It was decided to place the engines side-by-side within the fuselage, an arrangement automatically leading to a broad-beamed hull, which was not unwelcome as this would provide good longitudinal stability. It would be unnecessary to have a particularly tall hull to protect the engine intakes, since operations from sheltered water would not involve rough seas. Model tests were satisfactory, except for a tendency to porpoise when overloaded, which was easily cured by moving the step aft.

Power was to be provided by two Metropolitan-Vickers F.2/4 Beryl M.V.B.1 axial-flow turbojet engines, each providing 3,250 lb thrust, and there would be some space between them for fitters to work in. The horizontal oval-shaped air intake was situated fairly high in the nose, and to reduce the risk of taking in water it was fitted with a nozzle which automatically extended forward by ten inches when the wing floats were lowered. Separate exhausts were fitted in each wing root.

The overall length was 50 ft, and the tailplane was set half way up the tall rudder in order to keep out of the way of spray. Overall height was 16 ft 9 in, and the conventionally shaped wings had a span of 46 ft and an area of 415 sq ft. Proposed armament was four 20 mm Hispano cannon, two bombs of up to 1,000 lb or eight 60 lb rocket

The Saro SR.A1 prototype. (RAF Museum 6188-6)

projectiles.

The design had appeared too late in the war, however, to stand much real chance of operating in the Pacific before it ended, and after VJ-Day the project lost its immediate urgency. In January 1946 the Ministry of Supply approached Gouge informally about the possibility of cancelling the third machine. Gouge responded that all three boats were well advanced, but the real difficulty was that there was now barely sufficient work in the Saro shop to keep the team together. He was at that time awaiting definite news as to whether the large Princess flying boat could go ahead, and he was anxious to avoid discharges of men of the calibre he could ill afford to lose. He was therefore allowed to continue for the time being.

By the spring of 1947 the first machine was complete, and taxiing trials could commence. The first flight of TG263 took place in the evening of 16 July 1947, piloted by Geoffrey Tyson, the firm's Chief Test Pilot. He found a tendency to roll but this was easily cured by reducing the size of the rudder horn balance and fitting metal strips to the trailing edge of the rudder, and an acorn fairing at the junction of the tailplane and fin solved the problem of a tendency to snake at times. Otherwise no major difficulties emerged, either in the air or on the water. Tyson soon discovered that take-offs could be made quite short, if he retracted the wing-floats as soon as the machine became laterally stable.

Two months later TG263 was demonstrated at the annual Farnborough Show, but minor damage was caused on 16 December when the aircraft collided with a buoy. In May 1948 the transparent cockpit hood was lost in flight, being replaced by a new metal-framed one before going to the Marine Aircraft Experimental Establishment at Felixstowe on 11 June for hydrodynamic tests. Trials here proved the machine's capabilities, a take-off being possible in only 26 seconds, and the rate of climb was excellent for such a machine.

In November 1947 the company had let it be known that they were now prepared to cease work on the third aircraft, but this offer was not taken up. TG267 became airborne on 30 April 1948 powered by 3,500 lb thrust Beryl M.V.B.2s, followed on 17 August by TG271 with the fully rated Beryl 1 (M.V.B.2) delivering 3,850 lb thrust. In September, Tyson gave an impressive demonstration at Farnborough in TG271, including aerobatics and a low inverted pass for which the fuel system was specially adapted.

The prototype Saro SR.A1 flying inverted at Farnborough.

During trials this machine attained a maximum speed of 516 mph, and an initial climb of more than 4,000 ft/min.

Neither of these aircraft were to survive long, however. TG271 overturned after striking driftwood and sank in deep water while landing off Cowes on 12 August 1949, the pilot, Lt Cdr Eric 'Winkle' Brown, being rescued after getting clear by Geoffrey Tyson, who dived from a safety launch which was fortunately nearby. Then on 17 September 1949 TG267 went out of control while practising for a Battle of Britain display, and dived into the sea two miles off Felixstowe, the pilot, Sqn Ldr K.A. Major, being killed.

While neither of these incidents were due to design faults, they inevitably proved a major setback to the programme. The company thought things looked a little more hopeful, though, after the start of the Korean War in June 1950. Three months later they put forward a detailed submission, complete with drawings, with four possible options for the best use of fighter flying boats.

The first involved specially built ships of small length/beam ratio and shallow draft, equipped with ammunition, fuel and servicing gear, which would steam to the locality to be defended then drop anchor. They would be difficult to knock out, having their own AA guns and fighters, the latter being lowered alongside on to their mooring yokes ready for quick action.

Alternatively the aircraft could be harbour-based, though this would only be practicable where there was a small tidal run-out, such as a dredged channel extending almost to the sea wall. In this instance standard pontoons could be joined together to take any size of aircraft and to suit local conditions, riding up and down with tide. The inner pontoons would be connected to rails mounted on a landing ladder and the outer pontoons anchored to the sea bed. The ends of each aircraft would be made fast at bow and stern so that maintenance work could be effected without the use of launches. This concept was very much like modern-day marinas.

A variation of this was the use of suitable beaches. These would have to be shallow with a long run-out, the inner pontoons lying alongside the beach at low water to form a walkway. This method would have involved a single attachment point to the stern of the aircraft, released from the pilot's cockpit.

Finally, and rather optimistically, tunnels could be built in hills or cliffs. Initial cost would be high, but the aircraft would be invulnerable from air attack inside the tunnel, which would have two entrances each fitted with gates to prevent waves entering. The aircraft would be tied alongside anchored positions, with access over a drawbridge type gangway which would be raised when aircraft were taxying.

The SR.A1 now had another problem, however, that of engine supply, and in November the firm produced a design study for a Project P.122 development. Metropolitan-Vickers had decided to give up aircraft engine manufacture, their products to being taken over by Armstrong Siddeley, who abandoned the Beryl in the absence of orders from other aircraft manufacturers. Saro looked at an alternative layout with an engine still in production, and suggested that the advantages in flexibility of a twin-engine layout were outweighed by advantages of weight, cost and accessibility of a single-engined arrangement. The only turbojet in current production with requisite power seemed to be the Armstrong Siddeley Sapphire 2, which had a maximum static thrust of 7,500lb which was capable of being boosted to 9,450lb with afterburner equipment. There was also a weight advantage in that one Sapphire weighed 2,500lb compared with 3,570lb for two Beryls. It was proposed to fit one Sapphire in the central fuselage with the same nose air intake duct but dispensing with bifurcation, and also a single exit pipe running right aft, as opposed to the existing two exits half way along afterbody of hull. There would be improved access for maintenance, and it would avoid the necessity for two large bulges in the sides of the hull, with a consequent reduction in drag.

Disappointingly for the firm, the study met a cool reception, the Ministry not being optimistic that there could be any practical outcome of the firm's proposals for operational use. Saro were anxious to get them on record, but no work was undertaken to vet their figures, which simply remained on the file. On 2 December 1950 the Director

The prototype Saro SR.A1 bearing Class B registration G-12-1, and showing alterations to cockpit canopy and tail. (via M. Stroud)

Of Technical Development (Air) wrote to Sir Arthur Gouge informing him that there was definitely no interest in the project from the Air Ministry point of view. This effectively killed off the fighter flying boat concept, which in any event could not have got into service before the Korean war ended. Added to this advances in both land-based and carrier-borne fighters had made it largely superfluous.

TG263 was last seen in public when it was displayed on the Thames during the Festival of Britain celebrations in June 1951, resplendent by then with the Class B registration G-12-1. It was sold to Saro in February 1953, later going to the College of Aeronautics at Cranfield. One of the engines was removed to power Donald Campbell's ill-fated Bluebird, and G-12-1 joined the Skyfame Museum at Staverton in 1966, from where it went in 1978 to Duxford, being restored there as TG263 in the Imperial War Museum collection.

Chapter 30
SUPERSONIC SUCCESS STORY

Following cancellation of the Miles M.52, a new supersonic research programme was set in hand. One of the companies taking an interest was English Electric, which during and shortly after the war had built large numbers of aircraft under sub-contract, but had since set up an active design department, its first design being the A1, which would emerge to become the highly successful Canberra.

In August 1948 the firm received a contract from the Ministry of Supply for a design study relating to their proposals for a swept-wing aircraft with two engines buried in the fuselage. The power plants were to be mounted with the forward one lying centrally just above the bottom of the fuselage, whilst the other would be immediately to the rear of this below the top of the fuselage. It was considered that this arrangement would overcome any asymmetric thrust problems in the event of one of the engines failing in flight, with the added advantage of achieving twice the thrust of a single engine with only around 1.5 times the frontal area.

The design was submitted three months later, and in March 1949 permission was granted provisionally for design work to proceed as well as building of a mock-up and wind-tunnel models. By now the aircraft had become the P.1 under the new EEC project numbering system, and in March a formal contract was issued.

Wind tunnel tests with the models resulted in a number of changes. The original design envisaged a fairly pointed streamlined nose but incorporation of an engine air intake had resulted in a fuselage which was becoming somewhat tubular. Wing sweep was increased to 60 degrees, the tips being squared off at right angles to the fuselage, giving maximum effect to the ailerons. The original delta-shaped tailplane was dropped from the top of

the fin, first to its base and then to the lower fuselage. The main undercarriage wheels retracted outwards into the wings, whose highly swept design made it necessary to introduce a skewed pivot for the main undercarriage legs, this innovation being later adopted on a number of aircraft. In order not to obstruct the air intake, the nose wheel now pivoted through 90 degrees on retraction, so as to lie flat.

In September 1949 the Ministry of Supply issued Specification F.23/49, one of its last under the annual numbering system first instigated in 1920, and replaced at the beginning of 1950 by the system still in vogue with a single series commencing at 100. F.23/49 was based on Air Staff Requirement OR.268, drawn up two months earlier for a day fighter with supersonic performance. The specification was gradually refined and reissued, additional requirements including the ability to achieve supersonic speed in level flight without recourse to reheat, and provision for making daytime interceptions under ground control.

The EEC were ready for this, as all along they had in mind the possibility of developing the P.1 into a just such a machine. The design was soon accepted for F.23/49, and on 27 July 1950 serials WG760 and WG763 were issued for two aircraft to be delivered under contract number 6/Acft/5175/CB.7(c), a third unnumbered machine being also required for static test work.

On that same date a further serial number was issued, for a related aircraft. The Ministry had decided that the then unconventional design of the P.1 merited a separate investigation into its likely low speed handling characteristics. Specification ER.100 was therefore produced early in 1950, the first under the new numbering system, and also the first to bear the Experimental Research prefix. The resulting contract number 6/Acft/5347/CB.7(a) was awarded

The Short SB.5 in its original configuration. (RAF Museum 6521-3)

The Short SB.5 at Boscombe Down shortly after its maiden flight in the hands of Tom Brooke-Smith. (via M.J. Hooks)

on 2 August 1950 to Shorts Bros & Harland of Belfast, who produced the SB.5, bearing serial number WG768.

Despite all the EEC wind-tunnel tests at Warton, the Farnborough experts had reservations about the layout of the wing and tail surfaces of the P.1, preferring 50 degrees wing sweep and a high tailplane. The SB.5 was therefore designed so that it would be capable of being flown in a variety of wing and tail configurations. Wing sweep could be 50, 60 or 69 degrees, and the tailplane could be set either high or low.

Work proceeded meanwhile on the P.1, which was to have two Armstrong Siddeley Sapphire AS.Sa.5 turbojets producing 8,100 lb thrust without reheat, now mounted one below and one above the wing centre-section. By 1952 a decision had been reached to order prototypes of the P.1 fitted out as fighters. The two research prototypes then became retrospectively the P.1A, and the fighter version the P.1B, the latter type number being later applied also to all production models. Three fighter prototypes were ordered on 23 June 1952 under contract 6/Acft/CB.7(b), to

WG768

carry serial numbers XA847, XA853 and XA856.

The SB.5 flew for the first time at Boscombe Down on 2 December 1952, powered by a 3,600 lb thrust Rolls-Royce Derwent 8. It had a length of 47 ft 4 in, and in its initial configuration of 50 degree sweep wings and a high tailplane, the wing span was 35 ft 2 in. After a series of tests in this configuration, the wings were altered to 60 degrees sweep for further tests commencing in August 1953, then in January 1954 the tailplane was lowered, the sweep being left unchanged.

The final layout conformed with that of the P.lA, the first example of which was now nearing completion, and between February and August 1954 Roland Beamont, EEC's chief test pilot, made 22 flights in WG768. Neither of the first two layouts had proved satisfactory, thus substantiating EEC's design and wind-tunnel research, but the latest configuration produced handling characteristics which on the whole were very satisfactory. This pleased the company, which had never thought the expense of the SB.5 justified. The only difficulty encountered was of uneven aileron control forces at just above landing speed, this being cured by inserting a small notch in the leading edge of the wing. Even this shortcoming was really irrelevant to the P.lA, which would have powered controls, though the notch was retained.

Beamont also had the benefit, during the summer of

Dated December 1953, this photograph shows the Short SB.5 at Boscombe Down with horizontal stabilizer lowered and saw-tooth droop to a portion of the wing leading edge.

1954, of a cockpit simulator rig, one of the first in Britain, though later quite common. He also had a number of flights in a Hawker Hunter, and was therefore well ready for the first flight, which was to be made at Boscombe Down to take advantage of its long runway. After numerous checks, followed by taxiing trials and a short hop, WG760 finally took off for a full flight on 4 August 1954. Beamont was aloft for 40 minutes that day, and was especially impressed by the aircraft's manoeuvrability.

On 11 August, Beamont climbed to 30,000 ft and made a run at an indicated speed of Mach 0.98, but when the instrumentation results were analysed afterwards it was found that he had actually attained Mach 1.02, making the P.lA the first British aircraft to have attained a speed exceeding that of sound in level flight. This was pushed up to Mach 1.08 two days later, and by the end of the month the aircraft had been flown supersonic whilst manoeuvring. The climb to 30,000 ft took only four minutes, and a maximum height of 40,000 ft had been attained. By the time the aircraft was flown back to Warton on 23 September, it had amply demonstrated its capabilities, no handling problems had been encountered, and it was well capable of landing within the distance required in the Specification.

The designed maximum speed was Mach 1.2, but by the end of 1954 it had attained Mach 1.22. It was apparent that it was capable of going even faster, but this was considered inadvisable with WG760 due to some directional instability during manoeuvres at supersonic speeds, a problem which could easily be countered on the P.1B by fitting a larger fin.

The second machine, WG763, was now nearing completion, and on 18 July 1955 it made its maiden flight, again with Beamont at the controls, but this time at Warton, and two months later it appeared at the annual SBAC Show at Farnborough. Thereafter, WG763 was used for structural

and armament investigations, whilst WG760 undertook handling and performance trials. On 31 January 1956, WG760 made the first flight with reheated Sapphires, which each gave a thrust of 10,300 lb. There was now considerable loss of thrust without reheat, however, the fixed-area nozzles resulting in the normal 8,100 lb being reduced to only 4,100 lb, which meant that recovery after an engine failure would be in some doubt.

The trials were generally very satisfactory, but EEC were somewhat disconcerted by three separate incidents when a cockpit canopy came off in flight, the third time being at supersonic speed in August 1956 with Desmond de Villiers at the controls. The trouble was eventually traced to the locking mechanism becoming disengaged due to structural deflections in certain conditions of flight.

WG760 and WG763 continued to fly for a time, but as Lightning prototypes and then production machines emerged, their usefulness waned. WG763 eventually

Port side-view of the first prototype English Electric P.1.

A view of the classic Lightning planform illustrated by the second prototype English Electric P.1. (via J.D.Oughton)

achieved Mach 1.53 during supersonic research flying with RAE Bedford, but both aircraft eventually found their way to RAF Henlow as ground instructional machines, WG760 as 7755M and WG763 as 7816M, both later being preserved for exhibition.

The SB.5 in the meantime, following further experi-

ments at RAE Bedford on flow patterns over highly swept-wings, had returned to Belfast on 20 April 1958 to be been fitted in 1958 with 4,850 lb thrust Bristol Orpheus B.Or.3s against contract 6/Acft/13952/CB.5(b). The wings were set at 69 degrees sweep, reducing the wingspan to 25 ft $11\frac{3}{4}$ in, and it returned to Bedford on 6 December 1960 to continue the flow pattern trials. In March 1968 it too was relegated, to become 8005M at RAF Finningley, later going to the Cosford Aerospace Museum.

Chapter 31

THE TSR.2 SAGA

The history of the TSR.2 virtually began in October 1956, when English Electric started preliminary design work on a proposed replacement for their ageing Canberra. By that time it was becoming apparent that the Canberra concept was becoming obsolete, with its vulnerability to both supersonic fighters and ground-to-air guided missiles. By February 1957 the company's thoughts had developed to the stage of allocating a project number, P.17. Initial investigation had looked at a design with under-wing podded Rolls-Royce RB.134 engines, but this had been discarded in favour of a straight-winged machine with two fuselage mounted RB.133s.

Meanwhile official thinking led to the issue in September 1957 of General Operational Requirement No.339 for a two-seat high-speed bomber able to penetrate enemy territory to a distance of 1,000 miles at a sufficiently low-level as to avoid detection by radar, and to be in service by 1964. At a historic meeting that month attended by the heads of all the major British aircraft manufacturing companies it was made plain by the Government that the eventual contract would only be placed with a group of firms, one of which could act as leader. This effectively spelled the beginning of the end for the disparate collection of firms which had survived after the end of the First World War, and which ultimately led to British Aerospace being responsible for all major British fixed-wing aircraft production.

Ideas had to be submitted by the end of January 1958, and proposals were prepared by most of the firms attending the meeting, namely Avro, Blackburn & General, Bristol (Type 204), de Havilland, English Electric (P.17A), Fairey, Gloster, Handley Page, Hawker (P.1129), Shorts (P.D.17) and Vickers- Supermarine (571). English Electric had a head start on the other firms, having already put in nearly a year's work on the P.17 design study, now developed as the P.17A.

The two-man crew of the P.17A would be seated in tandem, in a fuselage 84 feet in length, the rear section of which would house two RB.142/3 engines fitted with reheat. The wings were to be delta shaped, with a span of only 35 feet. All-up weight would be 64,900 lb for a sortie radius of 600 nautical miles, increasing to 73,400 lb to achieve the 1,000 nautical miles laid down. An alternative fighter version was designated P.22, for long range attacks on both subsonic and supersonic bombers with rockets and guided missiles.

It was also proposed to give the P.17A auxiliary vertical take-off capability by mounting it on a special VTO platform, to be designed by Short Brothers as the P.17D. This was to be in the form of a compound delta, powered by no less then 70 RB.108 engines of 2,500 lb thrust, of which 44 would provide fixed lift, 16 give tilting lift, and 10 produce forward propulsion with jet deflection of 60 degrees. With the P.17A and P.17D in combination it would have been possible to operate from forward areas, the latter being also capable of airborne retrieval of the P.17A for a safe vertical landing.

The main contender for the contract emerged as the Type 571 from Supermarine, taken over by the Vickers-Armstrong parent at Weybridge. This was actually two designs, one being fitted with a single reheated 14,000 lb thrust RB.142 and the other with two engines of this type. The former weighed 40,000 lb and had slightly swept wings of 28 ft span, estimated low-level top speed being Mach 1.1, increasing to Mach 2.2 at height. Its scaled-up twin-engined stablemate weighed 81,000 lb and had a span of 41 ft 6 in. The smaller machine would meet the requirement, and at a much lower weight than the P.17A. This had

The prototype BAC TSR.2 under construction. (via M. Stroud)

been achieved by various advanced design and construction methods, including the use of alloys containing lithium, flap blowing and miniaturisation of electronic equipment.

By mid 1958 the contenders had been virtually reduced to the EEC and Vickers-Supermarine designs, both of which had their merits, and the possibility of VTOL capability was not being pursued. The obvious answer was to combine the two, but this presented problems for EEC as they had entered into an agreement that if either they or Shorts won the contract, they would work together on the resulting design.

The impasse was resolved by the issue of a completely new requirement, OR.343 being specifically drawn around the best aspects of the P.17 and the 571, but with added capabilities. Radius of action remained at 1,000 nautical miles, of which 200 nm had to be flown to and from the target area at a sea level speed of Mach 0.9 and 100 nm at supersonic speed at altitude. Non-operational ferry range had to be 2,800 nm, and the aircraft must achieve Mach 1.1 at 200 ft and over Mach 2 at medium altitudes. Take-off from rough strips had not to exceed 1,800 ft. Fully automatic navigation, automatic terrain following, high resolution radar and various other innovations were to be included in the resulting specification RB.192. The aircraft had to be capable of both nuclear and non-nuclear strike in all weathers, in addition to providing battlefield support

and various reconnaissance tasks.

By November 1958 discussions were taking place at Weybridge between the VA and EEC teams, and in January a formal announcement was made in Parliament that the two firms were to undertake the joint development of the new aircraft, now designed TSR.2. TSR stood for Tactical Strike Reconnaissance, though no mention was ever made of a TSR.1. Those with long memories recalled that there had been a previous TSR.2 – a Fairey-built Torpedo Spotter Reconnaissance aircraft (strictly TSR.II), developed into the legendary Swordfish.

The nominated main contractor was to be Vickers, which had the effect of placing the design leadership at Weybridge, where there was little experience of the engineering and aerodynamics involved in supersonic aircraft, recent designing and construction experience having been in the field of large subsonic aircraft. The EEC team, on the other hand, were fully experienced in this field, after all their successful work on the P.1 prototype and subsequent Lightning production.

The TSR.2 was to be an integrated weapons system, a now accepted concept, but one which at that time was an innovation in Britain. Thus the previous standard practice of building and proving an airframe and its engine before adding the various navigation and operational equipment was to be replaced, and these would now be designed in from the start. Unfortunately this had the effect of leading to a proliferation of official committees looking into every aspect of the design, often without reaching a firm decision, with consequent detriment to the programme. Added to this were the difficulties of communication and co-ordination between the EEC and VA teams, which at times left something to be desired.

In July 1960, a Government enforced merger between EEC, Vickers and Bristol, resulted in the British Aircraft Corporation. The following month specification RB.192D was issued in respect of TSR.2 development, and contract KD/2L/02/CB.42(a) was placed in October for nine development aircraft to be allocated serial numbers XR219 to XR227. By mid-1962 the design had been 'frozen'. The engines were to be two Olympus 22R each giving 19,600 lb thrust, which could be boosted to 30,600 lb with reheat. Length was 89 ft and span 37 ft, and take-off weight for a 1,000 nm sortie was 95,900 lb, but take-off distance for this had gone up to 2,870 ft on good surfaces and 3,000 to 4,500 ft on poor surfaces. Sea level cruising speed was estimated at Mach 0.9 to 1.1, and Mach 2 could be exceeded at altitude, with the possibility of development to achieve Mach 2.5.

Following planned trials with the prototype, it was envisaged that the second machine would be ready for

its first flight in January 1964, followed by XR221 in April of that year, then at two monthly intervals until April 1965 when XR227 should have flown. All of this turned out to be hopelessly optimistic.

A second batch of 11 aircraft, to carry serial numbers XS660 to XS670, was ordered on 14 June 1963 under contract KD/2L/013/CB.42(a), but by then the project was in trouble. Estimated costs had risen to nearly £200 million, and the earliest date it could be seen as entering squadron service was now 1969. Problems were being encountered with both the control system and the engines.

Despite everything, assembly of the first prototype XR219 was nearly complete at Weybridge by the end of 1963, and after some delay it was announced that it would make its first flight at Wisley, then fly to Boscombe Down for initial flight trials. The Warton technicians pointed out, however, that under Ministry's standard approval-to-test procedure, the requirements for the accelerate-stop test could not be met under experimental conditions within the length of the main runway at Wisley - and in fact the shorter Brooklands runway had already been ruled out for the same reason. As an alternative, they suggested the aircraft be transported by road to Warton, which did have a sufficiently long runway, as well as all the facilities required for the necessary testing. This was not acceptable to Weybridge, and Boscombe Down was finally selected. This had the advantage of a much longer main runway, but inevitably caused problems of both logistics and communications due to the distances involved between the site of the test flights and the location of the two factories concerned with the tests.

As a consequence it became necessary to build up at Boscombe Down a large reassembly and flight test facil-

The prototype BAC TSR.2 – photographed from a Lightning T.4 chase plane – seen with wheels down during its 15-minute first flight on 27 September 1954. (via M. Stroud)

ity, staffed by personnel drawn from both Weybridge and Warton. This probably caused a delay of about six months as compared with using Warton, and certainly added considerably to the cost involved. By April 1964, however, the first aircraft was ready to be transported by road in sections, then more delays due mainly to the scattered organisation and communication resulted in XR219 not being ready even for taxiing trials until August.

Meanwhile, problems had been encountered with undercarriage retraction, and a continuing series of major failures had occurred with the engine while under test at Bristol. Nevertheless, two pairs of engines were provided, to be used only for 25 hours, and at low power to avoid low-pressure compressor shaft resonance. On attempting to fit them, however, it was found that they would not go in at first due to alterations to the surrounding accessories. Further modifications were made, and limited taxiing trials finally began on 2 September with Roland Beamont and Ron Bowen at the controls.

Unexpectedly, it was found impossible to steer using differential brake action smoothly, a perfectly normal procedure, as the aircraft simply came to a halt without turning in the slightest. By trial and error, it was found that quick jabs would do the trick, though the results were rather rough and ready. Other problems were experienced with disengagement of double reheat, the oxygen supply and the cockpit heating, as well as a hydraulic leak. The sixth taxiing test, on 7 September, resulted in failure of the braking parachute at 145 knots, and the aircraft was well down the 10,000 ft runway before finally coming to a halt.

These snags were gradually overcome, but at a meeting of interested parties on 26 September it emerged that the problems with the engine were far from solved. No guarantee could be given that an engine failure would not result in parts exploding through the engine casing, which was potentially catastrophic. Nevertheless it was decided the risks were acceptable - especially as by this time the project was threatened with cancellation if there should be a change of Government in the forthcoming general election.

The following day, therefore, Roland Beamont, Deputy Chief Test Pilot of BAC, took off at 1528 hrs. Many restrictions had to be imposed at this stage, but despite all the doubts, the flight was very successful, the planned objectives being fully achieved. The aircraft handled beautifully, apart from some unexpected and disconcerting vibration on touchdown. Beamont commented afterwards that it was a fine aeroplane, and flying it was like the Warton simulator, only better.

It all came to nought, however, on 31 March 1965, XR219 made what turned out to be its last flight. The aircraft had achieved or exceeded all its main targets for the test programme, but was temporarily grounded while undercarriage vibration problems were cured. Six days later the Government announced cancellation of the whole programme, and it never flew again, being officially struck off charge on 28 February 1967. The aircraft were then mostly scrapped, but XR220, which was to have undertaken noise tests in the Boscombe Down detuner, was classified as a museum exhibit with the ground instructional number 7933M, being transported on 4 May 1975 to the Cosford Aerospace Museum. XR221 was used for a time by the Proof and Experimental Establishment at Shoeburyness on vulnerability trials, whilst XR222 went to the College of Aeronautics at Cranfield, being later used there by the fire fighting section before being presented to the Imperial War Museum at Duxford in 1977.

Supposedly the prototype BAC TSR.2 in flight – but far more likely a superimposed model.

Chapter 32

PROMISES UNFULFILLED

Among the many ideas being pursued in the early postwar years were two original lines of research which ultimately led nowhere. In both cases, however, one wonders what might have been the outcome if more time and money could have been expended on what appeared at the time to be promising objectives.

SARO SR.53

In 1950, Saros undertook a study to see if it was feasible to install a rocket motor in a small fighter aircraft, to enable it to climb to around 100,000 feet to intercept supersonic bombers. The concept was essentially the same as that already applied with a certain amount of success towards the end of the war in the Messerschmitt Me 163.

Although the Saro staff were unaware of the fact when they started work on the project, other companies had already received rocket contracts. These had been stimulated by the Me 163 and other German designs, and the attraction of a short range interceptor able to climb rapidly and make a single firing pass before its fuel was exhausted, then glide back to earth. Both Armstrong Siddeley Motors and de Havilland Engines were developing suitable rocket motors developing around 2,000 lb thrust.

Official thinking, based on these engines, had resulted in the formulation by August 1951 of Air Staff Requirement OR.301 for a high-speed rocket-propelled interceptor fighter. Development of this theme had progressed to the amended OR.301 Issue 2, by 21 January 1952, when Specification F.124T was issued. Firms taking an interest in this included Blackburns, Bristols and Shorts, but surprisingly Saros were not initially invited to tender, being regarded by the Ministry of Supply as purely flying boat designers. They learned of the requirement through de Havilland

Engines, however, and Sir Arthur Gouge, the firm's chief executive, made a formal request for a copy of the Specification. This was sent to him – but with the statement that they could not expect to be paid for any submission they made!

The original concept, probably based on the Me 163, called for a skid undercarriage so that the aircraft could land on a field if necessary. This was soon changed to a conventional undercarriage. It also became apparent that a rocket motor would not provide the necessary electrical power, so the Specification was altered to include a very small conventional turbojet.

The Saro proposals met the Specification, and were submitted in April 1952. The firm were far from satisfied that this was the best solution to the problem, however, and as an Addendum they proposed a quite different aircraft of a more conventional nature, which would have a much better performance and have the advantage of being capable of being refuelled and rearmed quickly after landing, so that it could undertake another sortie if necessary.

A month later they learned that the company's bid had been successful, and shortly afterwards they were asked to go ahead with the design set out in the Addendum. This meant, however, that they were out of line with the Specification as drawn up, and this therefore had to be amended. In the event two Specifications emerged, the second to appear being F.137D, issued on 16 July 1953 to OR.301 Issue 4 and awarded to Avros for a machine employing a combination of an Armstrong Siddeley Viper plus an Armstrong Siddeley Screamer rocket motor, to carry serial number XD696. Exactly a month earlier, OR.301 Issue 3 had appeared, together with Specification F.138D, and from this on 24 October 1952 came contract number

The first prototype Saro SR.53 taking off from Boscombe Down. (British Hovercraft Corporation)

The first prototype Saro SR.53 flying overhead, demonstrating the characteristic diamond pattern of the efflux of its Spectre rocket motor. (British Hovercraft Corporation)

6/Acft/8703/CB.7(a) for three prototypes, with the Saro type number SR.53, allocated serial numbers XD145, XD151 and XD153. The new design would be fitted with both an Armstrong Siddeley Viper turbojet and a de Havilland Spectre rocket motor. It would be fitted with radar, and able to carry Blue Jay missiles, the latter becoming the Firestreak on going into production.

As development proceeded, it became apparent that the radar was likely to prove a major stumbling block. The AI-23 was the most suitable equipment to meet requirements which were now changing rapidly in this field, but this was far too heavy for the small SR.53. It was proposed, therefore that the fuselage be enlarged to accommodate this. This led to a new design, referred to at that stage as Project P.177, fairly similar in general layout to the SR.53, but somewhat larger and fitted with a de Havilland Gyron Junior engine and a de Havilland Spectre rocket motor. It was targeted for flight in mid-1957, with an estimated all-up weight of 25,000 lb. Because of the prospects of the P.177, and to protect their interests, de Havilland acquired a substantial interest in Saunders-Roe during 1956.

Meanwhile SR.53 construction was proceeding rather slowly, partly because of the difficulty of working in such a small aircraft packed with equipment, but also due to delays in delivery of its Spectre rocket motor. A completed rear fuselage section sent de Havilland at the end of 1955 suffered damage when tested with a Spectre installed, but this setback was partially alleviated by the knowledge that as an economy measure work had been stopped on the rival Avro 720, which had cost the taxpayer around £1 million. On the other hand, the same economies caused the third SR.53 to be cancelled.

XD145 was taken to Boscombe Down in June 1956 for final assembly, and taxiing trials began there in May 1957, followed on 16 May by its first flight, piloted by Sqn Ldr John Booth, Saro's chief test pilot. The area-ruled fuselage had a pointed nose cone, the cockpit being well forward and equipped with a Martin-Baker ejector seat. The squat fin extended beyond the two exhausts, which were staggered, that of the Spectre rocket motor being set further forward than the one for the Viper. The wing was of delta outline with squared tips, the tailplane being a full delta and mounted at the extreme top of the fin, where it would be well clear of the combined exhausts. A tricycle undercarriage was fitted, with relatively small wheels. The machine had a span of 25 ft 1 in, length was 45 ft and wing area 274 sq ft.

Fitted with a 1,640 lb thrust Viper A.S.V.8, early tests revealed a fast rate of climb and a level speed of Mach 1.33 with the Spectre firing, this being eventually raised to Mach 2 at heights above 35,000 ft. Empty weight without fuel was 7,400 lb, the loaded weight being 19,000 lb. In September of that year it was able to show its paces at the Farnborough Show, XD151 being available by then for exhibition in the static display, powered by a Viper 101. Booth flew XD151 on 8 December, but sadly lost his life in the aircraft on 5 June 1958 when it overran after failing to take off from the Boscombe Down runway and exploded

upon hitting a concrete approach lighting pole.

The reason for the accident was never fully established, but the other machine was immediately grounded and never flew again. It was used for ground tests during Spectre development until December 1961 when it was released from Boscombe Down for static exhibition at the Rocket Propulsion Establishment at Westcott, eventually passing to the Cosford Aerospace Museum, where it can still be seen.

In the meantime, work was progressing with the P.177, by now known as the SR.177 (though more correctly SR.55). Both the RAF and the Royal Navy were interested, with respective requirements OR.337 and NR/A47 being drawn up, and combined Specification F.177D was written around it. An order was placed on 4 September 1956 for nine aircraft, XL905-907 being intended as prototypes, followed by XL920-922 for the RAF and XL923-925 for the Fleet Air Arm. A large production order was expected, with a distinct possibility of substantial numbers being sought by West Germany and maybe other countries.

A meeting was held in Bonn during July 1956, and in November 1956 the Ministry of Supply agreed to the West Germans being granted a license to manufacture the aircraft. Everything looked promising until the Defence White Paper in April 1957, which stopped almost all fighter development apart from the English Electric P.1. The naval version was allowed to continue for a time, but in August this too was cancelled. That was not quite the end of the project, however, as the following month the Ministry gave the firm permission to continue with construction of the first five aircraft in anticipation of a West German order, and to proceed on the assumption that a further 22 aircraft would be required, of which the last 18 were to be for planning purposes only at this stage and subject to confirmation at a later date. For the next two months redesign continued on the bases of installing two Rolls-Royce RB.133 engines and fitting thin wings, the latter being the responsibility of Armstrong Whitworth. Two senior Heinkel representatives paid a visit to Cowes during November, and a meeting was held in Bonn the same month in which it was stressed that the project was only being kept open for the German order. Shortly before Christmas 1957 the West Germans finally decided against the project, and on 24 December the Ministry of Supply advised Saro that they wished to stop the contract. There was some subsequent interest by the Japanese, who would have been willing to purchase SR.53 XD145 and two of the SR.177s, but there was no UK backing for this and the project finally came to an end in February 1958, thus bringing to a close the firm's involvement in fixed wing aircraft.

BRISTOL 188

During 1953, Specification ER.134T was drawn up for a research aircraft capable of maintaining sustained flight at speeds up to Mach 2, later updated to Mach 2.5, for the study of steady-state kinetic heating effects on its structure. Several firms took an interest in this advanced specifi-

The first prototype Bristol 188 resplendent in shiny stainless steel panelling.

The first prototype Bristol 188 seen during the 1962 Farnborough display. (via M.J. Hooks)

cation, but the contract, number 6/Acft/10144, was awarded in February 1953 to Bristol.

The aircraft was allotted type number 188, and the initial order was for three machines, one to be used as a static test bed, and two for flight testing. The latter were given constructor's sequence numbers 13518 and 13519, and the serials XF923 and XF926 were allocated on 4 January 1954 under contract KC/2M/04/CB.42(b). An order for three further machines, to have carried serial numbers XK429, XK434 and XK436, was later cancelled.

The aircraft was to be built of stainless steel, and the design developed as a long slender fuselage originally to be powered by two Rolls-Royce Avon RA.24R turbojet engines mounted at mid-point along a thin swept-wing.

The cladding material caused endless problems. It had to be strong and uniform in thickness, and due to the high temperatures likely to be generated all the fasteners had to be of compatible materials with a similar co-efficient of expansion. A new argon arc-welding system had to be devised by the firm, becoming known as 'puddle-welding', though this proved unsatisfactory, leading to long delays. The firm received considerable technical help from Armstrong Whitworth, who had experience in the techniques required and who were able to produce several of the more important components under sub-contract.

Wind tunnel tests and trials with high speed rocket-propelled scale models led to the inner wing sections being modified to become roughly rectangular. The chord of the fin was raised to provide better control in the event of an engine failure at take-off, and the all-moving tailplane was moved from near its base to the top. Five different engine combinations were tried, two involving Avon 200

This photograph of the first Bristol 188 shows well the extremely slim fuselage cross-section. (via M. Stroud)

series, two the Gyron Junior and one the Rolls-Royce AJ.65, the latter disintegrating on test. Finally the aircraft was fitted with two 10,000 lb thrust de Havilland Gyron Junior DGJ.10Rs which could develop 14,000 lb thrust with reheat at sea level, and 20,000 lb thrust at Mach 2 at 36,000 ft. It was the first British engine designed for sustained running at continuous supersonic speeds, and pioneered such features as stainless steel and titanium construction as well as high temperature oil and fuel systems. De Havilland Engines took advantage of the 188 and considered it an ideal test bed for supersonic research. Lessons learnt with this engine were later applied to the Olympus for the Concorde installation and also for the TSR.2 installation.

The design developed to have a fuselage measuring 71 ft, with wings of only 35 ft 1 in span and 396 sq ft in area. A large proportion of the oval-sectioned body was taken up with fuel tanks, the diameter being the smallest possible to accommodate the pilot and ejector seat. The main wheels retracted inwards, and twin nose wheels retracted into a well just aft of the cockpit, which was situated rather forward in the nose.

The first machine to be delivered was that for structural tests, which arrived at Farnborough in May 1960 and was at RAE Bedford by the end of the year. XF923 was rolled out on 26 April 1961, and undertook a number of taxiing trials, but various problems including difficulties with the intakes delayed the first flight until 14 April 1962, when

it was flown to Boscombe Down by the Chief Test Pilot, Godfrey Auty. It participated in the 1961 SBAC Show at Farnborough, then returned to Filton on 15 November 1962.

XF926 had its maiden flight on 29 April 1963, and on one flight managed to reach Mach 1.88 at 36,000 ft, but neither aircraft fulfilled their intended destiny. Problems were encountered with fuel leakage, and fuel consumption by the reheated Gyron Junior turned out to be badly underestimated, so that little flight time could be spent on the major objective of studying the effects of prolonged kinetic heating, which might otherwise have made it a useful tool in the Concorde development programme.

XF923 went into official storage at Filton on 19 November 1963, as did XF926 on 25 March 1964, which had made the last of its 51 flights on 11 January 1964. They both remained there until being struck off charge on 7 November 1966, when they were allotted to the Proof and Experimental Establishment at Shoeburyness for vulnerability trials as gunnery targets. XF926 was reprieved from and end at Shoeburyness, however, and reallotted in November 1974 for preservation at the Cosford Aerospace Museum with the ground instructional airframe number 8368M.

Chapter 33
FOR THE FUTURE

During the late sixties and throughout the seventies, very little practical military aviation research took place in Britain. The industry had become disillusioned by the repeated cycle of expending much time and effort on new projects, only to have them cancelled by the politicians just as they were beginning to show some promise. The TSR.2 cancellation in February 1965, accompanied as it was by the cancellation of the P.1154 and also the Hawker Siddeley HS.681 transport aircraft, sent a massive shockwave through the industry.

Much time and effort had been expended, not simply with airframes and engines, but with the advanced systems involved. The sweeping changes which followed as a consequence of the cancellations led to the loss of many young design people who left the industry for ever. The truncation of the Concorde programme added to the problems, as did the Government handling of the on/off purchase of F-111s and the eventual penny-pinching purchase of Phantoms. All of these left in their wake a disillusioned and somewhat shattered workforce, just at the point where rapid advances in computer technology would allow simulation, and therefore less need to produce to spend vast sums of money on an actual flying machine. All these factors led to a 'where to we go from here?' syndrome, which did not begin to dissipate until the changed political climate of the eighties brought about new and more hopeful attitudes in industry.

Early in the 1980s British Aerospace, Messerschmitt-Bölkow-Blohm (MBB) and Aeritalia got together, with Rolls-Royce, to produce the Agile Combat Aircraft (ACA), a full-scale mock-up of which was exhibited at the 1982 Farnborough Air Show. No official support was forthcoming for this, but in the same year the Ministry of Defence agreed to join with industry in an Experimental Aircraft Programme (EAP). This was to be an advanced-technology aircraft with outstanding performance characteristics.

It was to demonstrate for the first time in a single aircraft several recent technological developments. These included full authority digital fly-by-wire controls, an unstable canard delta configuration, electronic cockpit design, digital databus avionics, digital engine control, composite materials and new alloys and 'stealth'.

Initially the project was to be of a European nature, undertaken by the original three partners in ACA, but the German firm soon dropped out, which caused some difficulties, the centre fuselage having to be substantially redesigned as a consequence. Then the Italian Government withdrew its support from Aeritalia, but fortunately that firm put in some of its own funds to allow wing design to continue.

A formal announcement was made on 26 May 1983 that a contract had been signed for a demonstration aircraft, to carry serial number ZF534. Despite the setbacks work continued at Warton, and only three years after the contract had been signed the technology demonstrator was unveiled there on 16 April 1986.

The aircraft is of single-seat delta-canard layout, powered by two Turbo-Union RB.199D extended-reheat turbofan engines, each developing more than 17,000 lb thrust with reheat. Fuel is mainly carried in the wings, but 14 smaller tanks have been incorporated in the fuselage wherever space permits. The design incorporates components from numerous British, German and Italian firms, combining the latest technologies in the fields of aerodynamics, structure, cockpit layout and avionic integration. It was originally to have had twin fins and rudders, but in the interests of time and economy a single Tornado fin and rudder were fitted instead.

The latest developments in 'stealth', the need to reduce radar detection risks, have been incorporated, and agility in manoeuvring has been taken into account in the canard configuration. Including the canards, there are 15 control surfaces, and the makers claimed at the time of launch that these would enable it to out-manoeuvre anything then flying.

Overall length is 48 ft 3 in, and the fuselage has been area-ruled to minimise supersonic wave drag, the nose being drooped, providing good visibility, only slightly marred by the location of the canards. The wing is a compound delta of carbon fibre construction, with a span of 36 ft 8 in and an area of 560 sq ft. Carbon fibre has been used extensively throughout the aircraft, to save weight and increase strength, and the proportion would have been

The British Aerospace EAP a split-second after rotation. (BAe)

even higher if one of the partners had not dropped out, it being necessary to change to aluminium alloys for the centre and rear fuselages in order to keep on schedule.

The first flight was made on 8 August 1986 by David Eagles, Warton's Executive Director of Flight Operations, and the test team all reported it to have an exhilarating performance, which they were able to demonstrate a few weeks later at that year's Farnborough Show. Trials are continuing at the time of writing, and much of the technology involved in both the aircraft and its engine will be incorporated in the new European Fighter Aircraft (EFA).

INDEX

ABC Dragonfly engine, 9
Adam, Flt Lt M.J., 63
Aeritalia, 208
Aerodynamically stabilised rotor, 172
Aero-isoclinic wing, 156
Agile Combat Aircraft, 208
AI-23 radar, 205
Airborne Forces Experimental Establishment,
   43, 70, 73, 112, 117, 170, 172, 174
Airco D.H.9, 18
Air Ministry, 16, 17, 18, 29, 30, 32, 42, 47, 50,
   52, 58, 62, 66, 75, 77, 97, 172, 193
Air Observation Post squadrons, 69
Airspeed A.S.31, 54
Air Staff Requirements:
  OR.30, 53
  OR.69, 58
  OR.101, 160
  OR.107, 100
  OR.116, 103
  OR.170, 190
  OR.171, 142
  OR.182, 105
  OR.195, 105
  OR.207, 113
  OR.229, 120
  OR.241, 130
  OR.243, 165
  OR.252, 124
  OR.268, 194
  OR.282, 137
  OR.301, 203, 204
  OR.334, 179
  OR.337, 205
  GOR.339, 199
  OR.343, 200
  GOR.345, 150

Allright, H.J., 98
Aluminium alloys, 24
Alvis engines:
  Leonides, 173, 174, 178, 180, 181, 185
  Leonides Major, 183
Ames Flight Research Centre, 158
ANT-25, 66
A.R.III Construction (Hafner Gyroplane) Ltd, 39,
   170, 172, 173
Argus, HMS, 18
Arkell, Basil, 185
Ark Royal, HMS, 151
Armstrong-Siddeley engines:
  Adder, 139
  Cheetah, 173, 185
  Genet, 30, 32, 36, 44
  Genet Major, 32
  Jaguar, 16
  Lynx, 16, 31, 50, 52
  Mamba, 178
  Mongoose, 19
  Sapphire, 134, 137-139, 192, 195, 197
  Screamer rocket motor, 204
  Snarler rocket motor, 166-167
  Viper, 204, 205
Armstrong Whitworth Aircraft, 29, 103, 116, 117
Armstrong Whitworth aircraft:
  Ape, *15*, 15-16
  Armadillo, *13*, 13
  A.W.49, 116
  A.W.50, 116
  A.W.51, 116
  A.W.52, 7, *81*, 118, *118*, *119*
  A.W.52/G, 7, 116-117, *117*
  A.W.58, 134, 137-139, *138*
  B.11/41, 78
  B.35/46, 120

Whitley, 69, 111, 117
Army Air Corps, 69, 74
Austin Osprey, *12*, 13
Australian Aeronautical Research Council, 123
Australian Government, 168
Automotive Products Ltd, 176
Auty, Godfrey, 207
Avro aircraft:
  504, 25, 29
  574 (Cierva C.6C), 31, *38*
  575 (Cierva C.6D), 31
  576 (Cierva C.9), 31, *33*
  611 (Cierva C.8L-I), 31
  620 (Cierva C.19), 32
  698, 120-122
  707, 7, *82*, 120-124, *121-124*
  710, 120
  720, 205
  Athena, 121
  Lancaster, 117, 129, 143
  Tutor, 73
  Vulcan, 6, 118, 122, 156

Barnwell, Frank, 16, 25, 62
Baynes aircraft:
  Bee, 71
  Carrier Wing, 71, 73, *73*, 108
Baynes, L.E., 71, 159
Beamont, Roland, 196, 197, 202
Beardmore aircraft:
  Inflexible, 26-27, *27*, 52
  Inverness, 27-28, *28*
Beardmore, Sir William & Co Ltd, 26, 52
Bell aircraft:
  Airacobra, 162, *164*
  Bell X-1, 129
Bellanca aircraft, 64, 65

Bennett, Captain D.C.T., 67, 68,
Bennett, Dr J.A.J., 40, 42, 184, 186
Bentley B.R.2 engine, 9, 13, 29
Bentley car, 70
Bevan Brothers, 38
B.H.P. engine, 9, 13
Bishop, R.E., 113
Blackburn Aeroplane & Motor Co Ltd, 55, 75
Blackburn aircraft:
 B.20, 57-59, *58*
 B.40, 57
 B.44, 58
 Firebrand, 58
 R.5/39, 58
 YB.2, 155
Blackburne Tomtit engine, 25
Blacker, Lieutenant Colonel L.V.S., 61
Blaicher, Flg Off, 70
Bleriot-Zappata 110, 66
Blind Landing Experimental Unit, 150, 151
Bluebird car, 193
Blue Jay missile, 205
Boeing SST, 145
Bonnett, S.R., 61
Booth, Sqn Ldr John, 205
Boscombe Down, 74, 101, 104, 106, 117, 118, 121, 122, 125, 132, 134, 148, 150, 152, 158, 165, 168, 174, 179, 196, 201, 202, 205, 207
Boswell, R.O., 17
Boulton Paul aircraft:
 Bodeigre, 21
 Bodmin, 21-23, *22*
 Overstrand, 69
 P.6, 13, *14*
 P.111, *83*, 130-132, *130-131*
 P.120, 130-132, *131*
Boundary-layer suction control, 52, 157
Bowen, Ron, 202
Brabazon Committee, 78, 142
Brandt, Major, 98
Breguet XIX, 65
Brennan helicopter, 29, *30*
Brennan, Louis, 29
Brie, Wing Cdr Reggie, 170
Bristol Aeroplane Company, 140, 173
Bristol aircraft:
 92, *16*, 16-17
 138, *62*, 62-63, *63*
 151, 54
 171 Sycamore, 173-175, *173-175*, 180, 184
 173, *91*, 180-183, *181 183*
 185, 140
 188, 7, 205-207, *206-207*
 191, 183
 192 Belvedere, 183
 198, 145
 204, 199
 223, 145
 B.35/46, 120
 Badger, 16
 Bisley, 111
 Brabazon, 78, 128, 142-144, *143-144*
 Braemar, 21

Britannia, 144
Buckmaster, 143
Bullfinch, 16
E.20/45, 173
Fighter, 9, 17, 25
M.R.1, *24*, 25
Pullman, 21
Scout, 66
Ten-seater, 16
Tramp, 21, 22, *22*
Tramp Boat, 21
Bristol/Bristol Siddeley engines:
 Aquila, 173
 BS.100, 151
 Centaurus, 57, 78, 142-144, 160
 Cherub, 26, 36, 46, 47
 Hercules, 54
 Jupiter, 16, 17, 60, 62
 Olympus, 145, 146, 201, 207
 Orion, 150
 Orpheus, 157, 198
 Pegasus, 57, 60, 61, 62, 63, 67, 150, 151
 Phoenix, 66
 Pilot, 142
 Proteus, 143
 Theseus, 143
 Viper, 126
Bristol College of Advanced Technology, 156
British Aerospace BAC.221, *84*
British Aerospace EAP, 7, *96*, 208, *209*
British Air Commission, 170
British Aircraft Corporation aircraft:
 BAC-165, 158
 BAC-221, 136-137, *137*
 Concorde, *87*, 125, 126, 127, 137, 144-146, *146*, 207, 208
 TSR.2, 7, *94*, 199-202, *200-202*, 208
British Airways, 146
British European Airways, 144, 178, 181, 183, 186
British Government, 37
British Nieuport Fighter, 9
British Overseas Airways Corporation, 142, 144, 145-146
British Rotorcraft Museum, 179
Brooke-Smith, Tom, 148-150, 156
Broomfield, Duggie, 156
Brown, Lt Cdr Eric 'Winkle', 102, 112, 113-114, 162, 192
Bulwark, HMS, 152

Cable, Sqn Ldr 'Jeep', 177
Camm, Sir Sydney, 150
Caproni 161, 62, 63
Carbon fibre materials, 209
Carter, George, 97
Central Fighter Establishment, 153
Central Landing Establishment, 69
Chown, W.R., 75
Churchill, Winston, 99
Cierva Autogiro Company, 170, 171, 177
Cierva aircraft:
 C.6, 29-31, *31*, 32
 C.8L, *32*, 33

C.9, 31
C.10, 31, 32, *34*
C.19, 32, *35*, 38
C.30 (Rota I), 33, *35*, 38, 170
C.40 (Rota II), 33, *36*, 40, 42, 170
Gyrodyne, 42
Rota, 33
Skeeter, 172, 178
W.9, 7, 171-172, *171*, 176
W.11 Air Horse, 7, *90*, 172, 176-177, *177*
Cierva. Senor Juan de la, 6, 29-35, *31*, 38, 42
Civil Aviation Operational Requirements:
 CAOR.1/46, 180
 CAOR.2/46, 180, 184
 CAOR.3/46, 176, 180
Clerget engine, 9, 12, 30
Clydesdale, Lord, 61
Cobham, Sir Alan, 67
College of Aeronautics, 104, 132, 156, 193, 202
Colonial Office, 176, 177
Commonwealth Aircraft Corporation, 102
Controller of Research and Development, 142
Convair XC-99, 142
Conway, Hugh, 162
Copeland, SS, 148
Cosford Aerospace Museum, 124, 136, 140, 158, 168, 169, 187, 198, 202, 205, 207
Courtney, Captain Frank, 22, 29
Coventry Ordnance Works, 55, 60
Cox, Dr Roxbee, 98
Croydon Engineering engine, 159
Cunliffe-Owen Aircraft Ltd, 176
Cunningham, John, 115
Curtiss aircraft:
 Large America, 55
 Small America, 55
 Tanager, 19

Dalgoma, SS, 61
Dart Aircraft Ltd, 108
Dassault Mirage Balzac, 151
Daunt, Michael, 99
Davie, Sqn Ldr Douglas, 99
de Havilland aircraft:
 B.11/41, 78
 D.H.9A, 18
 D.H.106, 113
 D.H.108 Swallow, 7, *81*, 113-115, *114*, *115*
 Puss Moth, 61
 Sea Vampire, 102, 106, 162-163
 Spider Crab, 7, 100-103, *101*, *102*
 Tiger Moth, 69, 173
 Vampire, 7, 102, 113, 114, 115, 161-163, *162-163*
 Venom, 102
de Havilland (Canada) Otter, 157
de Havilland Engines, 203, 207
de Havilland engines:
 Ghost, 102, 104
 Gipsy, 47, 75
 Gipsy Major, 80, 108, 140, 157
 Gipsy Queen, 159
 Gipsy Six, 40, 154, 172
 Goblin, 100, 113-114

Gyron Junior, 206, 207
H.7, 178
Spectre rocket motor, 205
de Havilland, Geoffrey Jnr, 101, 113
de Havilland Propellers, 67, 178
Dennis, John, 187
Derry, John, 115
de Villiers, Desmond, 197
Dick, Kerr & Co Ltd, 55, 57
Directorate of Research, 21
Director(ate) of Scientific Research, 29, 108, 116, 118, 129
Director(ate) of Technical Development, 43, 64, 75, 97, 129, 143, 160, 161, 162, 193
Director of Military Aircraft Research and Development, 138
Dixon, F.H., 185
Douglas aircraft:
Boston, 53
DC-2, 33
Duke, Neville, 168
Dunlop's Aviation Division, 162
Dunlop wheels, 27
Dunne, John W., 45
Dunsfold, 121, 151, 152
Duxford, 156, 193, 202
Eagle, HMS, 18, 168, 181
Eagles, David, 209
Eassie, Jock, 149, 156
Electroscopic rudders, 47
English Electric aircraft:
Ayr, 55-57, *56*
Canberra, 55, 194, 199
Kingston, 56, 57,
Lightning, 134, 194-198, *197-198*, 201
M.1, 55
M.2, 55
M.3 Ayr, 55
P.1, *93*
P.17, 199, 200
P.22, 199
Esler, Eric, 121,
European Fighter Aircraft, 7, 209
Everest, Mount, 60-62, 156
Experimental Aeroplanes:
No.119, 40
No.126, 59
No.133, 75
No.137, 98
No.186, 110
No.205, 77
No.207, 70
No.217, 80
No.229, 113
No.233, 117
No.243, 112
No.248, 103

Fairey aircraft:
35/35, 54
F.B.1 Gyrodyne, 7, 184-185, *185*, 186, 188
F.D.1, 124-125, *125*, 132, 139
F.D.2, *83*, *85*, 125, *132*, *133*, 132-137, *135*, 139, 145

Gannet, 134
Gyrodyne, *92*
Jet Gyrodyne, *92*, 185-187, *186*
Long Range Monoplane, 64-66, *64*, *65*
R.1/36, 57
R.5/39, 58
Rotodyne, 7, *90*, *91*, 178-180, *178-180*, 185, 186
S.22/38, 40, 42
Swordfish, 200
Ultra Light Helicopter, 188
Falklands Campaign, 7, 153
Falk, Wing Cdr J.R., 121, 122
Farnborough, 17, 18, 29, 31, 32, 37, 39, 46, 47, 49, 52, 53, 57, 59, 63, 66, 73, 74, 75, 76, 80, 99, 102, 104, 105, 106, 111, 113, 114, 115, 116, 117, 118, 119, 121, 125, 126, 128, 132, 140, 144, 150, 162, 163, *164*, 165, 166, 168, 169, 174, 176, 177, 179, 191, 197, 205, 207, 208
Farren, W.S., 161
Fedden Flat-6 engine, 173
Felixstowe flying boats, 55
Fellowes, Air Commodore, 61
Fiat G.91, 151
Film Aviation Services, 140
Firestreak missile, 205
Fleet Air Arm Museum, 102, 127, 137, 146, 150, 152
Flexible rubber deck, 161-163
Flight Refuelling Ltd, 67, 152
Fokker aircraft:
F.VII/3m, 52, *52*
Fokker T.8W, 67
Fokker wing, 52
Folland aircraft:
E.28/40, 160, *161*
FO.116, 160
FO.117A, 160
Ford motor, 52
Forsyth, Captain A.G., 186
Fowler flaps, 50, 160
Franklin, Sqn Ldr Eric, 116, 118
French Government, 38
Frise-type ailerons, 43

Garroway, Derek, 185
Gayford, Sqn Ldr O.R., DFC, 66
Gellatly, Sqn Ldr Ron, 179, 188
Genders, Sqn Ldr George, 115
General Aircraft aircraft:
Cygnet, 53
GAL.28, 54
GAL.39 Fleet Shadower, 53
GAL.56, 110-113, *111*, *112*
GAL.61, 110, 113, *113*
Hamilcar, 71, 73
Hotspur, 108, 162
Monospar Tricycle, 53, *54*
Monospar Universal, 53
Owlet, 53
General Aircraft Ltd, 52, 75
Glendower design, 9
Gloster Aircraft, 52, 97

Gloster aircraft:
Ace, 103
E.1/44, 103-105, *103*, *104*
E.28/39, 6, 97-99, *98*, *99*, 100
F.5/34, 97
GA.1, 103
GA.2, 103
GA.3, 104
Meteor, 7, *86*, 100, 102, 103, 104, 116, 121, 140, *141*
Gotha bomber, 21
Gouge, Sir Arthur, 190, 191, 193
Gray, W.S., 75
Greater Manchester Museum of Science and Industry, 124
Green, J.R., 150
Grierson, John, 99
Griffiths, Professor A.A., 116-117
Guggenheim Safe Aeroplane Competition, 19
Gunn, 'Ben', 132

Hafner, Raoul, 38-39, 42, 69-71, 170, 172, 180
Hafner aircraft:
A.R.III, 38-39
A.R.V, *41*, 42
A.R.9, 39
H-8, 69
M-10, 69
P.D.6, 40, *41*, 42
P.D.9, 173
R.I Revoplane, 38
R.II Revoplane, 38
Rotabuggy, 70-71, *71*, *72*
Rotachute, 69-70, *70*, *71*
Rotaplane, 70-71
Haig, Squadron Leader de Haga, 27
Halford engines:
H.1, 103
H.1A, 101
H.2, 103
Halford, Major F.B., 100
Handley Page aircraft:
Gugnunc, 19-20, *19*, *20*
Halifax, 110-112
Hanley, 19
Harrow, 53, 67, *68*
Hendon, 19
H.P.17, *17*, 19
H.P.20 (X.4B), 18-19, *18*
H.P.80, 120
H.P.88, 7, 155-156, *155*
H.P.115, 7, *82*, 125-126, *126-127*
Manx, 108-110, *109*, *110*
Victor, 7, 118, 155
Handley Page, Frederick, 17
Handley Page slots, 17-20, 113-114
Hart, Stan, 147
Hatfield, 99, 100, 102, 113, 114, 115, 163
Hawker/Hawker Siddeley aircraft:
35/35, 54
B.11/41, 78
Harrier, 7, 152
Hart, 48

HS.681, 208
Hunter, 151, 165, 168, 196
Hurricane, 77, *77*, 78, 116, *119*
Kestrel, 7, 153
N.7/46, 163
P.1040, 165
P.1047, 165
P.1052, *89*, 121, 165-168, *166-168*
P.1078, 167
P.1081, 167-168, *167*
P.1121, 150
P.1127, 7, *88*, 150-153, *151-153*
P.1129, 199
P.1154, 151, 208
Sea Harrier, 7
Sea Hawk, 107, 163, 165, 167
Siddeley Aviation, 103
Supersonic transport, 145
Tempest, 105,
Typhoon, 99,
Head, Dr M.R., 157
Henderson, Sqn Ldr Jack, 126
Heston Aircraft Co, 159
Hill, Captain/Professor Geoffrey, 45, 49
Hiller UH-12, 177
Hillson aircraft:
    Bi-Mono, 75-76, *76*
    F.H.40, 77,
Hills, F. & Sons Ltd, 69, 77
Hislop, Dr G.S., 186
Hispano cannon, 101
Hispano guns, 103
Hispano-Suiza engines, 12, 25, 102
Hoare, Sir Samuel, 46
Home Office, 163
Hordern, Lebeus, 26
Houston, Lady, 61
Hubbard, Sqn Ldr S.J., 149
Hucknall, 147-148
Hunting H.126, *89*, 157-158, *158-159*
Hunting Jet Flap Research designs, 157
Hursley Park, 105, 106, 155, 168

Illustrious, HMS, 106, 169
Imperial Airways, 66, 67
Innes, T.Gordon, 169
Institute of Aviation Medicine, 140
International 100km Closed Circuit Record, 107
Isacco Helicogyre, 35-36, *42*
Italian Government, 208

Japan Air Lines, 179
J.A.P. engine, 74
Jenkins, Flt Lt N.H., OBE, DFC, DSM, 65
Jones-Williams, Sqn Ldr A.G., MC, 65
Junkers Jumo engine, 66

Kaman Aircraft Corporation, 179
Kay, David, 40, 42
Keep, Captain Stuart, 43
Kelly-Rogers, Capt J.C., 68
Kennedy Airport, 146
Kennedy, Hugh, 154

King-Joyce, Lt T.J.A., RN, 106
Kronfeld, Sqn Ldr Robert AFC, 73, 108, 110-113,

Lachmann, Gustav, 108
Lancaster, John, 119
Larson, Wg Cdr H.G., 148
Linton Hope hull, 55
Lippisch, 108
Lithgow, Mike, 106, 168
Little, Sqn Ldr I.M., 70
Lloyd, John, 16, 116
Lockheed aircraft:
    Hudson, 77
    Neptune, 66
    P-80A, 105
Lockspeiser, Sir Ben, 129
Long-range Weapons Establishment, 124
Long Range Development Flight, 66
Lyon, Col, 98

Major, Sqn Ldr K.A., 192
Malcolm ejector seat, 166
Malcolm, R. Ltd, 70
Manning, W.O., 55
Manton, Marcus, 56
Marine Aircraft Experimental Establishment, 26,
    59, 67, 192
Marshalls M.A.4, 157, *157*
Marsh, Sqn Ldr Alan, 171, 172, 177
Martin-Baker ejector seat, 106, 119, 126, 155, 205
Martin-Baker Ltd, 39
Martinsyde F.3, 9
Martlesham Heath, 22, 23
Mayo Composite Aircraft Co Ltd, 66, 75
Mayo, Major Robert, 66
MBB Helicopters, 178
McCulloch engine, 73
McGowan, Barry, 112,
McIntyre, Flt Lt D.F., 61
Menasco Buccaneer engine, 52
Mereweather, Hugh, 151
Messerschmitt aircraft:
    Me 163 Komet, 111, 161, 203
    Me 262, 129
Messerschmitt-Bolkow-Blohm, 208
Messier Aircraft Equipment Ltd, 162
Metropolitan-Vickers engines:
    Beryl, 190, 191
    F.2, 118
Middle Wallop, 53, 70, 74
Mignet Flying Flea, 108,
Miles Aeronautical Technical School, 78
Miles Aircraft, 128
Miles aircraft:
    Falcon Six, 154
    Gillette Falcon, 128, 154, *154*
    Libellula, 78, *79*, 80, *80*
    M.35, 78
    M.39, 78, 80
    M.52, 7, 128-129, *129*, 194
    Magister, 52
    Master, 52
    Messenger, 154

Peregrine, 52-53, *53*
Whitney Straight, 52
X-Minor, 77-78, *78*
X-series, 77-78
Miles, F.G., 77, 129
Miles, George, 78
Ministry of Agriculture and Fisheries, 176
Ministry of Aircraft Production, 59, 69, 80, 98, 100,
    105, 128, 142, 161, 162, 190
Ministry of Aviation, 126
Ministry of Civil Aviation, 176, 180
Ministry of Labour, 105
Ministry of Munitions, 29
Ministry of Supply, 115, 118, 120, 124, 129, 137, 143,
    158, 148, 176, 178, 184, 185, 187, 189, 191, 194
M.L. Utility, 73-74, *74*
Moffett Naval Air Station, 158
Mollart Engineering, 171
Monospar aircraft:
    S.T.1, 52
    S.T.2, 52
Mono-spar Wing Company, 52
Morris, H. & Sons, 70
Morris Motors, 173
Morton, Lt Cdr John, 179, 188
Muller-Rowland, Sqn Ldr J.S.R., 115
Muntz, Alan & Co Ltd, 71, 158-159
Museum of Army Flying, 70, 74
Mutual Weapons Development Programme, 150

Napier engines:
    Culverin, 66
    Eland, 179
    Lion, 21, 22, 23, 27, 43, 64
    Oryx, 187
    Rapier, 67
    Sabre, 78, 160
National Aeronautical and Space
Administration, 158
National Gas Turbine Establishment, 157
National Physical Laboratory, 55, 116
NATO Requirement NBMR.3, 151
Naval Requirement NR/A47, 205
Nepal Government, 61, 62
Nicholetts, Flt Lt G.E., AFC, 66
Noakes, Squadron Leader J., 27
North American aircraft:
    Sabre, 168, 186
    Super Sabre, 136
North Atlantic Treaty Organisation, 150
Nuffield Organisation, 173

Ocean, HMS, 102
Okanagan Helicopters, 179
Oliver, Stanley, 157-158
Olympia Aero Exhibition, 52

Packman, Flt R., 70
Paget, Louis, 48, 60
Pakistan Air Force, 107
Panavia Tornado, 145
Pandora Long Aerial Mine, 53
Paris Air Salon, 151, 158, 179

Parker, Lt Cdr D.G., 169
Parker, G.R.I., 155-156
Parker, J.Lankester, 26, 67
Parnall aircraft:
  C.10 (Cierva C.10), 32, *34*
  Parasol, 50, *51*
  Possum, 21, 23, *23*
Parnall, George & Co Ltd, 31, 50,
Pegg, Bill, 144
Penrose, Harald, 49, 61
Percival aircraft:
  P.46, 159
  P.74, 187-189, *188-189*
  P.94, 148
  P.113, 189
  Proctor, 158
Pest Control Ltd, 176, 177
Phillips and Powis Ltd, 52
Phoenix Dynamo Manufacturing Co Ltd, The, 55
Phoenix P.5 Cork, 55
Piper, H.L., 67
Pitcairn PA.39, 170
Pobjoy Aircraft and Engine Company, 42, 172
Pobjoy engines:
  Cataract, 39
  Niagara, 39, 53, 59
Porte Baby, 66
Porte, Colonel John C., 55
Power Jets Ltd, 97, 98
Power Jets W.2/700 engine, 128, 129
Pratt & Whitney engines:
  Wasp, 157
  Wasp Junior, 173
Preston, 56, 101, 113,
Pretoria Castle, HMS, 162
Principal Director of Scientific Research (Air), 134
Proof and Experimental Establishment, 105, 119,
  125, 202, 207
Pullin, C.G., 170, 171, 184

Quill, Jeffrey, 106

Radlett, 106, 108, 110, 112, 114, 185
R.A.E. Gas Starter, 50
R.A.E. Tailless Aircraft Committee, 110
R.A.F. Display, 27, 46, 48
R.A.F.1a engine, 13
R.A.F.15 wing section, 13
R.A.F. Museum, 124, 152, 183
R.A.F. Technical College, 181
Regent Motors, 97
Reid, W.T., 25
Reid and Sigrist aircraft:
  Bobsleigh, *86*, 140, *141*
  Desford, 140
Rennie, Major J.D., 57
Reynolds, Sqn Ldr J.McC., 97
Ripper, Dr, 176
R.N. Engineering College, 153
R.N. School of Aircraft Handling, 152
Rocket Propulsion Establishment, 205
Röhrbach, Dr Adolf, 26
Rolls-Royce engines:

A.J.65, 207
Avon, 134, 136, 137, 138, 206
Condor, 27
Crecy, 78
Dart, 178
Derwent, 121, 122, 124
Eagle, 27
Goshawk, 48
Griffon, 78
Kestrel, 42, 63, 77
Merlin, 54, 77, 78, 79, 176, 177, 186
Nene, 103, 104, 105, 106, 117, 147, 155
RB.108, 148, 157, 189
RB.133, 199
RB.134, 199
RB.142, 199
RB.176, 179
Tyne, 179
Vulture, 57
Welland, 99
Rolls-Royce Thrust Measuring Rig, 147-148, *148*
Roosevelt, President Franklin D., 68
Rose, Tommy, 78
Rowe, N.E., 161
Royal Aircraft Establishment Bedford, 122, 126, 136,
  137, 148, 149, 150, 151, 157, 158, 174, 198, 207
Royal Aircraft Establishment Farnborough, 15, 16,
  29, 32, 52, 53, 99, 100, 122, 132, 147, 148, 152,
  161, 162
Royal Aircraft Factory aircraft:
  B.E.2c, 66
  B.E.2d, 25
Royal Australian Navy, 102, 151
Royal Canadian Air Force, 68
Royal Geographical Society, 60
Royal Naval Air Service, 55
Royal Scottish Museum, 137
Russell, Dr A.E., 143

Salmson engine, 33
Saro aircraft:
  A.38, 58
  Lerwick, 55, 57
  London, 55
  P.122, 192
  P.177, 205
  R.1/36, 57
  R.14/40, 59
  Shrimp, 59, *59*
  SR.44, 190
  SR.53, *95*, 203-205, *204*
  SR.55, 205
  SR.177, 205
  SR.A1, *93*, 190-193, *191-193*
Saunders-Roe Ltd (Saro), 36, 177
Saunders, S.E. Ltd, 36
Saunders T.1, *12*, 12-13
Savoia-Marchetti S64, 64
Sayer, P.E.G., 98, 99,
SBAC Show, 106, 111, 113, 114, 115, 117, 118, 121, 126,
  150, 156, 169, 177, 179, 185, 191, 197, 205, 207,
  209
Schoultz, Mr, 98

Science Museum, 19, 46, 99, 148
Scottish Aircraft Manufacturing Co, 42
Sepecat Jaguar, 145
Shackleton, W.S., 26
Shepherd, Capt Ronnie, 147
Shorts aircraft:
  B.35/46, 120
  Belfast, 158
  Cockle, *25*, 25-26
  Empire Flying Boat, 67-68
  Maia, 67
  Mayo Composite, *66*, 66-68
  Mercury, 67,
  P.D.17, 199-200
  R.5/39, 58
  R.14/40, 59
  Satellite, 26
  SB.1, 156, *156*
  SB.5, 7, 195, 196, 198, *195-196*
  SC.1, 7, *88*, 148-150, *149-150*
  Scion Senior, 66
  Sherpa, 156-157, *156*
  Shetland, 57, 59
  Silver Streak, 25, *26*
  Stellite, 26
  Sturgeon, 156
  Sunderland, 55, 57, 58
Siddeley-Deasy gearbox, 21
Siddeley Puma engine, 21
Siddeley Sinaia, 9
Sikorsky helicopters:
  R-4 Hoverfly, 170, 176, 184, 187
  S.51, 184
  VS-300, 39, 170
Skyfame Museum, 156, 193
Slade, Gordon, 125
Slingsby Sailplanes Ltd, 71, 125
SNECMA, 145
Sopwith aircraft:
  Bulldog, 9, *10*
  Camel, 13
  Dolphin, 12
  Hippo, 9, *11*, 12
  Rhino, 9, *11*
  Snipe, 9, 13
Specifications:
  Type A.1(a), 13
  Type A.2(a), 9
  Type A.2(b), 9
  D of R Type 3, 21
  D of R Type 11, 21
  R.A.F. Type 1, 13
  Type VIII, 21
  1/20, 21
  9/20, 21, 22
  11/20, 21, 22
  6/21, 43
  12/21, 55
  13/21, 19
  29/22, 43
  48/22, 15
  18/23, 26
  20/24, 27

14/25, 29
3/26, 30
4/26, 30, 32
11/26, 31
23/26, 47
33/27, 64
2/28, 36
15/28, 50
16/29, 47
14/30, 65
F.3/32, 48
1/33, 49
F.5/33, 49
13/33, 66
27/33, 66
2/34, 62
35/35, 53-54
16/35, 33
R.1/36, 57
2/36, 33, 42
43/36, 40
S.29/37, 39
42/37, 77
R.3/38, 58
S.22/38, 40, 184
R.5/39, 58, 59
10/39, 40, 42
E.28/39, 7, 97-99
F.9/40, 98, 100
R.13/40, 57
R.14/40, 57
E.28/40, 160
E.6/41, 7, 100
B.11/41, 78, 80
E.5/42, 103
10/42, 70
11/42, 70
N.2/43, 58
E.16/43, 171
F.19/43, 160
E.24/43, 128
E.1/44, 103
2/44, 78
2/44, 142
E.6/44, 190
E.9/44, 118
E.10/44, 105, 168
E.1/45, 105
A.2/45, 184
E.18/45, 113
E.20/45, 173
2/46, 143
E.4/46, 184
N.7/46, 164, 166
E.19/46, 176
23/46P, 104
E.27/46, 130-131
34/46, 173
B.35/46, 118
E.38/46, 165
E.41/46, 168
E.4/47, 180, 181
A.6/47, 184

A.7/47, 184
E.10/47, 124
E.16/47, 185
E.1/48, 38
E.15/48, 120-121
E.10/49, 120-122
E.11/49, 120
E.16/49, 137, 138
F.23/49, 194
ER.100, 194
ER.103, 134
F.124T, 203
EH.125D, 187
ER.134T, 205
F.137D, 203
F.138D, 204
RH.142D, 179, 186
ER.143T, 148
F.177D, 205
ER.175D, 157
ER.184D, 157
ER.189D, 157
RB.192, 200, 201
ER.193D, 136
ER.197D, 125
X.197T, 126
ER.204D, 151
ER.221D, 136
Spithead, 168
Spriggs, Sir Frank, 103
Squadrons, R.A.F. :
    No.92, 53
    No.93, 53
    No.320, 67
    No.529, 171
Stainforth, George, 48
Steel Wing Company, The, 2
Stepan, August, 178
Stieger, H.J., 52, 75
Sud aircraft:
    Caravelle, 145
    Super Caravelle, 145
Sunbeam Nubian engine, 12
Supermarine aircraft:
    392, 105-107, *106*, *107*
    510, *90*, 168-169, *169*
    517, 169
    521, 155
    528, 169
    535, 169
    571, 199, 200
    Attacker, 106, 155, 165, 167, 169
    Jet Spiteful, 105
    N.9/47, 168
    S.6B, 48
    Scimitar, 165
    Seafang, 105, 106
    Seagull, 105
    Sea Attacker, 107
    Southampton, 65
    Spiteful, 105, 106, 119,
    Spitfire, 53, 78, 105, 111, 128
    Swift, 155, 165, 167

Supersonic Transport Advisory Committee, 125, 144
Swain, Sqn Ldr F.R.D., 63

Tailless Aircraft Advisory Committee, 108
Talbot, James, 110
Tayler, Dennis, 150
Thomas H.H., 12
Thunderer, HMS, 153
Townend ring, 17
Tripartite Evaluation Squadron, 153
Trubshaw, Brian, 146
Turbomeca Palas engine, 156
Turbo-Union RB.199D engine, 208
Turcat, André, 146
Turner-Hughes, Charles, 116-117
Twiss, Peter, 125, 136
Tyson, Geoffrey, 192

United States Army, 153
United States Government, 98, 99
United States Marine Corps, 153
United States Navy, 151, 153
Unsworth, H.J., 177
Uwins, Cyril, 60, 62

Vickers aircraft:
    B.35/46, 120
    Vespa, 60
    Vimy, 9, 43
    V.I.M., 9
    Wellesley, 66
Voyovodsky, 43

Wade, Sqn Ldr T.S., 165, 168
Wales, Sqn Ldr T.B., 122
Walter Mikron engine, 74
Warren-girder construction, 56
Warren spar, 52
Warrior, HMS, 163
Warton, 195, 197, 201, 202, 208
Waterton, Bill, 104, 105
Watson, Ken, 171, 172
Weir aircraft:
    W.1, *37*, 39
    W.2, *37*, *38*, 39
    W.3, *38*, 39, *39*
    W.4, 39, *39*
    W.5, 39, *39*, 170, 171
    W.6, 39, *39*, 40, 170, 171
    W.7, 40,
    W.8, 40, 171
Weir engine, 39,
Weir, G. & J. Ltd, 170-171
Weir, James, 170, 171
Weir organisation, 39,
Welsh, Flt Lt, 173
Westland aircraft:
    C.O.W.-gun fighter, 60
    Dragonfly, 184
    Dreadnought, 6, 43, *44*, 45
    Lysander, 111
    Pterodactyl, 6, *44-49*, 45-49

P.V.3, 60-62, *61*
Wallace, 61
Wapiti, 60
Westminster, 179
Wheeler, Group Capt A.H., 99
Whittle engines:
  W.1 engine, 97, 99

W.2 engine, 79, 97, 99, 102
Whittle, Sir Frank, 97
Wibault, Michel, 150
Willys Jeep, 70, 71, 73
Wilson, Wing Cdr H.J., 101
Wimperis, H.E., 29
Wolseley Viper engine, 16, 25

Wooller engine, 74

Yeovilton, 102, 127, 137, 146, 152
Youngman-Baynes high lift research aircraft,
  158-159, *159*

Zap flaps, 50
Zeppelin, 66